Buses
Restored
2007

Buses
Restored
2007

Ian Allan
PUBLISHING

Contents

Title page: Devon General 518 (CTT 518C), part of the Halifax Bus Museum collection, is a recently restored Willowbrook-bodied AEC Regent V. It is seen here in Exeter taking part in a running day in the summer of 2006.

First published 2007

ISBN (10) 0 7110 3211 4
ISBN (13) 978 0 7110 3211 8

© Ian Allan Publishing Ltd 2007

Published by Ian Allan Publishing

an imprint of Ian Allan Publishing Ltd, Hersham, Surrey KT12 4RG.
Printed by Ian Allan Printing Ltd, Hersham, Surrey KT12 4RG.

Code: 0703/A2

Visit the Ian Allan Publishing web site at:
www.ianallanpublishing.com

Note: Please be aware that vehicles on display can vary from time to time as not all museums display their entire 'fleet'. Visitors wishing to see a particular vehicle should make enquiries prior to their visit.

Part 2
Other Collections of Preserved Buses & Coaches

Part 3
Privately-Owned Vehicles

Part 4
Heritage Bus Services

Useful addresses
NARTM, PO Box 5141, Burton-upon-Trent DE15 OZF.
The Transport Trust, 202 Lambeth Road, London SE1 7JW.
British Bus Preservation Group, 25 Oldfield Road, Bexley
Heath, Kent DA7 4DX.
The PSV Circle, 26 Ashville Grove, Halifax HX2 OPN.

Classic Bus

This isn't just any bus magazine. This is the beautifully-designed, well-written bus magazine for anyone with an interest in understanding how we got to where we are today.

It is lovingly put together, gorgeously illustrated and deals with the subject matter with intelligence and passion.

buses
coaches
routes
places
people
profiles

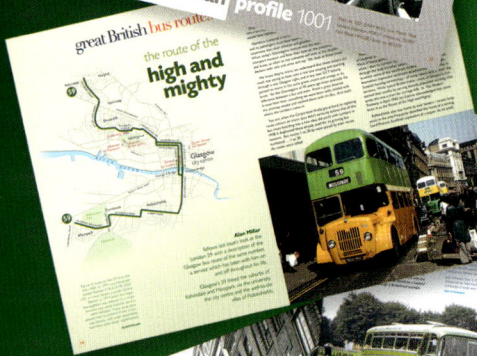

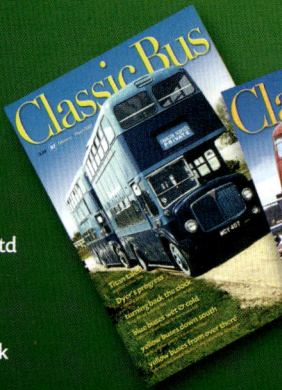

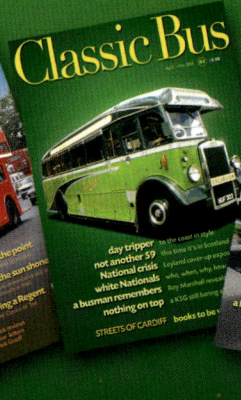

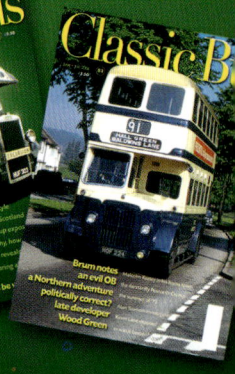

Introduction and Background

It is a pleasure once again to be writing the introduction to another edition of *Buses Restored*. This is the eighth edition and the biggest yet with around 2,500 buses and coaches listed. As we have stressed before, this is by no means all of the historic buses and coaches that exist in the UK today and the full total is probably around 5,000. The National Association of Road Transport Museums (NARTM) database now holds details of over 3,700 vehicles. The data in this book is an extract from the database, because while a number of owners are happy for NARTM to hold information about their vehicles, they understandably don't want all of their details to be published.

You will see that there are three main groups of collections listed in the book. The first are those museums and collections who are regularly open to the public and are obviously pleased to welcome visitors to their premises – that's why they exist after all. The second group includes collections that may be occasionally open to the public, or which are available to be seen by special appointment. However, there are some collections in this section that are never open; we ask our readers to respect the owner's privacy and not to visit or enter premises without the permission of the owners. Many of the vehicles from these collections do make regular appearances at the numerous historic vehicle rallies held all over the country each year, so you will be able to see them from time to time.

There is a third section to the book, listing those buses and coaches owned by members of the British Bus Preservation Group. Once again, we do not show the locations of these vehicles as many are kept at the owners' home addresses or on farms and other private premises.

In NARTM we try to represent all the owners of historic buses and coaches, from collections of over 100 vehicles in size, through smaller collections to the single bus or coach owned by a family. This is because all historic vehicle owners face the same issues, ranging from the difficulty of obtaining spares for elderly vehicles to the impact of proposed legislation on their continued operation. Finding secure accommodation for such large vehicles is another issue common to all of us. How often we have all thought how much simpler it would have been to collect something smaller! Even a classic car can usually be kept at home or in a nearby garage, but a double deck bus or 40 foot long coach is another matter.

Many of the museums listed in this book have come about by a group of owners looking for premises and discovering the ever-rising cost of housing a large vehicle. By working together, sometimes with the support of the local authority, but often without, owners have become 'museum-keepers' and have been drawn into the heritage 'industry'. Readers may know that I am involved with the Museum of Transport in Manchester and we have been open to the public for 28 years. Over the years we have had excellent support from the Greater Manchester Passenger Transport Authority and Executive and have built up a hard working core of volunteers. Together with our part time staff, we open the Museum on over 160 days each year.

There are several other museums listed that operate on similar lines, including some that have worked hard over many years to buy their own premises, giving a welcome extra degree of control and longer term stability. Opening to the public on a regular basis can be very rewarding; explaining how the buses and coaches were used, how they work and listening to visitors own experiences about the vehicles on which they used to travel. We can often help people trace their family trees by confirming employment details and are often a useful source for students and others engaged in research.

There are some downsides to running a museum – there is no option but to be open on every day advertised, there are some very quiet days and in contrast some very busy ones, plus the wet days when large families descend and appear to think that the museum is some alternative type of Wacky Warehouse or adventure playground… There are so many jobs to be done that have very little to do with the initial object of saving, restoring and using an old bus! These range from cleaning the toilets, buying food from the cash & carry and setting up special events to weekday meetings, book-keeping and website design. All the while the buses and coaches are safe and undercover, but their restoration doesn't always progress very fast…

Other collections are not open to the public and their members are freer to work on the vehicles, but have their own fund raising and property maintenance challenges to face if their projects are to succeed in the long term. Some of these collections, notably the Ribble Vehicle Preservation Trust and the Aycliffe and District Group have successfully combined the two approaches and have set up restoration centres which are never open to the public, but their vehicles make regular visits to events open to the public. This public benefit gives them the chance to apply for funding from various bodies, alongside the more 'conventional' museums, although this can be a very long process and can involve yet more hard work.

Quite rightly, public funding is not made available easily

and a good case has to be built with business plans and development plans, financial analysis of the project, collections management plans, training plans, sustainability reports and so on. All of these potentially wordy documents are required to ensure that public money (not just from the Heritage Lottery Fund) is going to be spent wisely and for the long term benefit of the public, as well as for the collection applying for the money. When faced with the stacks of paperwork (and a part-restored bus getting nowhere fast!) it is tempting to rely on your £1 a week stake in the National Lottery and to hope that your numbers come up as an alternative...

Having said that, it IS perfectly possible to get very substantial funding through the Heritage Lottery Fund (HLF) and some of the museums listed here have benefited handsomely. The Oxford Bus Museum has received a series of grants, allowing them to erect a second hand workshop building, two new display halls and some storage as well as surfacing the site and upgrading the visitor facilities. The Birmingham and Midland Motor Omnibus Trust, at Wythall, are going through a major expansion programme over this winter and their new facilities should be ready during 2007. Other collections have benefited from smaller amounts of funding to help with publicity, displays, computer equipment, educational materials and vehicle restoration.

Perhaps to an enthusiast, the latter is the most obvious activity to try and fund with grants. However, there must be a perceived public benefit and the project must have sufficient matching funding to complement any grant awarded. One of the strengths of a volunteer-run vehicle restoration is that it will be relatively cheap, with no labour costs involved, but often grant awarding bodies need to have a reasonably quick turn round on the projects they invest in, so restoration may have to be done professionally and up go the costs again. Once again, some collections have had grant funding for vehicle restoration and Ipswich Transport Museum are leading the restoration of an Eastern Counties Bristol K double decker at the present time.

Just which vehicles should and should not receive funding and support is another way in which NARTM may become involved. Regular readers of *Buses Restored* will know of the NARTM Scoring System which attempts to assess the importance of a particular coach or bus in national, local, social and technical terms. Applicants for funding will often contact NARTM to assess the vehicle in question and the system can help the funding body to decide if the vehicle is a worthy recipient of funding. At the same time, the group owning the vehicle and their long term prospects are assessed just as keenly as the vehicle itself. This is another means of checking that public money is spent wisely. In the case of the Bristol mentioned above, it

is in the care of Ipswich Transport Museum, who have a long track record of successfully operating a museum that is readily accessible to the public and, having got all the paperwork in order, they were in with a good chance of obtaining funding.

The other tool that NARTM has to help it assess the importance of a particular vehicle is the NARTM database. This has grown yet again by another couple of hundred buses and coaches since last year; some newly preserved out of service and others whose owners have decided to record their details on the database. It is some years since we published a breakdown by age of the vehicles on the database so here it is, by decade for the last century and before. Not surprisingly, all the nineteenth century vehicles are horse drawn! The age of the vehicle is taken as the date of its first registration, where appropriate.

Pre 1900	6
1900 to 1909	10
1910 to 1919	51
1920 to 1929	208
1930 to 1939	251
1940 to 1949	394
1950 to 1959	827
1960 to 1969	901
1970 to 1979	781
1980 to 1989	310
1990 to 1999	21

It is encouraging that all decades of the twentieth century now have more vehicles recorded on the database than even a year ago, showing that interest is spread across the whole age range of public service vehicles. How long this can continue is perhaps open to debate; there must be a finite number of elderly buses and coaches lurking in the undergrowth (and even inside houses!) waiting to be discovered. At the other end of the range, newer vehicles continue to be purchased for preservation; usually following the traditional reason "I used to go to school on those buses". And why not? While museums will have a more specific collecting policy as mentioned above, history did not end in 1973 even if the Government's 'Historic Vehicle' Taxation category does! Most museums continue to collect significant vehicles from more recent years and that is good, but it does add to the already huge pressure on storage and display space that is well-known to most of us.

It must be a function of getting older, but buses from the early 1990s really don't seem that old to me, and probably have several years life ahead of them. Back in the 1970s, with the Government's bus grant encouraging operators to buy shiny new buses, fifteen year old buses were getting to seem quite long in the tooth and several twelve and thirteen

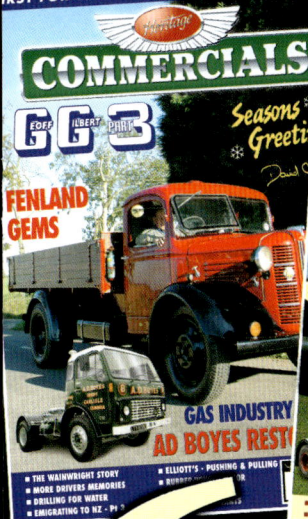

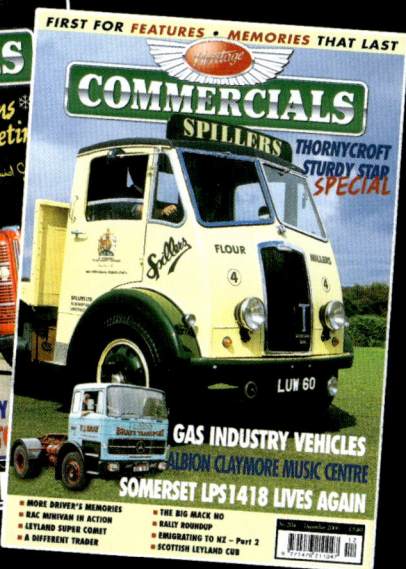

year old Leyland Titans joined the Manchester Museum of Transport in its early years after a relatively short life. Other buses, such as the AEC Swifts and Leyland Panthers of the late 1960s had very short lives in some fleets and relatively few have survived into preservation.

In the earlier years of motor buses, roads had much rougher surfaces, tyres were solid rather than pneumatic and their bodywork was usually made of timber. In Britain's damp climate, all this bumping over rough roads and streets meant that the bodies often only lasted a few years and it was not unusual for the chassis to carry two or even three different bodies during its life. As technology improved in the 1920s and early 1930s, older models were superseded by stronger, more powerful (and safer) types, so the vast majority passed to the scrap man, leaving just those examples we see today.

At the time, it was popular to have a 'holiday home' and many redundant bus bodies were taken to seaside camp sites and inland beauty spots such as the Severn Valley where quite large developments sprawled across the countryside, giving great enjoyment to their new owners and giving bus preservationists sixty years later the chance to salvage the remains as the basis on which to recreate some of those buses and coaches from the past.

Other vehicles survived into preservation through various later uses. Obvious second uses are as driver training vehicles and breakdown vans, while others were used by bus companies as tree lopping platforms, as street lamp maintenance lorries, traction pole carriers and clothing issue vans. Some were used as ambulances in the Second World War, as mobile canteens and later as offices, stores and even as toilets at special events. All of these thrifty second-uses have given that chance for more vehicles to join the ranks of those in preservation today.

I hope that the above notes have given an indication of the range of vehicles available for you to go and see, and even to ride on at the various museums and events up and down the country. Don't forget the regular open top bus tours, often using quite elderly vehicles in good condition that operate in many cities and rural areas too.

I hope also that my notes have given a brief look behind the scenes at what is involved in keeping a public service vehicle on the road, and most importantly, providing a roof over its head and some long-term security. At the same time as mentioning all the different activities, I hope I haven't deterred you from getting involved yourself. I can't think of a collection listed in the book that would not be glad of some extra support, whether that is to help polish the vehicles before an event, do some of the more specialised maintenance and restoration, take on some of the administration or even just go along for a chat and brew up for them! As my first manager used to say, "A job that won't stand a cup of tea isn't worth doing!"

More seriously, if you think that you can help in any way, working from home or at one of the sites listed here, do contact one of the collections direct, or get in touch with

Left: The SELNEC Preservation Society has examples of most modern vehicles to have operated with SELNEC and its immediate successors, Greater Manchester PTE and GM Buses. From the last named is 5320 (D320 LNB), one of the only batch of MCW Metrobuses to be bodied by Northern Counties.

NARTM at the addresses given in the next section. I am sure that you will be most welcome.

Finally, yet another aspect of NARTM activities is to keep an eye on forthcoming legislation to make sure that it does not (often unintentionally) restrict the future operation of our historic coaches and buses. In this field we work closely with our friends in the Federation of British Historic Vehicle Clubs (FBHVC). The FBHVC also represents the owners of many thousands of historic cars, motorcycles, lorries and other vehicles. It was instrumental in obtaining a Derogation from the UK Government to allow us to use our coaches and buses without tachographs under certain circumstances. This took place almost 20 years ago and if this had not been arranged, all our vehicles would have had to have had tachographs fitted, regularly inspected and used on every journey they made at a substantial cost to the owners.

The tachograph debate has come to the fore again recently and we are all keen to be able to continue to use our historic vehicles in a responsible manner, covering a limited distance each year. One way forward is to try and introduce a simple, standard definition of a Historic Vehicle which could then be used when other future legislation is being drafted and which would take these vehicles out of the scope of such legislation – in the same way as Showman's Vehicles have been for many years. This work is on going at the time of writing and the consultation period for the new tachograph regulations will have ended before you read this, so please keep an eye on the enthusiast press for any updates.

Both NARTM and the FBHVC support new legislation designed to improve road safety, and the Federation recently issued a voluntary driving code for the drivers of historic vehicles. Thankfully, historic vehicles in non-commercial use have a very good safety record in the UK and we all want to work to keep things that way. With very few exceptions, our vehicles are driven carefully and considerately and only take to the road relatively infrequently, so to include them in the scope of new legislation on drivers' hours, vehicle emissions and construction issues will add very little to their already good safety record on Britain's roads.

Please enjoy reading this book and try to visit as many of the locations listed as you can.

Dennis Talbot,
Chairman, NARTM.
January 2007.

What is NARTM ?

The National Association of Road Transport Museums (NARTM) is an informal organisation of museums and collections. Volunteers operate many of them, although others, such as the Glasgow and London Transport Museums, are managed by full-time staff. This mix of museum types gives the opportunity to share ideas and experiences and the volunteers involved each bring their own professional skills to their projects and best practices can then be shared by all the member collections.

NARTM has been in existence for almost 20 years and now has around 30 member organisations, with more joining each year. The buses and coaches that form part of the NARTM collections are generally regarded as forming the nucleus of the National Collection of Buses and Coaches. However, it must be stressed that many important examples are in private hands outside the scope of NARTM and its members.

What does NARTM do?

Many of the people involved in running transport museums are busy people and have little spare time after making significant contributions to their own projects, such as the Museum in Manchester. This is why NARTM only holds two meetings each year at the various member museums and in recent years we have visited Devon, Lincoln, Glasgow, Oxford and Portsmouth. In between meetings, the quarterly *Bulletin* keeps members in touch with each other and we are often in touch. Indeed, one of the main functions of NARTM is to put people in touch with each other and there are many instances of restoration projects progressing and spare parts being located through NARTM contacts. Discussion topics at recent meetings have included the encouragement and role of Junior members, bus services, grant applications, museum registration, visitor facilities, risk assessment, documentation and links with other bodies.

NARTM's unique service to its members is also as an information exchange about running museums — after all, as so many of our members are volunteers, their skills and experiences are not within the heritage and leisure industry. It is often the case that another project in another area has already been faced with exactly the same issues as we have today, and by sharing ideas and pooling resources, progress can be made more quickly.

Over the years NARTM has also taken a lead role in campaigning on new legislation to lessen its impact on the historic bus preservation movement. Vehicle licensing, driver licensing, tachographs and the retention of original registration numbers have all received our attention, with some success in each case through our work in conjunction with other groups within the movement. NARTM is also a club authorised to endorse applications from historic vehicle owners to retain, or regain, the original registration of their vehicle.

The future

NARTM is currently working closely with the Transport Trust to define the bus preservation sector of the heritage transport industry. It is also addressing the major issues currently facing the movement — storage, documentation, human resources and skills, public access and the future of vehicles in preservation. A database is now maintained which lists all vehicles in NARTM and associated collections and this will eventually form part of a decision-making process to ensure that the most historically important vehicles have a secure long-term future.

For more information about NARTM please contact:
NARTM, PO Box 5141, Burton-upon-Trent,
Staffordshire, DE15 0ZF.
Website: **www.nartm.org.uk**
e-mail: **email@nartm.org.uk**

Useful addresses

The Transport Trust, 202 Lambeth Road, London SE1 7JW.

British Bus Preservation Group, 25 Oldfield Road, Bexley Heath DA7 4DX.

The PSV Circle, 26 Ashville Grove, Halifax HX2 0PN.

How to Use this Book

This book lists both formal museums and the more informal types of collection, and gives details of opening times, contact addresses and the facilities available, together with a list of the buses, trolleybuses and coaches on display. Many of the sites are open to the public on a regular basis. Admission fees vary and some are even free to visitors, although donations towards the upkeep of the collections are always welcome. Please be aware that the vehicles on display can vary from time to time. Not all museums are able to display their entire 'fleet', and some practise the regular rotation of exhibits for added interest. In addition, some of the vehicles may be in the process of restoration in a workshop off-site, and there is always the possibility that a bus may be on loan to another museum! Visitors wishing to see a particular vehicle should make enquiries prior to the visit.

Some collections are not normally available for public access. However, the owners usually welcome visitors and will arrange for viewing by prior application. In addition, many such groups do have open or public days from time to time. Contact addresses are provided in this book, and those wishing to visit a particular site are asked to contact the address given. Please bear in mind that most are run by volunteers — please enclose a stamped self-addressed envelope when writing and respect the privacy of individuals. This book does not grant or imply any permission whatsoever to enter premises to look at old buses except by the agreement of the group involved. Note that, where buses are licensed for use on public passenger-carrying services, the use of individual vehicles will vary from time to time, as the demands of their preservation dictate.

Whilst some of the restored vehicles detailed here have been 'officially' preserved by their former operators, the majority have been restored and conserved by volunteers, often working in difficult conditions with limited resources of time, money and materials. That there are so many buses and coaches fully restored is a testimony to the

dedication of bus enthusiasts over the last 40 years or more, and it is intended that the vehicles will have a long and secure future.

The information used in this book is as provided by the organisations listed, for which the authors express their thanks. Any information on further collections not included in the current edition will be most welcome. If you own vehicles, or are associated wih such an organisation, please contact NARTM at the address given on page 7.

For each vehicle, details given include the present registration number, year first registered, brief chassis and body details (including seating) and original operator. Standard PSV Circle body codes are used, as outlined below.

Body type (before seating capacity):

A	articulated
B	single-deck bus
C	coach (single-deck)
CH	double-decker coach
Ch	charabanc
CO	convertible open-top double-decker
DP	dual-purpose (eg coach seats in bus shell)
F	full-front (where not normal for chassis)
H	Highbridge double-decker
L	Lowbridge double-decker (ie with sunken side gangway upstairs; all other types — with conventional gangways — are 'H', regardless of overall height)
O	open-top double-decker
OB	open-top single-decker
PO	partially-open-top double-decker
R	single-decker with raised rear saloon (eg over luggage compartment)
T	Toastrack

Seating capacity:

For double-deckers this is shown with the upper-deck capacity first, eg 43/31

Door position (after seating capacity):

C	centre entrance/exit
D	dual doors (usually front entrance and centre exit)
F	front or forward entrance/exit
R	open rear platform
RD	rear entrance/exit with doors
RO	open rear platform with open staircase
T	triple doors (eg on articulated vehicles)

Suffix:

t	fitted with toilet
l	fitted with wheelchair lift

The restoration state is given in accordance with the following code:

R	restored;
RP	restoration in progress;
A	awaiting restoration.

Left: Delaine 47 (MTL 750) is a 1958 Leyland Tiger Cub with Yeates coach bodywork, and is based at the Abbey Pumping Station in Leicester.

Right: The Mike Sutcliffe Collection houses some of the earliest British omnibuses in the world, one of which is Barnsley & District Electric Traction Co Ltd No 5 (HE 12), a 1913 Brush-bodied Leyland.

Part 1

Museums
Normally Open
to the Public

Manchester Corporation 3629 (UNB 629) is a
1960 Leyland Atlantean with Metro-Cammell
bodywork. It is housed in the Manchester
Museum of Transport at Cheetham.
Philip Lamb

Key to facilities

A	Audio/visual displays	H	Baby-changing facilities
B	Bus rides (regular)	L	Lecture theatre
B(e)	Bus rides (at events)	M	Band stand
C	Children's information pack	P	Car parking
D	Access for disabled	R	Refreshments
E	Picnic facilities	S	Enthusiasts' shop
F	School activity pack	T	Toilets
G	Gift shop		

Note: Please be aware that vehicles on display can vary from time to time as not all museums display their entire 'fleet'. Visitors wishing to see a particular vehicle should make enquiries prior to their visit.

Abbey Pumping Station
Leicester

Contact address: Corporation Road, Leicester LE4 5PX

Phone: 0116 299 5111

Fax: 0116 299 5125

Brief description: The Museum is a Victorian pumping-station dating from 1892 with four beam-engines. The vehicle collection is on view on special open days. On these occasions, one of the beam-engines is steamed.

Events planned: Opening times for special events: Saturdays 11.00-14.30, Sundays 13.00-17.00

31 March, 5 May, 2 June, 7 July, 4 August, 1 September, 6 October 2006 — Railway Running Days;

15 April 2007 — Inventors and Inventions Steam Day

6 May 2007 — Classic Vehicles

23/24 June 2007 — Urban Rally Weekend

9 September 2007 — Pastimes Steam Day with Crafts

29 October 2007 — Ghostly Engineer Evening

9 December 2007 — Christmas Toys and Steam Day

12 January 2008 — Meccano Day

3 February 2008 — Steam Toys in Action

Please see the enthusiast press for further details.

Opening days/times:

1 February-31 November, plus 9 December and 12 January 2008. Saturday, Monday to Thursday 11.00-16.30; Sundays 13.00-13.60. Museum closed December and January except for above dates

Directions by car: A6 (north of Leicester) joins Abbey Lane at Redhill Island. Corporation Road is off Abbey Lane.

Directions by public transport: From City Centre (Charles Street) take bus 54 to top of Corporation Road.

Charges: Free except on special open days.

Facilities: C D E G H P R (on open days) T

Registration	Date	Chassis	Body	New to	Fleet No	Status
CBC 921	1939	AEC Renown O664	Northern Counties H32/32R	Leicester City Transport	329	R
MTL 750	1958	Leyland Tiger Cub PSUC1/2	Yeates DP43F	Delaine Coaches of Bourne	47	R
TBC 164	1958	Leyland Titan PD3/1	Willowbrook H41/33R	Leicester City Transport	164	R
OUM 727P	1976	Bedford J2SZ10	Caetano C16F	Anderton Tours of Keighley		R
B401 NJF	1984	Ford Transit 190D	Rootes B16F	Midland Fox	M1	R

Notes:

CBC 921	On view at Snibston Discovery Park
B401 NJF	On view at Snibston Discovery Park

Note: Please be aware that vehicles on display can vary from time to time as not all museums display their entire 'fleet'. Visitors wishing to see a particular vehicle should make enquiries prior to their visit.

Amberley Working Museum

Contact address: Amberley, Arundel, West Sussex, BN18 9LT
Phone: 01798 831370
Fax: 01798 831831
E-mail: office@amberleymuseum.co.uk
Brief Description: The industrial museum has a wide range of attractions, including rail and bus operations. Some buses in the collection are museum-owned and others are owned by the Southdown Omnibus Trust or are in private hands.
Events planned:
16 September 2007 — Annual Bus Show, theme based on several 80th anniversaries 'Ride 8 Decades.'
Opening days/times:
March to October: Weds to Sun (also Mon and Tues during school holidays)
Directions by car: Situated close to Amberley railway station on the B2139. Approach from the north and west via the A29 and from the east via the A24 and A283.
Directions by public transport: Hourly rail service calls at Amberley station which is adjacent to the museum.
Charges: Adults £8, OAP £7.20.
Facilities: A B B(e) C D E F G H L P R T

Registration	Date	Chassis	Body	New to	Fleet No	Status
IB 552	1914	Tilling Stevens TS3 Petrol Electric	Newman O22/16R	Worthing Motor Services	52	R
CD 5125	1920	Leyland N	Short O27/24R	Southdown Motor Services	125	R
CD 4867	1923	Tilling Stevens TS3A Petrol Electric	(chassis only) Ch32	Southdown Motor Services	67	RP
BP 9822	1924	Shelvoke & Drewery Freighter	Hickman (replica) B18F	Tramocar of Worthing	1	R
MO 9324	1927	Tilling Stevens B9A	Brush B32R	Thames Valley Traction Co	152	R
UF 1517	1927	Dennis 30cwt	Short B19R	Southdown Motor Services	517	R
BR 7132	1929	Leyland Lion LT1	Leyland B34F	Sunderland Corporation	2	R
UF 4813	1929	Leyland Titan TD1	Brush O27/24R	Southdown Motor Services	813	A
UF 6473	1930	Leyland Titan TD1	Leyland H24/24R	Southdown Motor Services	873	R
UF 6805	1930	Tilling Stevens B10A2	Short B31R	Southdown Motor Services	1205	RP
UF 7428	1931	Leyland Titan TD1	Short H26/24R	Southdown Motor Services	928	R
ECD 524	1937	Leyland Cub KPZ2	Park Royal B20F	Southdown Motor Services	24	RP
EUF 184	1938	Leyland Titan TD5	Leyland -	Southdown Motor Services	0184	R

Notes:

IB 552	Petrol-electric Transmission. Body new 1909.
CD 5125	Restored using a P or Q 5- or 6-ton chassis. Rebodied 1928
CD 4867	Petrol-electric. Replica charabanc body under construction
BP 9822	Solid tyres. Replica body built at Amberley
UF 1517	All-metal body.
MO 9324	Mechanical Transmission. Restored at Amberley
BR 7132	Stored off-site
UF 4813	On loan from Southdown Motor Services Ltd
UF 6805	Mechanical Transmission.
EUF 184	Converted from bus 184; fitted with breakdown vehicle body ex Leyland TD1 872 (UF 6472)

Aston Manor Road Transport Museum

Contact address: The Old Tram Depot, 208-216 Witton Lane, Aston, Birmingham B6 6QE
Phone: 0121 322 2298
Fax: 0121 449 4606
Web site: www.amrtm.org
Affiliation: NARTM

Brief description: The 19th-century former tram depot houses a selection of buses, coaches, commercial vehicles and tramcar bodies in an authentic setting — the depot still has tram tracks and stone sets in situ. There are also many small exhibits, working model layouts and video presentations.

Events planned:

24 June 2007 — Two Museums Running Day. Bus service linking Aston Manor and Wythall.

8 July 2007 — Open day/Outer Circle running day.

8/9 Sept 2007 — Heritage Open Days.

25 Nov 2007 — Collectors' fair with free bus rides.

Please see the enthusiast press for other events.

Opening days/times:

Saturdays, Sundays and Bank Hols 11.00 to 17.00. Other times by arrangement.

Opening times may vary over Christmas/New Year period.

Directions by car: Easy access from M6 junction 6.

Directions by public transport: Rail to Witton Station and a short walk (170yd)

Bus No 7 from Birmingham City Centre or bus No 11, outer circle to Witton Square.

Charges:

Adults £1.50, Child and Concessions 75p, Family £4.00.

Admission charges may vary on special event days.

Facilities: A B(e) D H P R S T

Other information: Not all of the vehicles listed are on display at the museum. To view any vehicle not normally accessible, visitors should enquire at the museum as to arrangements for viewing.

Registration	Date	Chassis	Body	New to	Fleet No	Status
note z	1925	AEC S	Buckingham	Birmingham Corporation Tramways	215	A
OP 237	1926	(no chassis)	Short H32/26R	Birmingham Corporation Tramways	208	A
EA 4181	1929	Dennis E	Dixon B32F	West Bromwich Corporation	32	RP
HA 4963	1930	SOS RR	(chassis only)	BMMO ('Midland Red')	963	A
JF 2378	1931	AEC Regal 662	Burlingham C32R	Provincial of Leicester	R1	R
OJ 9347	1933	Morris Commercial Dictator	Metro-Cammell B34F	Birmingham Corporation Tramways	47	RP
AOG 679	1935	Daimler COG5		Birmingham Corporation Tramways	83	A
EHA 775	1938	SOS SON	(chassis only)	BMMO ('Midland Red')	2207	A
RC 7927	1940	BMMO SON	Willowbrook DP34F	Trent Motor Traction Co	417	R
FON 630	1942	Leyland Titan TD7	(chassis only)	Birmingham City Transport	1330	A
KHA 301	1948	BMMO C1	Duple C30C	BMMO ('Midland Red')	3301	R
KTT 689	1948	Guy Vixen	Wadham FC29F	Court Cars of Torquay		R
ARC 515+	1949	Sunbeam F4	Brush H30/26R	Derby Corporation	215	R
GUJ 608	1950	Sentinel STC4	Sentinel B40F	Sentinal demonstrator		R
JOJ 222	1950	Leyland Titan PD2/1	Park Royal H29/25R	Birmingham City Transport	2222	RP
JOJ 526	1950	Guy Arab IV	Metro-Cammell H30/24R	Birmingham City Transport	2526	A
JOJ 548	1950	Guy Arab IV	Metro Cammell H30/24R	Birmingham City Transport	2548	RP
KHA 352	1950	BMMO CL2	Plaxton C26C	BMMO ('Midland Red')	3352	RP
SB 8155	1950	Guy Wolf	Ormac B20F	Alexander MacConnacher of Ballachulish		R
JOJ 847	1952	Daimler CVG6	Crossley H30/25RD	Birmingham City Transport	2847	A
LOG 301	1952	Guy Arab IV	Saunders Roe H30/25R	Birmingham City Transport	3001	RP
LJW 336	1953	Guy LUF	Saunders Roe B44F	Guy Demonstrator		R
LOG 302	1954	Daimler CLG5	Metro Cammell H30/25R	Birmingham City Transport	3002	R
MOF 90	1954	Guy Arab IV	Metro Cammell H30/25R	Birmingham City Transport	3090	RP
TOB 377	1956	AEC Reliance MU3RV	Burlingham C37C	Flights of Birmingham		R
XDH 72+	1956	Sunbeam F4A	Willowbrook H36/34RD	Walsall Corporation	872	RP
773 FHA	1958	BMMO D9	BMMO H40/32RD	BMMO ('Midland Red')	4773	A
1294 RE	1959	Guy Arab LUF	Burlingham C41F	Harper Bros of Heath Hayes	60	R
WLT 506	1960	AEC Routemaster R2RH	Park Royal H36/28R	London Transport	RM506	R
264 ERY	1963	Leyland Titan PD3A/1	Park Royal O41/33R	Leicester City Transport	264	R
3035 HA	1963	BMMO D9	BMMO O40/32RD	BMMO ('Midland Red')	5035	RP
334 CRW	1963	Daimler CVG6	Metro Cammell H34/29R	Coventry City Transport	334	RP
6479 HA	1963	BMMO S17	Willowbrook B52F	BMMO ('Midland Red')	5479	R
6370 HA	1964	BMMO D9	BMMO H40/32RD	BMMO ('Midland Red')	5370	R
KOX 663F	1967	AEC Swift MP2R	MCW B37D	Birmingham City Transport	3663	RP
LHA 870F	1967	BMMO S21	BMMO DP49F	BMMO ('Midland Red')	5870	R
XNX 136H	1970	Leyland Leopard	Alexander DP49F	Stratford-upon-Avon Blue Motors	36	R

Registration	Date	Chassis	Body	New to	Fleet No	Status
XON 41J	1971	Daimler Fleetline CRG6LX	Park Royal H43/33F	West Midlands PTE	4041	R
JOV 714P	1976	Bristol VRTSL6LX	MCW H43/33F	West Midlands PTE	4714	R
OOX 825R	1977	Leyland National 11351A/1R	Leyland National DP45F	West Midlands PTE	6825	RP
SOA 658S	1977	Leyland National 11351A/1R	Leyland National B49F	Midland Red Omnibus Co	658	RP
WDA 700T	1979	Leyland Fleetline FE30AGR	MCW H43/33F	West Midlands PTE	7000	A
WDA 986T	1978	Leyland Fleetline FE30AGR	MCW H43/33F	West Midlands PTE	6986	R
BVP 784V	1979	Leyland Leopard PSU3E/4R	Plaxton C53F	Midland Red Omnibus Co	784	A
A110 WVP	1984	MCW Metrobus GR133/1	MCW H43/30F	West Midlands PTE	8110	RP
F685 YOG	1988	MCW Metrorider MF150/113	MCW B23F	West Midlands PTE	685	A
G292 EOG	1990	Leyland Lynx	Leyland Lynx B49F	West Midlands Travel	1292	RP

+ Trolleybus

Notes:

note z	Registration not known
HA 4963	Chassis only
OJ 9347	Renumbered 77 in 1935
AOG 679	Originally bus 679 with Northern Counties H26/22R body; rebodied 1947 as a van
EHA 775	Chassis only
RC 7927	On loan from Trent Motor Traction
KHA 352	Rebodied 1963
LOG 302	Chrome-plated chassis exhibited 1952 Commercial Motor Show
XDH 72	Last Walsall trolleybus. Owned by British Trolleybus Society.
3035 HA	Originally H40/32RD; converted to open-top by Marshall ('Obsolete Fleet') London (OM6)
264 ERY	Originally H41/33R
OOX 825R	Volvo engine fitted by WM PTE
A110 WVP	Guided wheel experimental vehicle

Black Country Living Museum Transport Group
Dudley

Contact address: Tipton Road, Dudley, West Midlands DY1 4SQ
Phone: 0121 557 9643
Web site: wwww.bclm.co.uk
Brief description: Tramway operation daily. Trolleybus operation on Sundays and Bank Holidays.
Opening days/times: Summer: daily 10.00-17.00. Winter: Wednesdays to Sundays 10.00-16.00. Some evening openings
Directions by car: M5 (jct 2) signposted on Motorway. follow signs on A4123 to 'Black Country Living Museum'.
Directions by public transport: Central Trains to Tipton station. Travel West Midlands 224, 263, 270, 311-313 to Museum.
Facilities: A, B, B(e)C, D, E, F, G, H, L, P, R, T
Contact (Transport Group): Black Country Museum Transport Group, 28 Farm Close, Etchinghill, Rugeley, Staffs WS15 2XT.

Registration	Date	Chassis	Body	New to	Fleet No	Status
UK 9978+	1931	Guy BTX	Guy H26/24R	Wolverhampton Corporation	78	A
HA 8047	1933	SOS REDD	Metro Cammell H26/26R	BMMO ('Midland Red')	1047	A
DKY 735+	1946	Karrier W	East Lancs H37/29F	Bradford Corporation	735	RP
DUK 833+	1946	Sunbeam W	Roe H32/28R	Wolverhampton Corporation	433	R
FEA156	1949	Daimler CVG5	Metro Cammell B38R	West Bromwich Corporation	156	RP
GEA 174	1952	Daimler CVG6	Weymann H30/26R	West Bromwich Corporation	174	RP
TDH 912+	1955	Sunbeam F4A	Willowbrook H36/34RD	Walsall Corporation	862	R
2206 OI+	1958	Sunbeam F4A	Harkness H36/32R	Belfast Corporation	246	R
SCH 237+	1960	Sunbeam F4A	Roe H37/28R	Derby Corporation	237	R
UCX 275	1961	Guy Wulfrunian	Roe H43/32F	County Motors of Lepton	99	R

Note: Please be aware that vehicles on display can vary from time to time as not all museums display their entire 'fleet'. Visitors wishing to see a particular vehicle should make enquiries prior to their visit.

Registration	Date	Chassis	Body	New to	Fleet No	Status
VRD 186+	1961	Sunbeam F4A	Burlingham H38/30F	Reading Corporation	186	RP
6342 HA	1963	BMMO D9	BMMO H40/32RD	BMMO ('Midland Red')	5342	R
GHA 327D	1965	Leyland Leopard PSU4/4R	Plaxton -	Midland Red Omnibus Co	5827	R
XDH 519G	1969	Daimler Fleetline CRG6LX	Northern Counties H41/27D	Walsall Corporation	119	RP
+ Trolleybus						

Notes:

HA 8047	Sole surviving SOS double decker
DKY 735	Rebodied 1959
DUK 833	Rebodied 1959
2206 OI	On Loan from East Anglia Transport Museum
UCX 275	On loan from Dewsbury Bus Museum
VRD 186	Operated at Teeside 1968-71 and currently in their livery
GHA 327D	Converted to breakdown vehicle in 1979.

British Commercial Vehicle Museum
Leyland

Contact address: King Street, Leyland, Lancashire, PR25 2LE
Phone: 01772 451011
Fax: 01772 451015
Brief description: A unique line-up of historic commercial vehicles and buses spans over a century of truck and bus building. More than 50 exhibits are on display in this national collection.
Events planned: Please see the enthusiast press for details.
Opening days/times:
April to end of September: Sundays, Tuesdays, Wednesdays, Thursdays and Bank Holiday Mondays, 10.00 to 17.00
October: Sundays only, 10.00 to 17.00
Directions by car: Close to the M6 Junction 28.
Directions by public transport:
By train to Leyland station (on West Coast main line).
Buses from Preston and Chorley bus stations.
Charges: Adult £4, Child/OAP £2, Family £10.
Facilities: A B(e) D F G L P R S T

Registration	Date	Chassis	Body	New to	Fleet No	Status
note t	1896	Horse bus	O14/12R	Edinburgh & District Tramways		R
XW 9892	1925	Tilling Stevens TS7	Tilling B30R	Thomas Tilling	0172	R
YT 3738	1927	Leyland Lioness PLC1	Thurgood C22F	King George V		R
KGU 284	1949	Leyland Titan 7RT	Park Royal H30/26R	London Transport	RTL325	R
JRN 29	1956	Leyland Tiger Cub PSUC1/2	Burlingham C41F	Ribble Motor Services	963	R
OED 217	1956	Foden PVD6	East Lancs H30/28R	Warrington Corporation	112	R
301 LJ+	1962	Sunbeam MF2B	Weymann H37/28D	Bournemouth Corporation	301	R
+ Trolleybus						

Notes:

note t	Unregistered
301 LJ	On loan from Bournemouth Heritage Transport Collection

Note: Please be aware that vehicles on display can vary from time to time as not all museums display their entire 'fleet'. Visitors wishing to see a particular vehicle should make enquiries prior to their visit.

Castle Point Transport Museum
Canvey Island

Contact address: 105 Point Road, Canvey Island, Essex SS8 7TP
Phone: 01268 684272
Affiliation: NARTM
Brief description: This historic former Canvey & District bus depot, built in 1935, houses approximately 35 commercial vehicles spanning the years 1944 to 1988. Exhibits include buses, coaches, lorries, fire engines and military vehicles. They can be seen in varying stages from the totally restored to those in need of complete restoration. Completely run by volunteers, membership of the society is available at £10 per annum.
Events planned: Please see enthusiast press for details
Opening days/times: Open on 1st/3rd Sundays, April to mid October.
Directions by car: A130 to Canvey Island; follow brown tourism signs on reaching the island.
Directions by public transport: By rail to South Benfleet, then by bus to Leigh Beck, Canvey Island.
Charges: Free admission. Donations welcome. A charge is made on the Transport Show day in October.
Facilities: B(e) P T
Other information: Hot drinks available.

Registration	Date	Chassis	Body	New to	Fleet No	Status
FOP 429	1944	Daimler CWA6	Duple O33/26R	Birmingham Corporation Tramways	1429	R
JVW 430	1944	Bristol K5G	ECW L27/28R	Eastern National Omnibus Co	3885	R
MPU 52	1947	Leyland Titan PD1A	ECW L27/26R	Eastern National Omnibus Co	3991	RP
CFV 851	1948	Bedford OB	Duple C29F	Seagull Coaches of Blackpool		R
LYR 997	1949	AEC Regent III O961 RT	Weymann H30/26R	London Transport	RT2827	RP
NEH 453	1949	Leyland Titan OPD2/1	Northern Counties L27/26RD	Potteries Motor Traction Co	L453	R
ONO 49	1950	Bristol L5G	ECW B35R	Eastern National Omnibus Co	4029	R
PTW 110	1950	Bristol L6B	ECW FC31F	Eastern National Omnibus Co	4107	RP
WNO 478	1953	Bristol KSW5G	ECW O33/28R	Westcliff-on-Sea Motor Services		R
XVX 19	1954	Bristol Lodekka LD5G	ECW H33/25R	Eastern National Omnibus Co	4208	R
381 BKM	1957	AEC Reliance MU3RV	Harrington C41F	Maidstone & District Motor Services	C381	RP
PHJ 954	1958	Leyland Titan PD3/6	Massey L35/32R	Southend Corporation	315	RP
217 MHK	1959	Bristol MW6G	ECW DP41F	Eastern National Omnibus Co	480	R
236 LNO	1959	Bristol Lodekka LDL6LX	ECW H37/33R	Eastern National Omnibus Co	1541	R
VLT 44	1959	AEC Routemaster	Park Royal H36/28R	London Transport	RM44	RP
SGD 407	1960	Leyland Titan PD3/2	Alexander H41/31F	Glasgow Corporation	L405	RP
373 WPU	1961	Guy Arab IV	Massey L34/33R	Moore Bros of Kelvedon		R
138 CLT	1962	AEC Routemaster R2RH	Park Royal H36/28R	London Transport	RM1138	R
28 TKR	1962	AEC Reliance 2MU3RV	Harrington C29F	Maidstone & District Motor Services	C28	R
918 NRT	1963	AEC Regent V MD3RV	Massey H33/28R	Lowestoft Corporation	8	RP
SDX 57	1963	AEC Regent V 2D2RA	East Lancs Neepsend H37/28R	Ipswich Corporation	57	RP
CUV 233C	1965	AEC Routemaster R2RH/1	Park Royal H36/29RD	London Transport	RCL2233	R
NTW 942C	1965	Bristol Lodekka FLF6G	ECW H38/32F	Eastern National Omnibus Co	2849	R
AVX 975G	1968	Bristol Lodekka FLF6LX	ECW H38/32F	Eastern National Omnibus Co	2614	R
CPU 979G	1968	Bristol VRTSL6LX	ECW H39/31F	Eastern National Omnibus Co	3000	R
GNM 232N	1975	Bristol LHS6L	Plaxton C33F	Epsom Coaches		RP

Notes:

JVW 430	Renumbered 1274 in 1954
FOP 429	Originally H33/26R; later operated by Eastern National Omnibus Co and Southend Corporation (244)
MPU 52	Renumbered 1121 in 1954
LYR 997	In Osbornes of Tollesbury livery
ONO 49	Renumbered 309 in 1954 and 1107 in 1964
PTW 110	Renumbered 328 in 1954
WNO 478	Built as H33/28R; numbered 1423 in 1954; passed to Eastern National Omnibus Co in 1955; renumbered 2380 in 1964 and converted to open-top in 1965/6

XVX 19	Renumbered 1431 in 1954 and 2400 in 1964
VLT 44	In Southend Transport livery
236 LNO	Renumbered 2510 in 1964
217 MHK	Renumbered 1402 in 1964
AVX 975G	Delivered as CH37/18F; fitted with bus seats and renumbered 2946 in 1969

Cavan & Leitrim Railway
Dromod

Contact address: Cavan & Leitrim Railway, Narrow Gauge Station, Station Road, Dromod, Co Leitrim, Eire
Phone/fax: 00353 71 9638599
E-mail: dromod@eircom.net
Web site (railway): http://www.irish-railway.com
Brief description: Half mile 3ft gauge steam railway with a collection of railway vehicles (steam, diesel, carriages, wagons and railcars) together with a selection of vintage road vehicles, military equipment and vintage aircraft.
Opening days/times:
Open Saturday, Sundays and Mondays April-September. Rest of year by request, please phone, write or e-mail
Directions by car: to Dromod on N4 from Dublin. R202 from Dromod, 500yds.
Directions by public transport: Train to Dromod Irish Rail station from Dublin Connolly (Dublin-Sligo line). Narrow gauge station next to main line
Charges: Adult 8 Euro, Child 5 Euro, Family 17 Euro, OAP 5 Euro
Facilities: B(e) C D E G R (on request) S T

Registration	Date	Chassis	Body	New to	Fleet No	Status
KID 154	1947	Leyland Tiger PS1	Northern Ireland Road Transport Board B34R	Northern Ireland Road Transport Board	A8520	A
FCI 323	1950	Bristol LL5G	ECW B39R	Crosville Motor Services	KG156	RP
ZJ 5904	1950	Leyland Tiger OPS3/1	CIE	CIE	P164	R
IY 7383	1951	GNR Gardner	Park Royal/GNR B33R	Great Northern Railway (Ireland)	G389	R
IY 8044	1952	GNR Gardner	Park Royal/GNR B33R	Great Northern Railway (Ireland)	G396	A
ZO 6960	1953	Leyland Titan OPD2/1	CIE H37/31R	CIE	R541	RP
ZU 5000	1953	Leyland Royal Tiger PSU1/9	Saunders Roe B44C	Irish Army		RP
ZY 1715	1955	AEC Regal IV 9622E	Park Royal/GNR B40F	Great Northern Railway (Ireland)	345	R
ILI 98	1958	Bristol SC4LK	ECW B35F	Eastern National Omnibus Co	455	RP
OST 502	1959	AEC Reliance 2MU3RV	Alexander B41F	Highland Omnibuses	B24	RP
3945 UE	1960	Leyland Tiger Cub PSUC1	Park Royal B45F	Stratford-upon-Avon Blue Motors	45	A
71 AHI	1960	Leyland Tiger Cub PSUC1/2	Metro Cammell B41F	Western Welsh Omnibus Co	1274	A
AZD 203	1964	Leyland Leopard L2	CIE B45F	CIE	E140	R
BLH 123B	1964	Bedford VAS2	Duple (Midland) B30F	London County Council		RP
EZH 155	1965	Leyland Leopard PSU3/4R	CIE B—F	CIE	C155	A
EZH 170	1966	Leyland Leopard PSU3/4R	CIE B45F	CIE	C170	R
UZH 258	1966	Leyland Leopard PSU3/4R	CIE B55F	CIE	C258	R
ZS 8621	1971	Daimler Fleetline CRG6LX	Park Royal H—/—F	West Midlands PTE	4130	A
177 IK	1972	Leyland Leopard PSU5/4R	CIE B48F	CIE	M177	A
78 D140	1978	Bedford SB5	Marshall B40F	Royal Navy		R
78 D824	1978	Bristol RELL6G	Alexander (Belfast) B52F	Ulsterbus	2193	R
85 D2412	1978	Bedford SB5	Marshall B40F	Royal Air Force		A
643 MIP	1980	Volvo B58	Duple C53F	North West Coachlines		A

Notes:

KID 154	Originally registered GZ7588	AZD 203	Worked on hire to County Donegal Railways
FCI 323	Originally registered LFM737	EZH 155	Converted to mobile workshop
ZJ 5904	Converted to recovery vehicle by CIE in 1971	ZS 8621	Converted to Playbus. Originally registered YOX130K.
ZU 5000	Spent 28 years as garden shed	177 IK	Daf engine fitted early 1980s.
ZO 6960	Sole survivor of a batch of 6 Airport buses	78 D140	Originally registered 42 RN 98
ZY 1715	Converted to 3ft gauge railway carriage 1971	85 D2412	Originally registered 48 AC 14
ILI 98	Originally registered 9579 F	78 D824	Originally registered POI 2193
71 AHI	Originally registered UKG 274	643 MIP	Originally registered GRN 896W

Cobham Bus Museum

Contact address: Redhill Road, Cobham, Surrey, KT11 1EF
Phone: 01932 868665
Web site: www.lbpt.org
E-mail: info@lbpt.org
Affiliation: AIM, NARTM
Brief description: This well-established museum is home to the London Bus Preservation Trust. It was formed by a small group of enthusiasts in 1966. The collection has steadily grown over the years and now over 30 preserved buses, coaches and service vehicles are located at Cobham.
Events planned: 1 April 2007 — Annual Open Day, for other events please see the enthusiast press for details.
Opening days/times: Open days as advertised.
Viewing possible at weekends 11.00 to 17.00 but please telephone in advance to confirm.
Directions by car: From M25 junction 10 take A3 north and turn left on to A245. Museum is 1 mile on left.
Directions by public transport: Museum bus service from Weybridge station on main events. Network of special services on annual open day. Infrequent bus service at other times to Brooklands Road/Byfleet.
Charges: £5 but higher charges on Annual Open Days.
Facilities: B B(e) G P R(limited) S T

Registration	Date	Chassis	Body	New to	Fleet No	Status
XO 1048	1923	AEC 405 (NS)	(chassis only)	London General Omnibus Co	NS174	RP
XX 9591	1925	Dennis 4 ton	Dodson O24/24RO	Dominion Omnibus Co		R
UU 6646	1929	AEC Regal 662	LGOC B30R	London General Omnibus Co	T31	R
GJ 2098	1930	AEC Regent 661	Thomas Tilling H27/25RO	Thomas Tilling	ST922	R
GN 8242	1931	AEC Regal 662	Weymann B30F	Queen Line Coaches of London	T357	A
GO 5170	1931	AEC Renown 664	LGOC B35F	London General Omnibus Co	LT1059	A
AXM 693	1934	AEC Regent 661	LPTB H30/26R	London Transport	STL441	RP
CGJ 188	1935	AEC Q O762	Birmingham RC&W B35C	LPTB	Q83	R
CXX 171	1936	AEC Regal O662	Weymann C30F	LPTB	T448	RP
DLU 92	1937	AEC Regent O661	LPTB H30/26R	LPTB	STL2093	A
EGO 426	1937	AEC Regent O661	LPTB H30/26R	LPTB	STL2377	R
ELP 228	1938	AEC Regal O662	LPTB C30F	LPTB	T504	R
HGC 130	1945	Guy Arab II	Park Royal UH30/26R	LPTB	G351	R
HLX 410	1948	AEC Regent III O961 RT	Weymann H30/26R	London Transport	RT593	R
JXC 288	1949	Leyland Tiger PS1	Mann Egerton B30F	London Transport	TD95	R
KGK 803	1949	Leyland Titan 7RT	Park Royal H30/26R	London Transport	RTL139	R
KGU 142	1949	AEC Regent III O961 RT	(chassis only)	London Transport	RT2213	R
MYA 590	1949	Leyland Comet CPO1	Harrington C29F	Scarlet Pimpernel of Minehead		R
LUC 210	1951	AEC Regal IV 9821LT RF	Metro Cammell DP35F	London Transport	RF10	RP
LYR 826	1952	AEC Regent III O961 RT	Park Royal H30/26R	London Transport	RT2775	RP
LYR 910	1952	AEC Regent III O961 RT	Park Royal H30/26R	London Transport	RT3491	R
MLL 740	1953	AEC Regal IV 9822E	Park Royal RC37C	British European Airways		R
MXX 334	1953	Guy Special NLLVP	ECW B26F	London Transport	GS34	R
NLE 672	1953	AEC Regal IV 9821LT RF	Metro Cammell B41F	London Transport	RF672	R
CDX 516	1954	AEC Regent III 9613E	Park Royal H30/26R	Ipswich Corporation	16	R
SLT 58	1958	Leyland Routemaster	Weymann H34/30R	London Transport	RML3	R
461 CLT	1962	AEC Routemaster	Park Royal H32/25RD	London Transport	RMC1461	R
EGN 369J	1971	AEC Swift 4MP2R	Park Royal B33D	London Transport	SMS369	R
JPA 190K	1972	AEC Reliance 6U2R	Park Royal DP45F	London Country Bus Services	RP90	R
OJD 172R	1976	Leyland Fleetline FE30GR	(chassis only)	London Transport	DMS2172	R
WYW 6T	1979	MCW Metrobus DR101/8	MCW H43/28D	London Transport	M6	R

Note: Please be aware that vehicles on display can vary from time to time as not all museums display their entire 'fleet'. Visitors wishing to see a particular vehicle should make enquiries prior to their visit.

Notes:

XX 9591	Restored as London General Omnibus Co D142	MYA 590	Converted from petrol to diesel in 1966
GJ 2098	On loan to BMMO during World War 2	JXC 288	Toured Europe and USSR 1963-1967
CXX 171	Used as an ambulance during World War 2	LYR 910	Fitted with AEC 11.3 litre engine in 1998
DLU 92	Original metal-framed Park Royal body replaced in 1949	LYR 826	Toured USA and Canada when new
ELP 228	Used as an ambulance during World War 2	SLT 58	Prototype Leyland Routemaster; renumbered RM3 in 1961
HGC 130	Only remaining example of a London utility bus	OJD 172R	Shortened chassis only

Coventry Transport Museum

Contact address: Coventry Transport Museum, Millenium Place, Hales Street, Coventry CV1 1PN
Phone: 024 7623 4270
Fax: 024 7623 4284
E-mail: enquiries@transport-museum.com
Brief Description: The museum has over 250 cars and commercial vehicles, over 100 motorcycles and around 300 bicycles. Various tableaux chart the development of the motor vehicle from the early years and Coventry's contribution to this can be seen in the many marques on display. Other exhibits include the Thrust 2 and Thrust SSC land speed record car, several thousand die-cast models and a walk through audio visual display of the Coventry Blitz experience.
Opening days/times:
Open all year, 10.00-17.00 (last admission 016.30) except 24/25/26 December.
Directions by car: Coventry ring road circles the city centre and is encountered whichever direction you come from. Once on it follow the brown 'Transport Museum' signs and turn off at junction 1. Nearest car park (pay & display) is signposted and is in Tower Street at the back of the Museum.
Directions by public transport: The Museum is opposite Pool Meadow bus/coach station. Use Travel West Midlands bus 17 or 27 from Coventry railway station to Broadgate (5min walk downhill to Museum from Broadgate).
Facilities: R, T, L, D, S, G, F, Be, H
Note: The vehicles are frequently stored off site while new developments are built. Please phone to check which vehicles are on display

Registration	Date	Chassis	Body	New to	Fleet No	Status
SR 1266	1916	Maudslay Subsidy A	(chassis only)			A
EKV 966	1944	Daimler CWA6	Roe H31/25R	Coventry Corporation	366	R
JNB 416	1948	Maudslay Marathon II	Trans-United C33F	Hackett's of Manchester		R
KOM 150	1950	Daimler CVD6	Wilsdon -	Birmingham Post & Mail		R
SRB 424	1953	Daimler CD650	Willowbrook L27/28RD	Tailby & George ('Blue Bus Services') Willington		R
PBC 734	1954	Karrier Bantam Q25	Reading C14F	Mablethorpe Homes of Leicester		R
333 CRW	1963	Daimler CVG6	Metro Cammell H34/29R	Coventry Corporation	333	R
PDU 125M	1973	Daimler Fleetline CRG6LX	East Lancs O44/30F	Coventry Corporation	125	R
K232 DAC	1993	Peugeot J5	C11F	Peugeot UK		A

Notes:

SR 1266	To be restored as replica of 1921 Hickman bodied bus for Coventry Corporation
EKV 966	Rebodied 1951; converted to mobile repair workshop (O2) in 1960
KOM 150	Built as mobile print shop for the Birmingham Post and Mail and currently used as museum promotional vehicle
PBC 734	Welfare bus
PDU 125M	Originally H44/30F; converted to open-top in 1986
K232 DAC	Prototype electric minibus

Dover Transport Museum
Whitfield

Contact address: Willingdon Road, Port Zone White Cliffs Business Park, Whitfield, Dover, CT16 2HJ
Phone: 01304 822409
Affiliation: NARTM, Transport Trust, AIM, ASTRO
Brief description: The museum displays local transport and social history. Road vehicles of all types. A maritime room, railway room, bygone shops and a garage. Hundreds of transport models including a working model tramway.
Events planned: Please see the enthusiast press for details.
Opening days/times: All year round — Sundays 10.00 to 17.00 (except when Chrisatmas Day falls on a Sunday)
Easter to end September — Sundays and Bank Holidays 10.00 to 17.00; Wednesday,Thursdays and Fridays 14.00 to 17.00.
Last entry 45 minutes before closing
Open at other times for pre-arranged groups.
Directions by car: Approximately one mile from the A2 Whitfield roundabout on the Dover bypass.
Directions by public transport: Dover Priory station then bus to Old Park, Whitfield.
Charges: Adult £3, Senior Citizen £2.50, Child £1.50, Family £7.
Facilities: B(e) D E G P R T

Registration	Date	Chassis	Body	New to	Fleet No	Status
CC 9305	1930	Dennis G	Roberts T19	Llandudno UDC	4	R
569 KKK	1960	AEC Reliance 2MU3RA	Duple C41C	Ayers Coaches of Dover		R
WFN 912	1961	Ford 570E	Duple C41F	Seath Coaches		A
GJG 751D	1966	AEC Regent V 2D3RA	Park Royal O40/32F	East Kent Road Car Co		R
NPD 145L	1973	Leyland National	Leyland National B30D	London Country Bus Services	LNC45	A

Notes:
GJG 751D   Originally H40/32F; used as promotional vehicle
NPD 145L   Converted to rally control/hospitality unit.

East Anglia Transport Museum
Carlton Colville

Contact address: Chapel Road, Carlton Colville, Lowestoft, Suffolk, NR33 8BL
Phone: 01502 518459
Web site: www.eatm.org.uk
Affiliation: NARTM, London Trolleybus Preservation Society, Transport Trust.
Brief description: A working transport museum on a fiver-acre site, first opened in 1972 and run entirely by volunteers. Tram and trolleybus services operate regularly within a developing street scene and the tramway has a woodland section. There is also a narrow-gauge railway. A wide variety of other vehicles on display and sometimes operated includes buses, lorries, steam rollers, battery-electrics, tower wagons and a London taxi. The museum is a registered charity.
Events planned:
28/29 April 2007 — Steam & Vintage Weekend. Also unveiling of Portsmouth trolleybus No 313
7/8 July 2007 — Eastern Coach Works Event 2007.
8/9 September 2007 — Trolleybus Weekend. Free bus service to Lowestoft and Beccles.

Note: Please be aware that vehicles on display can vary from time to time as not all museums display their entire 'fleet'. Visitors wishing to see a particular vehicle should make enquiries prior to their visit.

Opening days/times: April to end of September:
Sundays and Bank Holidays — 11.00 to 17.00;
Thursdays and Saturdays (June to Sept) — 14.00 to 17.00;
Daily, except Mondays (late July and Aug) — 14.00 to 17.00.
Last entry 1 hour before closing.
Directions by car: Situated just off the A1384. Follow the brown signs from the A12, A146 and A1117. Free car parking.
Directions by public transport:
Monday to Saturday: First Eastern Counties bus 111 or 112 from Lowestoft bus station to Carlton Colville Church.
X2 (Monday-Saturday), X71 (Sundays) Lowestoft to Norwich, to Carlton Crown PH then 5min walk.
By train to Oulton Broad South then 35min walk or bus 606 or 607.
Bus service 606 or 607 links Oulton Broad North and Oulton Broad South railway stations with the museum (Chapel Road bus stop daily), also gives a direct link to Great Yarmouth (Mondays to Saturdays only). For more details of this or other public transport information please ring the travel line on 08459 583358.
Charges: £6 adults, £5 Senior Citizens, £4.50 children. Admission includes free rides within the museum.
Facilities: B(e) D E F G H P R S T
Other information: Regular tram, train and trolleybus rides

Registration	Date	Chassis	Body	New to	Fleet No	Status
AH 79505+	1926	Garrett O type	Strachan & Brown B26D	NESA Copenhagen	5	RP
KW 1961	1927	Leyland Lion PLSC3	Leyland B35F	Blythe & Berwick of Bradford		A
WX 3567	1930	Gilford 168SD	Fielding & Bottomley C26D	Oade of Heckmondwike		RP
ALJ 986+	1935	Sunbeam MS2	Park Royal O40/29R	Bournemouth Corporation	202	R
CUL 260+	1936	AEC 664T	Metro Cammell H40/30R	London Transport	260	R
EXV 201+	1938	Leyland LPTB70	Leyland H40/30R	London Transport	1201	R
FXH 521+	1940	Metro Cammell	Metro Cammell H40/30R	London Transport	1521	R
GBJ 192	1947	AEC Regent II O661	ECW H30/26R	Lowestoft Corporation	21	R
BDY 809+	1948	Sunbeam W	Weymann H30/26R	Hastings Tramways Co	34	RP
KAH 408	1948	Bristol L4G	ECW B35R	Eastern Counties Omnibus Co	LL108	A
note d+	1948	Berna	Hess B37D	Biel (Switzerland)	39	R
LLU 829	1950	Leyland Titan 7RT	Park Royal H30/26R	London Transport	RTL1050	R
NBB 628+	1950	BUT 9641T	Metro Cammell H40/30R	Newcastle Corporation	628	A
ERV 938+	1951	BUT 9611T	Burlingham H28/26R	Portsmouth Corporation	313	R
SG 2030+	1952	Henschel ,HIII/s	Uerdingen B32T	Solingen (Germany)	1	R
DRC 224+	1953	Sunbeam F4	Willowbrook H32/28R	Derby Corporation	224	R
LCD 52+	1953	BUT 9611T	Weymann H30/26R	Brighton Corporation	52	R
ONE 744+	1956	BUT 9612T	Burlingham H33/26R	Manchester Corporation	1344	R
YTE 826+	1956	BUT 9612T	Bond H32/28R	Ashton-under-Lyne Corporation	87	A
YLJ 286+	1959	Sunbeam MF2B	Weymann H35/28D	Bournemouth Corporation	286	R
557 BNG	1962	Bristol Lodekka FL6G	ECW H37/33RD	Eastern Counties Omnibus Co	LFL57	R
AEX 85B	1964	AEC Reliance 2MU3RA	Pennine B39F	Great Yarmouth Corporation	85	RP
YRT 898H	1969	AEC Swift 2MP2R	ECW B45D	Lowestoft Corporation	4	R
OCK 985K	1972	Bristol VRTSL6LX	ECW H39/31F	Ribble Motor Services	1985	R
D103 DAJ	1986	Mercedes L608D	Reeve Burgess B20F	Hartlepool Transport	13	R

+ Trolleybus

Notes:

AH 79505	Danish registration
ALJ 986	Converted to open top 1958
note d	Swiss Trolleybus; unregistered
SG 2030	German registration
LCD 52	Built 1950. First used 1953; Preserved in colours of subsequent operator Maidstone Corporation
OCK 985K	Acquired by Eastern Counties Omnibus Co (VR385) in 1985
D103 DAJ	Restored in Lincolnshire Road Car (Roadrunner) livery

Grampian Transport Museum
Alford

Contact address: Alford, Aberdeenshire AB33 8AE
Phone: 01975 562292
Fax: 01975 562180
E-mail: info@g-t-m.freeserve.co.uk
Web site: www.gtm.org.uk
Brief description: Dramatic displays, working exhibits and video presentations trace the history of travel and transport.
Opening days/times: April to October inclusive, 10.00 to 17.00 (10.00-16.00 in October).
Directions by car: On A944 west from Aberdeen (27 miles).
Directions by public transport: Stagecoach bus services from Aberdeen.
Charges: £5 Adults, £4.40 Senior Citizens, £2.40 Children, £13.Family.
Facilities: A B(e) C D E FG H L M P R S T

Registration	Date	Chassis	Body	New to	Fleet No	Status
JFM 238D	1966	Bristol Lodekka FS6G	ECW H33/27RD	Crosville Motor Services	DFG238	R
NRG 154M	1974	Leyland Atlantean AN68/1R	Alexander H45/29D	Grampian Regional Transport	154	R

Notes:
JFM 238D	Last rear-entrance Bristol ever built
NRG 154M	Used as a video theatre

Imperial War Museum
London

Contact address: Lambeth Road, London SE1 6HZ
Phone:
020 7416 5320
0891 600140 (Recorded information)
E-mail: website: www.iwm.org.uk
Brief description: Revel in the history of the nation, through the world wars and much more besides. Regular exhibitions and displays of considerable educational value. The one bus in the collection fills a significant gap in transport history and is on display in museum atrium.
Opening days/times: Daily 10.00 to 18.00 (closed 24, 25 and 26 December)
Directions by car: South of Waterloo Station, close to the Elephant & Castle. Parking difficult but Coach Park at Vauxhall Bridge and disabled parking by prior arrangement only — phone 020 7416 5397.
Directions by public transport:
Underground to Lambeth North, Waterloo or Elephant & Castle.
Rail to Waterloo.
Bus routes 1, 3, 12, 53, 59, 68, 148, 155, 159, 168, 171, 172, 176, 188, 344, 453, 468 and C10 with 45, 63, 100 nearby.
Charges: Free entry to main displays.
Facilities: A C D G H R T

Registration	Date	Chassis	Body	New to	Fleet No	Status
LN 4743	1911	LGOC B	LGOC O18/16RO	London General Omnibus Co	B43	R

Notes:
LN 4743	Named 'Ole Bill' after wartime cartoon character

Note: Please be aware that vehicles on display can vary from time to time as not all museums display their entire 'fleet'. Visitors wishing to see a particular vehicle should make enquiries prior to their visit.

Ipswich Transport Museum

Contact address: Old Trolleybus Depot, Cobham Road, Ipswich IP3 9JD
Phone: 01473 715666
E-mail: www.ipswichtransportmuseum.co.uk.html
Affiliation: NARTM, ASTRO, SEMS, AFSM
Brief description: The collection includes most forms of road transport from the last 200 years, including bicycles, horse-drawn vehicles, trucks and service vehicles. There are displays of vehicles and other products of Ipswich engineering companies including six mobile cranes.
Events planned: Please see enthusiast press for details
Opening days/times: April to November: Sundays and Bank Holidays 11.00 to 16.00. School holidays, Monday to Friday 13.00 to 16.00
Directions by car: From A12/A14 junction with A1189 (Nacton and Ipswich East) head towards Ipswich on Nacton Road. Turn right into Lindburgh Road. Museum is on left in Cobham Road.
Directions by public transport: By train to Ipswich. Take any bus to Tower Ramparts bus station. Then Ipswich Buses route 6.
Charges: Adult £3.50, Child £2.50, Concessions £2.50, Family £9.50. Special event rates may apply
Facilities: A B(e) D G P R T, picnic area

Registration	Date	Chassis	Body	New to	Fleet No	Status
DX 3988+	1923	Railless	Short B30D	Ipswich Corporation	2	R
DX 5610+	1926	Ransomes Sims & Jefferies D	Ransomes Sims & Jefferies B31D	Ipswich Corporation	9	A
DX 5629+	1926	Garrett O type	Strachan & Brown B31D	Ipswich Corporation	26	A
DX 6591	1927	Tilling Stevens B9B	Eastern Counties B36R	Eastern Counties Road Car Co	78	A
VF 2788	1928	ADC 425A	Eastern Counties B36R	United Automobile Services	J379	A
DX 7812	1929	Tilling Stevens B10A2	(chassis only)	Eastern Counties Road Car Co	116	R
VF 8157	1930	Chevrolet LQ	Bush & Twiddy C14D	Final of Hockwold	4	R
WV 1209	1932	Bedford WLB	Waveney B20F	Alexander of Devizes		A
PV 817+	1933	Ransomes Sims & Jefferies	Ransomes Sims & Jefferies H24/24R	Ipswich Corporation	46	A
CVF 874	1939	Bristol L5G	ECW B35R	Eastern Counties Omnibus Co	LL574	A
CAH 923	1940	Dennis Ace	ECW B20F	Eastern Counties Omnibus Co	D23	A
PV 8270+	1948	Karrier W	Park Royal H30/26R	Ipswich Corporation	105	RP
KAH 407	1949	Bristol L4G	ECW B35R	Eastern Counties Omnibus Co	LL407	R
KNG 374	1949	Bristol K6B	ECW L27/28R	Eastern Counties Omnibus Co	LK374	RP
PV 9371	1949	Bedford OB	Duple C27F	Mulleys Motorways	26	R
ADX 1	1950	AEC Regent III 9612E	Park Royal H30/26R	Ipswich Corporation	1	R
ADX 196+	1950	Sunbeam F4	Park Royal H30/26R	Ipswich Corporation	126	R
MAH 744	1951	Bristol LSX4G	ECW B42F	Eastern Counties Omnibus Co	LL744	R
BPV 9	1953	AEC Regal IV 9822E	Park Royal B42D	Ipswich Corporation	9	A
ADX 63B	1964	AEC Regent V 2D2RA	Massey H37/28R	Ipswich Corporation	63	R
APW 829B	1964	Bristol MW6G	ECW C39F	Eastern Counties Omnibus Co	LS829	R
GNG 125C	1965	Bristol Lodekka FS5G	ECW H33/27RD	Eastern Counties Omnibus Co	LFS125	RP
DPV 68D	1966	AEC Regent V 2D2RA	East Lancs Neepsend H37/28R	Ipswich Corporation	68	A
JRT 82K	1971	AEC Swift 2MP2R	Willowbrook B40D	Ipswich Corporation	82	R
MRT 6P	1976	Leyland Atlantean AN68/1R	Roe H43/29D	Ipswich Borough Transport	6	R
XNG 770S	1978	Leyland National 11351/1R	Leyland National B53F	Eastern Counties Omnibus Co	LN770	A

+ Trolleybus

Notes:

DX 3988	Believed the oldest trolleybus on display in the world	PV 817	First Ipswich double-decker
DX 5610	Changed from solid to pneumatic tyres in 1930	CVF 874	Originally numbered LL74
DX 6591	New with charabanc body; rebuilt in 1934	CAH 923	Originally fitted with Gardner 4LK engine
VF 2788	Original United body replaced in 1934	PV 8270	Originally fitted with wooden seats
DX 7812	Rebodied twice while with Eastern Counties	KNG 374	Engine changed Gardner 5LW by Eastern Counties
VF 8157	Body swapped with VF 9126; acquired by	ADX 1	Ipswich Corporation's first motor bus
	Mulleys Motorways of Ixworth in 1940	MAH 744	Bristol LS prototype

Right: Routemaster RM1 (SLT 56) is owned by London's Transport Museum and often comes out to perform at rallies. It is seen on 28 August 2006 about to take visitors to Cobham Bus Museum from a small display area carved out of the once-massive Brooklands site. *Matthew Wharmby*

Below: TD95 (JXC 288) dates from 1949 and is now owned by Cobham Bus Museum. On 16 April 2006 it made a very rare appearance in service on a running day held in the Hackney and Clapton areas, as part of which former London Transport routes and workings were re-created. *Matthew Wharmby*

Isle of Wight Bus Museum
Newport (IoW)

Contact address: Seaclose Quay, Newport, Isle of Wight, PO30 2EF
Phone: 01983 533352
Affiliation: NARTM
Brief description: The collection ranges from a 1927 Daimler CK to a 1979 Ford R-series. Many of the vehicles are of Southern Vectis origin.
Events planned: 15th October 2006 — Running day.
Opening days/times: 8-23 April: daily 10.30-16.00 then Tuesdays only until 23 May;
28 May-28 September: Tuesdays, Wednesdays, Thursdays and Sundays 10.30-16.00
27 May-4 June and 22 July-3 September: daily 10.30 to 16.00
October: Sundays 10.30-16.00
Directions by car: Bus museum is adjacent to Boat Museum (both signposted) off Fairlee Road through Sea Close Park to Quay past Travel Inn.
Directions by public transport: Bus to Newport bus station. Walk 12min to north of town.
Charges: £3 Adult, £2.50 Senior Citizen, £1.50 child.
Facilities: B(e) D G S
Other information: Car parking nearby. Refreshments and toilets at adjacent Boat Museum.
Some vehicles are stored away from the museum. Please enquire for details.

Registration	Date	Chassis	Body	New to	Fleet No	Status
DL 5084	1927	Daimler CK	Dodson B26R	Dodson Bros ('Vectis')	11	A
NG 1109	1931	Reo Pullman	Taylor Ch26D	Reynolds of Overstrand		R
JT 8077	1937	Bedford WTB	Duple C25F	South Dorset Coaches		R
DDL 50	1940	Bristol K5G	ECW O30/26R	Southern Vectis Omnibus Co	703	R
EDL 657	1947	Bristol K5G	ECW L27/28R	Southern Vectis Omnibus Co	721	RP
FDL 676	1949	Bedford OB	Duple C29F	Southern Vectis Omnibus Co	216	R
GDL 764	1950	Leyland Titan PD2/1A	Leyland L27/26R	Seaview Services		R
ODL 400	1957	Bedford SBG	Duple C41F	Moss Motor Tours of Sandown		RP
PDL 515	1958	Bristol MW6G	ECW C39F	Southern Vectis Omnibus Co	315	RP
PDL 519	1958	Bristol Lodekka LD6G	ECW CO33/27R	Southern Vectis Omnibus Co	559	R
VJW 882	1958	Commer Avenger TS3	Duple C37F	Don Everall of Wolverhampton		R
SDL 268	1959	Bristol Lodekka LD6G	ECW H33/27R	Southern Vectis Omnibus Co	563	R
ADL 459B	1964	Bedford SB3	Duple C41F	Paul's Tours of Ryde	9	RP
CDL 479C	1965	Bristol Lodekka FLF6G	ECW H38/32F	Southern Vectis Omnibus Co	611	R
FDL 927D	1966	Bristol MW6G	ECW B43F	Southern Vectis Omnibus Co	806	R
KDL 885F	1968	Bristol RESH6G	Duple C45F	Southern Vectis Omnibus Co	301	R
SDL 638J	1971	Bristol VRTSL6LX	ECW H39/31F	Southern Vectis Omnibus Co	628	R
TDL 564K	1971	Bristol RELL6G	ECW OB53F	Southern Vectis Omnibus Co	864	R
VDL 264K	1972	Bedford YRQ	Plaxton B47F	Seaview Services		R
NDL 637M	1973	Bristol VRTSL6LX	ECW H43/31F	Southern Vectis Omnibus Co	637	R
MDL 880R	1976	Leyland National 11351A/1R	Leyland National B52F	Southern Vectis Omnibus Co	880	A
YDL 135T	1979	Ford R1014	Duple B47F	Isle of Wight County Council	5809	A
A700 DDL	1984	Leyland Olympian ONLXB/1R	ECW H45/32F	Southern Vectis Omnibus Co	700	A

Notes:

DDL 50	Converted to open-top 1959, became tree-lopper in 1969
PDL 519	Originally H33/27R

Keighley Bus Museum
Keighley

Contact address: 47 Brantfell Drive, Burnley, Lancs BB12 8AW
Phone: 01282 413179
Web site: www.kbmt.org.uk
Affiliation: AIM, FBHVC, NARTM, Y&HMC
Brief description: A collection of 50 buses, coaches and ancillary vehicles. Some 50% are owned by the Trust and others by private individuals. The Trust aims to establish a permanent home for the collection in central Keighley.
Events planned:
2007 events not yet finalised. Please see enthusiast press.
Opening days/times: Tuesday evenings 19.00-22.00, and most Saturdays and Sundays (please check in advance) at Riverside, off Dalton Lane adjacent to railway station.
Car parking: Dalton Lane.
Directions by public transport: Keighley (5min from main line station) and 10min walk from bus station. Frequent buses from Keighley (zone routes 708/711, alight at Dalton Mills).
Charges: Special events: £2 Adult, £1 concession. Otherwise free but donations welcome.
Facilities: B(e) P T

Registration	Date	Chassis	Body	New to	Fleet No	Status
WT 7101+	1924	Straker Clough	Brush H50R	Keighley Corporation Tramways	5	R
KW 2260	1927	Leyland Lion PLSC3	Leyland B35R	Bradford Corporation	325	A
KY 9106	1931	AEC Regent I O661	MCW	Bradford Corporation	046	A
TF 6860	1931	Leyland Lion LT3	Leyland B36R	Rawtenstall Corporation	61	RP
ANW 682	1934	AEC Regent 661	Roe H30/26R	Leeds City Transport	139	R
CWX 671	1938	Bristol K5G	Roe L27/28R	Keighley West Yorkshire Services	KDG26	R
FWX 914+	1948	Sunbeam F4	East Lancs H37/29F	Mexborough & Swinton Traction Co		R
MNW 86	1948	Leyland Tiger PS1	Roe B36R	Leeds City Transport	28	R
LFM 767	1950	Bristol LL6B	ECW B39R	Crosville Motor Services	SLB186	RP
JWU 886	1951	Bristol LL5G	ECW B39R	West Yorkshire Road Car Co	SGL16	R
LYR 533	1951	AEC Regent III O961 RT	Park Royal H30/26R	London Transport	RT3314	R
MTE 635	1951	AEC Regent III 6812A	Weymann H33/26R	Morecambe & Heysham Corporation	73	RP
UUA 214	1955	Leyland Titan PD2/11	Roe H33/25R	Leeds City Transport	214	RP
GJX 331	1956	Daimler CVG6	Roe H37/26R	Halifax Corporation	119	R
VTU 76	1956	Daimler CVG6	Northern Counties H35/23C	SHMD Board	76	R
XLG 477	1956	Atkinson Alpha PL745H	Northern Counties B34C	SHMD Board	77	A
7514 UA	1959	Daimler CVG6-30	Roe H38/32R	Leeds City Transport	514	A
XYJ 418	1961	AEC Routemaster	Park Royal H36/28R	London Transport	RM736	R
PJX 232	1962	Leyland Leopard L1	Weymann B44F	Halifax Joint Omnibus Committee	232	R
WJY 758	1962	Leyland Atlantean	MCW O44/31F	Plymouth Corporation	158	R
WBR 246	1963	Atkinson Alpha PM746HL	Marshall B45D	Sunderland Corporation	46	RP
6203 KW	1964	AEC Regent V 2D3RA	Metro Cammell H40/30F	Bradford Corporation	203	A
6204 KW	1964	AEC Regent V 2D3RA	Metro Cammell H40/30F	Bradford Corporation	204	A
6220 KW	1964	AEC Regent V 2D3RA	MCW H40/30F	Bradford Corporation	220	R
CUB 331C	1965	Leyland Atlantean PDR1/1	MCW H41/29F	Leeds City Transport	331	RP
ENW 980D	1966	AEC Regent V 2D2RA	Roe H39/31R	Leeds City Transport	980	RP
HNW 131D	1966	Daimler Fleetline CRG6LX	Roe H45/33F	Leeds City Transport	131	R
KVH 473E	1966	Daimler Fleetline CRG6LX	Roe H44/31F	Huddersfield Corporation	473	R
KWT 642D	1966	Bristol Lodekka FS6B	ECW H33/27RD	West Yorkshire Road Car Co	DX210	R
NWU 265D	1966	Bristol Lodekka FS6B	ECW H33/27RD	York - West Yorkshire	YDX221	R
TWW 766F	1967	Bristol RELH6G	ECW C47F	West Yorkshire Road Car Co	CRG6	R
YLG 717F	1967	Bristol RESL6G	Northern Counties B43F	SHMD Board	117	A
LAK 309G	1969	Leyland Titan PD3A/12	Alexander H41/29F	Bradford Corporation	309	R
LAK 313G	1969	Leyland Titan PD3A/12	Alexander H41/29F	Bradford Corporation	313	RP

Note: Please be aware that vehicles on display can vary from time to time as not all museums display their entire 'fleet'. Visitors wishing to see a particular vehicle should make enquiries prior to their visit.

Registration	Date	Chassis	Body	New to	Fleet No	Status
TKU 467K	1971	Leyland Atlantean PDR2/1	Alexander H47/29D	Bradford Corporation	467	RP
WFM 801K	1972	Leyland National 1151/2R/0403	Leyland National B44D	Crosville Motor Services	SNL801	R
XAK 355L	1972	Daimler Fleetline CRL6	Alexander H43/31F	Bradford Corporation	355	RP
GWY 690N	1975	Leyland Leopard PSU4B/4R	Plaxton C45F	West Yorkshire PTE	64	A
OJD 192R	1977	Daimler Fleetline	MCW H45/32F	London Transport	DMS2192	A
DNW 840T	1978	Leyland National 10351B/1R	Leyland National B44F	West Yorkshire Road Car	1002	R
JUM 505V	1980	MCW Metrobus	MCW H43/30F	West Yorkshire PTE	7505	A
NKU 245X	1981	Leyland National 2	Leyland National B52F	Yorkshire Traction	245	RP
D275 OOJ	1987	Freight Rover Sherpa	Carlyle B20F	Carlyle Works Demonstrator		RP
+ Trolleybus						

Notes:

WT 7101	Solid tyres		XYJ 418	Original registration WLT736
KY 9106	Former double-decker converted to gritter. On loan from Bradford Museums Service		WJY 758	Converted to open-top in 1975. Restored as Keighley Corporation Tramways 59
TF 6860	Used as a tow bus and snow plough 1950-63		NWU 265D	Renumbered 3821 in 1971
CWX 671	Rebodied 1950		KWT 642D	Renumbered 1810 in 1971
FWX 914	Originally single-deck. Rebodied as double-decker by Bradford Corporation 1963		TWW 766F	Renumbered 1019 in 1971; restored in later guise as 2508
JWU 886	Single-block experimental Gardner engine		WFM 801K	Second production Leyland National; operated single-door with Greater Manchester Buses (South)
UUA 214	Leeds City Transport driver trainer 1972-78			

Lincolnshire Road Transport Museum
North Hykeham

Contact address: Whisby Road, North Hykeham, Lincoln LN6 3QT
Phone: 01522 689497
Web site: www.lvvs.org.uk
Affiliation: NARTM
Brief description: An impressive collection of over 50 vehicles including classic cars, commercials, buses and motor cycles, mostly with Lincolnshire connections. Sixty years of road transport history is represented in the museum hall, which was built in 1993. An extension to the hall is planned.
Events planned: Please see enthusiast press and web site.
8 April 2007 — Easter Sunday open day
4 November 2007 — Autumn open day
Opening days/times:
May to October: Monday to Friday 12.00 to 16.00; Sunday 10.00 to 16.00;
November to April: Sunday 13.00 to 16.00. Other times by appointment.
Directions by car: Just off A46 Lincoln by-pass on Whisby Road, which links A46 to B1190.
Directions by public transport:
1 mile from North Hykeham railway station.
Whisby Road is just off Doddington Road, served by several bus routes from city centre.
Charges: £2 adult. Accompanied children free. Other charges may apply at special events — please see web site.
Facilities: A B(e) D P T
Other information: Refreshments available on open days. Please check beforehand if you wish to se aparticular vehicle as a few are rotated with other accommodation.

Registration	Date	Chassis	Body	New to	Fleet No	Status
KW 474	1927	Leyland Lion PLSC1	Leyland B31F	Blythe & Berwick of Bradford		R
TE 8318	1929	Chevrolet LQ	Spicer C14D	Jardine of Morcambe		R
VL 1263	1929	Leyland Lion LT1	Applewhite B32R	Lincoln Corporation	5	R
WH 1553	1929	Leyland Titan TD1	Leyland L27/24RO	Bolton Corporation	54	R
KW 7604	1930	Leyland Badger TA4	Plaxton B20F	Bradford Education Committee	023	R

Registration	Date	Chassis	Body	New to	Fleet No	Status
TF 818	1930	Leyland Lion LT1	Roe B30F	Lancashire United Transport	202	R
FW 5698	1935	Leyland Tiger TS7	Burlingham B35F	Lincolnshire Road Car Co	1411	R
RC 2721	1935	SOS DON	Brush B—F	Trent Motor Traction Co	321	R
FHN 833	1940	Bristol L5G	ECW B35F	United Automobile Services	BG147	RP
BFE 419	1941	Leyland Titan TD7	Roe H30/26R	Lincoln Corporation	64	R
VV 8934	1945	Daimler CWD6	Duple UH30/26R	Northampton Corporation	129	RP
AHE 163	1946	Leyland Titan PD1	Roe H31/25R	Yorkshire Traction	726	RP
DBE 187	1946	Bristol K6A	ECW H30/26R	Lincolnshire Road Car Co	2115	R
GUF 727	1947	Leyland Tiger PS1/1	ECW B32R	Southdown Motor Services	677	R
DFE 383	1948	Guy Arab III	Guy H30/26R	Lincoln Corporation	23	R
HPW 133	1949	Bristol K5G	ECW H30/26R	Eastern Counties Omnibus Co	LKH133	R
OHK 432	1949	Daimler CVD6	Roberts H30/26R	Colchester Corporation	4	R
ONO 59	1949	Bristol K5G	ECW L-/-R	Eastern National Omnibus Co	4038	R
FFU 860	1950	AEC Regal III 9621E	Willowbrook DP35F	Enterprise of Scunthorpe	60	R
FDO 573	1953	AEC Regent III 9613E	Willowbrook H32/28RD	J W Camplin & Sons ('Holme Delight') of Donington		RP
OLD 714	1954	AEC Regent III O961 RT	Weymann H30/26R	London Transport	RT4494	R
LFW 326	1955	Bristol Lodekka LD6B	ECW H33/25RD	Lincolnshire Road Car Co	2318	R
OVL 465	1960	Bristol MW5G	ECW B45F	Lincolnshire Road Car Co	2245	R
RFE 416	1961	Leyland Titan PD2/41	Roe H33/28R	Lincoln Corporation	89	R
952 JUB	1964	AEC Regent V 2D2RA	Roe H39/31R	Leeds City Transport	952	RP
CVL 850D	1966	Bristol RELH6G	ECW C47F	Lincolnshire Road Car Co	1431	RP
EVL 549E	1967	Leyland Panther PSUR1/1R	Roe DP45F	Lincoln Corporation	41	RP
UVL 873M	1973	Bristol RELL6L	Alexander B48F	Lincoln Corporation	73	RP
NFW 36V	1980	Bristol VRT/LL3/6LXB	East Lancs H50/36F	Lincoln City Transport	36	A
PFE 542V	1980	Bristol VRTSL3/6LXB	ECW H43/31F	Lincolnshire Road Car Co	1958	R

Notes:

KW 474	Restored as Lincoln Corporation No 1
FW 5698	Originally fleet No 368. Rebodied in 1949
FHN 833	Originally fleet No BLO133
DBE 187	Originally fleet No 661. Rebuilt by ECW in mid 1950s.
DFE 383	Ruston Hornsby air-cooled engine
ONO 59	Renumbered 1427 in 1954 and 2255 in 1964; subsequently converted to caravan
FFU 860	Passed to Lincolnshire Road Car Co (860) in 1950
CVL 850D	Later renumbered 2231

London's Transport Museum
London

Contact address: 39 Wellington Street, London WC2E 7BB.

Phone: 020 7565 7299 — 24hr recorded information; 020 7379 6344 — Admin etc

Fax: 020 7565 7250

E-mail: resourcedesk@ltmuseum.co.uk

Web site: www.ltmuseum.co.uk

Affiliation: HRA, NARTM, TT

Brief description: The £20 million re-build and re-display project for London's Transport Museum in Covent Garden is fully underway. Over 400 objects have been moved to the Museum Depot in Acton since the Museum closed in September 2005. The new, transformed Museum will open in autumn 2007. The Museum's popular shop remains open throughout the refurbishment at Unit 26 Covent Garden Piazza; it will re-open in its new Museum site in April 2007.

Note: Please be aware that vehicles on display can vary from time to time as not all museums display their entire 'fleet'. Visitors wishing to see a particular vehicle should make enquiries prior to their visit.

Opening days/times: Closed until autumn 2007.
Access by public transport: Tube: Covent Garden, Holborn, Leicester Square stations
Main line: Charing Cross
Bus: to Strand or Aldwych
Facilities for the disabled: Full disabled access including toilets. Reduced admission for registered disabled and person accompanying them.

Registration	Date	Chassis	Body	New to	Fleet No	Status
note m	1829	Horse bus	LGOC	George Shillibeer		R
note n	1875	Horse bus	Thomas Tilling -24-	Thomas Tilling		R
LA 9928	1911	LGOC B	LGOC O18/16RO	London General Omnibus Co	B340	R
FJJ 774	1939	Leyland FEC	LPTB B34F	London Transport	TF77	R
737 DYE	1963	AEC Routemaster 2R2RH	Park Royal H36/28R	London Transport	RM1737	R
EGP 1J	1970	Daimler Fleetline CRG6LXB	Park Royal H44/24D	London Transport	DMS1	R

Notes:
note m   Unregistered reconstruction
note n   Unregistered; Knifeboard type

Manchester Museum of Transport
Cheetham

Contact address: Boyle Street, Cheetham, Manchester M8 8UW
Phone/Fax: 0161 205 2122
E-mail: emai@gmts.com
Web site: www.gmts.co.uk or www.manchester.bus.museum
Affiliation: NARTM
Brief description:
The museum houses over 70 buses and coaches from the Greater Manchester area, from an 1876 horse bus to a 1990 Metrolink tram. Travel back to a time of twopenny singles and coach trips to Blackpool. Extensive displays of photos, uniforms and models complement the vehicles, and visitors may enter many of the vehicles and view the museum's workshop.
Events planned:
24/25 March 2007 — Spring Transport Festival
22 April 2007 — London Bus Event
12/13 May 2007 — Simply Red Weekend
10 June 2007 — Morris Register Event
17 June 2007 — Accessible Transport Event
8 July 2007 — Book & Postcard Fair
29 July 2007 — Standard Car Club Event
2 September 2007 — Trans-Lancs Rally
8/9 September 2007 — Heritage Open Days Weekend
6/7 October 2007 — free bus service to Manchester Model Railway Exhibition
20/21 October 2007 — Leyland PD2/60 Event
1/2 December 2007 — Christmas Cracker
Opening days/times: Wednesdays, Saturdays, Sundays & Bank Holidays: 10.00-17.00 March to October, 10.00 to 16.00 November-February inclusive (please phone for Christmas/New Year opening)
Directions by car:
From M62/M60 junction 18, follow 'Castlefields' signs to Cheetham Hill; from City, follow A665 (Cheetham Hill Road) — Museum signposted.
Due to limited parking on special event days it is suggested to park at eithe MEN Arena, or any other central arew car park and travel on one of the free buses linking Victoria station with the museum
Directions by public transport:
Bus 135 or 59 to Queen's Road; Metrolink tram to Woodlands Road (10min walk)
Charges: £4 adult, £2 concession (5-15, over 60, students and unemployed), £9 family. Free under 5 and registered disabled. Season tickets available. School parties free
Facilities: B(e) C D F G H P R S T
Other information: Archives available for study by arrangement.

Registration	Date	Chassis	Body	New to	Fleet No	Status
note b	1876	Horse bus	Manchester Carriage Co O18/14RO	Manchester Carriage Co	2	R
DB 5070	1925	Tilling-Stevens TS6 Petrol Electric	Brush O54RO	North Western Road Car Co	170	R
CK 3825	1927	Leyland Lion PLSC1	Leyland B31F	Ribble Motor Services	295	R
VM 4439	1928	Leyland Tiger TS1	Metro Cammell/Crossley B—R	Manchester Corporation	138	A
VY 957	1929	Leyland Lion PLSC1	Ribble B32R	York Corporation	2	R
VR 5742	1930	Leyland Tiger TS2	Manchester Corporation Car Works B30R	Manchester Corporation	28	R
ANB 851	1934	Crossley Mancunian	Crossley/MCT H28/26R	Manchester Corporation	436	A
AXJ 857	1934	Leyland Titan TD3	(chassis only)	Manchester Corporation	526	R
JA 7585	1935	Leyland Tiger TS7	English Electric B35C	Stockport Corporation	185	A
RN 7824	1936	Leyland Cheetah LZ2	Brush C31F	Ribble Motor Services	1568	RP
EFJ 92	1938	Bedford WTB	Heaver C25F	Taylor of Exeter		RP
AJA 152	1939	Bristol K5G	Willowbrook L27/26R	North Western Road Car Co	432	R
BBA 560	1939	AEC Regent O661	Park Royal H26/22R	Salford Corporation	235	R
JP 4712	1940	Leyland Titan TD7	Leyland L24/24R	Wigan Corporation	70	RP
FTB 11	1941	Leyland Titan TD7	Northern Coachbuilders UL27/26R	Leigh Corporation	84	A
BJA 425	1946	Bristol L5G	Willowbrook B38R	North Western Road Car Co	270	R
HTB 656	1946	Leyland Tiger PS1	Roe B35R	Ramsbottom UDC	17	R
HTF 586	1947	Bedford OB	Scottish Motor Traction C29F	Warburton Bros of Bury		R
CDB 224	1948	Leyland Titan PD2/1	Leyland L27/26R	North Western Road Car Co	224	R
CWH 717	1948	Leyland Titan PD2/4	Leyland	Bolton Corporation	367	R
DBU 246	1948	Leyland Titan PD1/3	Roe H31/25R	Oldham Corporation	246	RP
JND 791	1948	Crossley DD42/8S	Crossley H32/26R	Manchester Corporation	2150	R
JNA 467	1949	Leyland Titan PD1/3	Metro Cammell H32/26R	Manchester Corporation	3166	RP
LMA 284	1949	Foden PVSC6	Lawton C35F	Coppenhall of Comberbach		R
BEN 177	1950	AEC Regent III 9613A	Weymann H30/26R	Bury Corporation	177	R
CWG 206	1950	Leyland Tiger PS1	Alexander C35F	W. Alexander & Sons	PA164	R
FBU 827	1950	Crossley DD42/8	Crossley H30/26R	Oldham Corporation	368	RP
LTC 774+	1950	Crossley Empire TDD42/2	Crossley H30/26R	Ashton-under-Lyne Corporation	80	RP
EDB 549	1951	Leyland Titan PD2/1	Leyland O30/20R	Stockport Corporation	295	R
EDB 562	1951	Leyland Titan PD2/1	Leyland H30/26R	Stockport Corporation	308	A
EDB 575	1951	Crossley DD42/7	Crossley H30/26R	Stockport Corporation	321	R
JND 646	1951	Leyland Titan PD2/3	Metro Cammell H32/26R	Manchester Corporation	3245	R
JVU 755+	1951	Crossley Dominion TDD64/1	Crossley H36/30R	Manchester Corporation	1250	R
NNB 125	1953	Leyland Royal Tiger PSU1/13	Northern Counties B41C	Manchester Corporation	25	R
UTC 672	1954	AEC Regent III 9613S	East Lancs L27/28RD	Bamber Bridge Motor Services	4	R
UMA 370	1955	Atkinson PD746	Northern Counties H35/24C	SHMD Board	70	R
JBN 153	1956	Leyland Titan PD2/13	Metro Cammell H34/28R	Bolton Corporation	77	R
NDK 980	1956	AEC Regent V D2RA6G	Weymann H33/28R	Rochdale Corporation	280	R
PND 460	1956	Leyland Titan PD2/12	Metro Cammell H36/28R	Manchester Corporation	3460	R
DJP 754	1957	Leyland Titan PD2/30	Northern Counties H33/28R	Wigan Corporation	115	R
NBU 494	1957	Leyland Titan PD2/20	Roe H31/29R	Oldham Corporation	394	R
116 JTD	1958	Guy Arab IV	Northern Counties H41/32R	Lancashire United Transport	21	R
122 JTD	1958	Guy Arab IV	Northern Counties H41/32R	Lancashire United Transport	27	R
SDK 442	1958	Leyland Worldmaster RT3/2	Plaxton C41F	Ellen Smith of Rochdale		RP
TNA 496	1958	Leyland Titan PD2/40	Burlingham H37/28R	Manchester Corporation	3496	R
TNA 520	1958	Leyland Titan PD2/34	Burlingham H37/28R	Manchester Corporation	3520	R
UNB 629	1960	Leyland Atlantean PDR1/1	Metro Cammell H45/33F	Manchester Corporation	3629	R
YDK 590	1960	AEC Reliance 2MU3RA	Harrington C37F	Yelloway Motor Services of Rochdale		R
HEK 705	1961	Leyland Titan PD3A/2	Massey H41/29F	Wigan Corporation	57	A
3655 NE	1962	Leyland Tiger Cub PSUC1/12	Park Royal DP38D	Manchester City Transport	55	A

Note: Please be aware that vehicles on display can vary from time to time as not all museums display their entire 'fleet'. Visitors wishing to see a particular vehicle should make enquiries prior to their visit.

Registration	Date	Chassis	Body	New to	Fleet No	Status
TRJ 112	1962	Daimler CVG6	Metro Cammell H37/28R	Salford City Transport	112	R
414 CLT	1963	AEC Routemaster 2R2RH	Park Royal H36/28R	London Transport	RM1414	R
4632 VM	1963	Daimler CVG6K	Metro Cammell H37/28R	Manchester Corporation	4632	R
REN 116	1963	Leyland Atlantean PDR1/1	Metro Cammell H41/33F	Bury Corporation	116	A
8860 VR	1964	AEC Regent V 2D3RA	East Lancs/Neepsend H41/32R	A. Mayne & Son of Manchester		R
BND 874C	1965	Leyland Panther Cub	Park Royal B43D	Manchester Corporation	74	R
DBA 214C	1965	Leyland Atlantean PDR1/1	Metro Cammell H43/33F	Salford City Transport	214	R
DDB 174C	1965	Daimler Fleetline CRG6LX	Alexander H44/31F	North Western Road Car Co	174	R
PTC 114C	1965	AEC Renown 3B3RA	East Lancs H41/31F	Leigh Corporation	15	R
PTE 944C	1965	Leyland Titan PD2/37	Roe H37/28F	Ashton-under-Lyne Corporation	44	R
FRJ 254D	1966	Leyland Titan PD2/40	Metro Cammell H36/28F	Salford City Transport	254	R
HVM 901F	1968	Leyland Atlantean PDR1/1	Park Royal H45/28D	Manchester City Transport	1001	R
KDB 408F	1968	Leyland Leopard PSU4/1R	East Lancs B43D	Stockport Corporation	408	RP
KJA 871F	1968	Leyland Titan PD3/14	East Lancs H38/32R	Stockport Corporation	71	R
MJA 891G	1969	Leyland Titan PD3/14	East Lancs H38/32R	Stockport Corporation	91	R
MJA 897G	1969	Leyland Titan PD3/14	East Lancs O38/32F	Stockport Corporation	97	R
TTD 386H	1969	Leyland Titan PD3/14	East Lancs H41/32F	RamsbottomU DC	11	R
SRJ 328H	1970	Leyland Atlantean PDR2/1	MCW H47/31D	SELNEC PTE	1205	RP
TXJ 507K	1972	Leyland National 1151/2R/0202	Leyland National B46D	SELNEC PTE	EX30	R
VNB 101L	1972	Leyland Atlantean AN68/1R	Park Royal H43/32F	SELNEC PTE	7001	R
XVU 352M	1974	Seddon Pennine IV-236	Pennine B19F	Greater Manchester PTE	1722	R
GNC 276N	1975	Seddon Lucas	Pennine B19F	Greater Manchester PTE	EX62	R
HVU 244N	1975	AEC Reliance 6U3ZR	Plaxton C49F	Yelloway Motor Services of Rochdale		R
XBU 17S	1978	Leyland Fleetline FE30AGR	Northern Counties H43/32F	Greater Manchester PTE	8017	A
ORJ 83W	1981	MCW Metrobus DR102/21	MCW H43/30F	Greater Manchester PTE	5083	A
A706 LNC	1984	Leyland Atlantean AN68D/1R	Northern Counties H43/32F	Greater Manchester PTE	8706	A
B65 PJA	1984	Leyland Olympian ONLXB/1R	Northern Counties H43/30F	Greater Manchester PTE	3065	A
C208 FVU	1986	MCW Metrobus DR132/8	Northern Counties CH43/29F	Greater Manchester PTE	5208	RP
C255 FRJ	1986	Leyland Olympian ONLXB/1R	Northern Counties CH43/26F	Greater Manchester PTE	3255	A
D63 NOF	1986	Freight Rover 400 Special	Carlyle B18F	Manchester Minibuses of Rochdale		A
D676 NNE	1987	MCW Metrorider MF151/3	MCW B23F	Greater Manchester Buses	1676	R
M939 XKA	1994	Mercedes Benz 609D	Mercedes/Devon Conversions	Greater Manchester Accessible of Rochdale		R

+ Trolleybus

Notes:

note b	Largest surviving horse bus.	TNA 520	Fully auto transmission when new and converted to semi-auto in 1963
DB 5070	Petrol Electric transmission		
CK 3825	Body rebuilt 1981	SDK 442	New body fitted 1970
VM 4439	Body new 1935	UNB 629	H43/34F when new. Reseated in 1954 using ex-trolleybus seats
VY 957	Body rebuilt 1983; restored to Ribble livery		
VR 5742	Rebodied 1937	414 CLT	Loaned to Manchester Corporation when new in February 1963
ANB 851	Rebodied 1938		
BBA 560	Training bus with dual controls 1948-70. Renumbered 98 in 1950	HVM 901F	First 'Mancunian' double-decker
		KJA 871F	Restored as GMPTE 5871
AJA 152	Rebodied 1951	MJA 897G	Originally H38/32F; converted to open-top in 1982
FTB 11	Originally L27/28R. Refurbished by Thurgood in the 1950s	MJA 891G	Last open-rear-platform double-decker delivered to a British operator
BJA 425	Originally numbered 125; rebodied 1958 with 1952 body	TTD 386H	Last half-cab double-decker delivered to a British operator
CWH 717	Originally H30/26R; converted to tower wagon 1963.	SRJ 328H	Mancunian style ordered originally by Salford City Transport
LMA 284	Body new 1954		
EDB 562	Used as training bus 1968-78	VNB 101L	First SELNEC Standard double-decker
EDB 549	Originally H30/26R. Converted to open top in 1968.	TXJ 507K	First production Leyland National
UMA 370	Only Atkinson double-decker bodied. Originally H35/25C	GNC 276N	Battery-powered
		M939 XKA	Wheelchair lift at rear
122 JTD	Gardner 6LX from new		

Midland Road Transport Group — Butterley

Contact address: 21 Ash Grove, Mastin Moor, Chesterfield S43 3AW
Phone: Midland Road Transport Group — 01246 473619
Midland Railway 01773 747674, Visitor Information Line (01773) 570140.
Brief Description: A large purpose-built museum building housing a collection of buses, lorries and fork lift trucks fully or partially restored. Situated at the Swanwick Junction site of the Midland Railway Centre. All vehicles are all privately-owned by individual preservaionists who co-operated together to provide finances to build the museum which was completed in 2004
Events planned:
8 July 2007 — 3rd Annual Road Transport Rally (date to be confirmed)
Opening days/times:
See Railways Restored for details
Directions by car: To Swanwick Junction.
From the north, M1 Jcn 28, follow A38 southbound to B600, turn left to Somercotes, right on to B6016 through Riddings. Follow signs to Codnor/Heanor and turn right onto Coach Road at the bottom of descent from Riddings. Half mile along this narrow lane, take right fork after speed bumps.
From the south, M1 Jcn 26, follow A610 northbound to Codnor, turn right and right again onto B6016 Alfreton/Somercotes. Travel along for three miles and turn left onto Coach Road at bottom of hill after wooded areas on B6016.
Directions by public transport: Trent Barton service H1 from Derby, Heanor or Alfreton. Half mile walk from end of Coach Road, ask for Riddings Dale
Facilities: R, S, T

Registration	Date	Chassis	Body	New to	Fleet No	Status
ESV 811	1947	AEC Regal III O963	Weymann B30D	Carris of Lisbon	141	R
HVO 937	1947	AEC Regent II O661	Weymann H30/26R	Mansfield District	126	R
KRR 255	1949	AEC Regal III 9621E	Weymann B35F	Mansfield District	9	R
NRA 78F	1968	Bedford TK	Reeves Burgess	Derbyshire County Council		RP
BNU 679G	1969	Bristol VRTSL6LX	ECW H43/32F	Midland General Omnibus Co		RP
PNU 114K	1971	Leyland Atlantean PDR1A/1	Northern Counties H44/28D	Chesterfield Corporation	114	RP
RCH 629L	1972	Bristol VRTSL6LX	ECW H43/34F	Trent Motor Traction Co	629	R
NNU 123M	1973	Daimler Fleetline CRL6-30	Roe H42/29D	Chesterfield Corporation	123	R
NNU 124M	1973	Daimler Fleetline CRL6-30	Roe H42/29D	Chesterfield Corporation	124	R
SHN 80L	1973	Bristol RELH6G	ECW DP49F	United Automobile Services	6080	R
UOA 322L	1973	Leyland National 1151/1R/0401	Leyland National B52F	Eastern National Omnibus Co	1702	RP
LRA 801P	1975	Bristol VRTSL3/501	ECW H43/34F	Midland General Omnibus Co	801	R

Notes:

ESV 811	Original Portugese registration II-14-49
NRA 78F	Library bus
UOA 322L	Originally registered WNO 551L
LRA 801P	Original Leyland 501 engine replaced by Gardner unit in 1980

Note: Please be aware that vehicles on display can vary from time to time as not all museums display their entire 'fleet'. Visitors wishing to see a particular vehicle should make enquiries prior to their visit.

Museum of Transport
Glasgow

Contact address: Kelvin Hall, 1 Bunhouse Road, Glasgow G3 8DP
Phone: 0141 287 2720 (school bookings on 0141 565 4112/3)
Fax: 0141 287 2692
Web site: www.glasgowmuseums.com
Affiliation: NARTM
Brief description: The museum displays many items of transport history dating from the 1860s.
Opening days/times: Monday to Thursday and Saturday, 10.00 to 17.00; Friday and Sunday 11.00 to 17.00 (closed 25/26, 31 December and 1/2 January)
Directions by car: From M8 junctions 17 or 19
Directions by public transport: Buses 9, 16, 18, 62, from City Centre (Dumbarton Road) to Kelvin Hall; Underground to Kelvin Hall; nearest main-line railway station is Partick.
Charges: Free admission
Facilities: D F G H R T
Other information: Guided tours, exhibitions and events also held.

Registration	Date	Chassis	Body	New to	Fleet No	Status
EGA 79	1949	Albion Venturer CX37S	Croft H30/26R	Glasgow Corporation	B92	R
FYS 988+	1958	BUT RETB1	Burlingham B50F	Glasgow Corporation	TBS13	R
FYS 998	1958	Leyland Atlantean PDR1/1	Alexander H44/34F	Glasgow Corporation	LA1	R
+ Trolleybus						

Notes:
FYS 988   Exhibited at the 1958 Commercial Motor Show

National Museum of Science and Industry
Wroughton

Contact address: Exhibition Road, London SW7 2DD
Phone: 0207 942 4105 or 01793 814466
E-mail: s.evans@nmsi.ac.uk
Brief description: The bus collection is located at Wroughton
airfield (hangar 4), near Swindon, Wiltshire.
Events planned: Open days are held and details of these may be found in the enthusiast press.
Opening days/times: Open only on Transport Festival and Open Days.
Directions by car: On A4361 approx 4 miles south of Swindon.
Directions by public transport: Publicised for Open Days
Charges: Published for each event.

Registration	Date	Chassis	Body	New to	Fleet No	Status
LMJ 653G	1913	Fiat 52B		(operator unknown) Yugoslavia		RP
JCP 60F	1928	Leyland Lion PLSC1	Leyland B31F	Jersey Railways & Tramways		A
DR 4902	1929	Leyland Titan TD1	Leyland L51RO	National Omnibus & Transport Co	2849	A
DX 8871+	1930	Ransomes Sims & Jefferies D	Ransomes Sims & Jefferies B31D	Ipswich Corporation	44	A
GW 713	1931	Gilford 168OT	Weymann C30D	Valliant of Ealing		A
VO 6806	1931	AEC Regal 662	Cravens B32F	Red Bus of Mansfield		A
JN 5783	1935	AEC Q 762	(chassis only)	Westcliff-on-Sea Motor Services		A
CPM 61+	1939	AEC 661T	Weymann H28/26R	Brighton Hove & District	6340	A
FR 1347	1940	Saurer CRD		GFM (Switzerland)	52	A

Registration	Date	Chassis	Body	New to	Fleet No	Status
DHR 192	1943	Guy Arab II	Weymann UH30/26R	Swindon Corporation	51	A
KPT 909	1949	Leyland Titan PD2/1	Leyland L27/26R	Weardale Motor Services of Frosterley		R
LTA 772	1951	Bristol LWL5G	ECW B32R	Western National Omnibus Co	1613	A
HET 513	1953	Crossley DD42/7	Crossley H30/26R	Rotherham Corporation	213	A
NLP 645	1953	AEC Regal IV 9822E	Park Royal RDP37C	British European Airways	1035	A
OTT 55	1953	Bristol LS5G	ECW B41F	Southern National Omnibus Co	1701	A
OLJ 291	1954	Bedford CAV	Bedford B12	Non-psv use		A
VLT 140	1960	AEC Routemaster R2RH	Park Royal H36/28R	London Transport	RM140	R
504 EBL	1963	Bedford VAL14	Duple C52F	Reliance Motor Services of Newbury	87	A
note u	1970	Moulton MD	Moulton C23F	Moulton Development vehicle		A
BCD 820L	1973	Leyland National 1151/1R/0102	Leyland National B49F	Southdown Motor Services	20	A
+ Trolleybus						

Notes:

LMJ 653G	Yugoslavia origins
JCP 60F	Originally registered J 4601
FR 1347	Displays original Swiss registration FR1347
note u	Eight wheeled integral development vehicle (unregistered)

North of England Open Air Museum
Beamish

Contact address: Beamish, Co Durham, DH9 0RG
Phone: 0191 370 4000
Fax: 0191 370 4001
E-mail: museum@beamish.org.uk
Web site: www.beamishmuseum.co.uk
Brief description: Beamish is an open-air museum which vividly recreates life in the North of England in the early 1800s and early 1900s Buildings from throughout the region have been brought to Beamish, rebuilt and furnished as they once were. Costumed staff welcome visitors and demonstrate the past way of life in The Town, Colliery Village, Home Farm, Railway Station, Pockerley Manor and 1825 Railway. A one-mile circular period tramway carries visitors around the Museum and a replica 1913 Daimler bus operates between The Town and Colliery Village.
Events planned: Please see web site for details

Opening days/times: 2005
Summer: 31 March to 28 October: (open every day)
Winter 30 October to 29 March 2008: 10.00 to 16.00 (closed Mondays and Fridays); also closed 9 December to 1 January 2007inclusive (inclusive).
Reduced operations in winter.
Last admission always 15.00.
Directions by car: Follow A1(M) to junction 63 (Chester-le-Street exit). Take A693 towards Stanley and follow Beamish Museum signs.
Directions by public transport: Buses 709 from Newcastle, 720 from Durham and 775/778 from Sunderland all serve Beamish.
Charges: — 2007 rates, under 5s free
Summer: Adult £16, Child £10, Over 60s/Students £12.50.
Winter: £6 per person.
Group rates available in summer for parties of 20 or more.
Facilities: B E F G H M P R T
Other information: Free leaflet available in advance for visitors with disabilities and mobility limitations.
Some vehicles not on display. Please telephone for information

Note: Please be aware that vehicles on display can vary from time to time as not all museums display their entire 'fleet'. Visitors wishing to see a particular vehicle should make enquiries prior to their visit.

Registration	Date	Chassis	Body	New to	Fleet No	Status
WT 7108+	1924	Straker Clough T29	Brush B32F	Keighley Corporation Tramways	12	A
UP 551	1928	BMMO SOS QL	Brush Replica B37F	Northern General Transport Co	338	RP
VK 5401	1931	Dodge UF30A	Robson of Consett B14F	Batey of Rookhope		RP
LTN 501+	1948	Sunbeam S7	Northern Coachbuilders H39/31R	Newcastle Corporation	501	R
J 2503	1988	Renault	Osborne O18/14RO	Beamish of the North of England Open Air Museum		R

+ Trolleybus

Notes:

UP 551	Replica body has been constructed
VK 5401	Undergoing restoration off-site
LTN 501	On loan to the Trolleybus Museum at Sandtoft
J 2503	Replica of 1913 Daimler

North West Museum of Road Transport

Contact address: The Old Bus Depot, 51 Hall Street, St Helens, WA10 1DU
Phone: 01744 451681
E-mail: email@hallstreetdepot.co.uk
website: www.hallstreetdepot.co.uk
Affiliation: NARTM
Brief description: A collection of over 65 historic vehicles representing the transport heritage of the northwest of England.
Events planned: Please see the enthusiast press for details
Opening days/times: Saturdays, Sundays and bank holidays 12.00-16.00
Facilities: Fully disabled access including toilets, drinks machine, shop

Registration	Date	Chassis	Body	New to	Fleet No	Status
AFY 971	1934	Leyland Titan TD3	English Electric O26/25R	Southport Corporation	43	A
ATD 683	1935	Leyland Lion LT7	Massey B30R	Widnes Corporation	39	A
RV 6360	1935	Leyland Titan TD4	English Electric O26/24R	Portsmouth Corporation	117	R
EWM 358	1945	Daimler CWA6	Duple UH30/26R	Southport Corporation	62	A
ANQ 778	1946	AEC Regent III O961	Commonwealth Engineering H-/-RD	Dept of Road Transport & Tramways of Sydney	1984	A
DED 797	1946	Leyland Titan PD1	Alexander H30/26R	Warrington Corporation	16	A
HLW 159	1946	AEC Regent III O961 RT	Park Royal H30/26R	London Transport	RT172	R
FFY 404	1947	Leyland Titan PD2/3	Leyland O30/26R	Southport Corporation	87	R
KTD 768	1948	Leyland Titan PD2/1	Lydney L27/26R	Leigh Corporation	16	R
GFY 406	1950	Leyland Titan PD2/3	Leyland H30/26R	Southport Corporation	106	RP
NTF 466	1952	Daimler CVG5	Northern Counties B32F	Lancaster City Transport	466	R
RFM 641	1953	Guy Arab IV	Massey H30/26R	Chester Corporation	1	R
CDJ 878	1954	Leyland Titan PD2/9	Davies H30/26R	St Helens Corporation	E78	A
RFM 644	1954	Guy Arab IV	Guy/Park Royal H30/26R	Chester Corporation	4	R
434 BTE	1957	Crossley Regent V D3RV	East Lancs H31/28RD	Darwen Corporation	17	R
GDJ 435	1957	AEC Regent V MD3RV	Weymann H33/26R	St Helens Corporation	H135	A
KRN 422	1957	Leyland Titan PD2/10	Crossley H33/29R	Preston Corporation	31	R
FHF 456	1959	Leyland Atlantean PDR1/1	Metro Cammell H44/33F	Wallasey Corporation	6	A

Note: Please be aware that vehicles on display can vary from time to time as not all museums display their entire 'fleet'. Visitors wishing to see a particular vehicle should make enquiries prior to their visit.

Above: Chesterfield Daimler Fleetline 124 (NNU 124M) alongside former Trent Bristol VR 629 (RCH 629L). Both are Midland Transport Group vehicles.

Below: Seen here at the Black Country Living Museum, Maidstone 56 (GKP 911), a 1944 Sunbeam W with 1962 Roe body, is normally to be found at The Trolleybus Museum at Sandtoft.

Registration	Date	Chassis	Body	New to	Fleet No	Status
KDJ 999	1959	AEC Regent V 2D3RA	East Lancs H41/32F	St Helens Corporation	K199	A
LDJ 985	1960	Leyland Titan PD2A/27	Weymann H30/25RD	St Helens Corporation	K175	A
562 RTF	1961	Leyland Titan PD2/40	East Lancs H37/28R	Widnes Corporation	31	R
574 TD	1962	Guy Arab IV	Northern Counties H41/32R	Lancashire United Transport	110	R
PSJ 480	1962	Leyland Titan PD2A/27	Massey H37/27F	Wigan Corporation	35	RP
TRJ 109	1962	AEC Reliance 2MU3RV	Weymann B45F	Salford City Transport	109	RP
201 YTE	1963	Leyland Titan PD2/37	East Lancs O37/28F	Lancaster City Transport	201	R
TDJ 612	1963	AEC Reliance 2MU3RA	Marshall B45F	St Helens Corporation	212	R
4227 FM	1964	Bristol Lodekka FS6G	ECW H33/27RD	Crosville Motor Services	DFG157	R
AJA 139B	1964	Bedford VAL 14	Strachan B52F	North Western Road Car Co	139	RP
HTF 644B	1964	Leyland Titan PD2/40	East Lancs H37/28R	Widnes Corporation	38	R
JTD 300B	1964	Guy Arab V	Northern Counties H41/32F	Lancashire United Transport	166	A
BCK 367C	1965	Leyland Titan PD3/6	Leyland/Preston Corporation H38/32F	Preston Corporation	61	A
BED 731C	1965	Leyland Titan PD2/40 Special	East Lancs H34/30F	Warrington Corporation	50	R
FFM 135C	1965	Guy Arab V	Massey H41/32F	Chester Corporation	35	A
UTC 768D	1966	Leyland Leopard L2	Plaxton C43F	Lancashire United Transport	216	R
MDJ 555E	1967	Leyland Titan PD2A/27	East Lancs H37/28R	St Helens Corporation	55	A
RFM 453F	1967	Leyland Tiger Cub PSUC1/11	Massey B40D	Chester Corporation	53	A
SMK 701F	1967	AEC Routemaster	Park Royal H40/32R	London Transport	RML2701	R
KJA 299G	1968	Bristol RESL6G	Marshall B43F	North Western Road Car Co	299	R
TVT 127G	1968	Leyland Leopard PSU4/4R	Marshall B38FL	Potteries Motor Traction Co	SN1127	R
DFM 347H	1969	Guy Arab V	Northern Counties H41/32F	Chester Corporation	47	R
EFM 181H	1970	Bristol RELL6G	ECW B53F	Crosville Motor Services	SRG181	A
JFM 650J	1970	Daimler Fleetline CRG6LX	Northern Counties H43/29F	Chester Corporation	50	A
EDJ 248J	1971	AEC Swift 2MP2R	Marshall B44D	St Helens Corporation	248	R
DKC 301L	1972	Leyland Atlantean AN68/1R	Alexander H43/32F	Merseyside PTE	1301	A
NWA 257K	1972	Daimler Fleetline CRG6LXB	Alexander H43/31F	Sheffield Corporation	257	A
PDJ 269L	1972	AEC Swift 3MP2R	Marshall B42D	St Helens Corporation	269	A
RTC 645L	1972	Leyland National 1151/1R/0101	Leyland National B52F	Widnes Corporation	1	R
LED 71P	1976	Bristol RESL6G	East Lancs B41D	Warrington Corporation	71	R
CWG 696V	1979	Leyland Atlantean AN68A/1R	Alexander	South Yorkshire PTE	1696	R
GEK 14V	1980	Leyland Atlantean AN68A/1R	East Lancs H45/31F	Warrington Corporation	14	A
XLV 140W	1980	Leyland National 2 NL116AL11/1R	Leyland National B49F	Merseyside PTE	6140	R
YMA 99W	1981	Dennis Dominator DD	Northern Counties H43/29F	Chester City Transport	99	RP
A323 GLV	1983	Leyland Atlantean AN68D/1R	Alexander H43/32F	Merseyside PTE	1003	R
A910 SYE	1983	Leyland Titan TNLXB2RR	Leyland H44/26D	London Transport	T910	R

Notes:

AFY 971	Originally H26/25R
RV 6360	Originally H26/24R; renumbered 6 following open-top conversion
HLW 159	Acquired by Bradford City Transport (410) in 1958
FFY 404	Originally H30/26R
PSJ 480	Originally registered JJP 502
201 YTE	Originally H37/28F
BCK 367C	Rebuilt from Leyland PD2 by Preston Corporation
DFM 347H	Last Guy Arab delivered to a British operator

Nottingham Transport Heritage Centre
Ruddington

Contact address: Mere Way, Ruddington, Nottingham NG11 6NX
Phone: 0115 940 5705
E-mail: aecley@aol.com
Web site: http://www.nthc.co.uk
Affiliation: NARTM
Brief description: The centre offers exhibits covering road and rail transport, and provides the opportunity to experience travel of a bygone age.
Events planned: Please see enthusiast press for details.
Opening days/times: Easter to mid-October: Sundays and Bank Holiday Mondays (10.45-17.00).
Directions by car: 3 miles south of Nottingham just off A52 ring-road and main A60 road via small roundabout at Ruddington.
Directions by public transport: Buses from Nottingham pass near museum
Charges: Not finalised at time of publication, all rides inclusive of steam train rides.
Facilities: B B(e) D E G H P R S T

Registration	Date	Chassis	Body	New to	Fleet No	Status
VO 8846	1932	Leyland Lion LT5	Willowbrook DP32F	South Notts Bus Co of Gotham	17	A
DJF 349	1947	Leyland Titan PD1	Leyland H30/26R	Leicester City Transport	248	RP
JVO 230	1948	Leyland Titan PD1A	Duple L29/26F	Barton Transport of Chilwell	507	R
MAL 310	1951	Leyland Royal Tiger PSU1/11	Duple DP45F	South Notts Bus Co of Gotham	42	A
APR 167A	1953	Leyland Titan PD2/12	no body	Barton Transport of Chilwell	732	RP
OTV 161	1953	AEC Regent III 9613E	Park Royal H30/26R	Nottingham City Transport	161	R
PFN 865	1959	AEC Regent V 2LD3RA		East Kent Road Car Co		R
866 HAL	1960	AEC Reliance 2MU3RV	Plaxton C41F	Barton Transport of Chilwell	866	RP
80 NVO	1962	Leyland Titan PD3/4	Northern Counties L33/32F	South Notts Bus Co of Gotham	80	RP
YRC 194	1962	Leyland Tiger Cub PSUC1/1	Alexander DP41F	Trent Motor Traction Co	194	R
CUV 218C	1965	AEC Routemaster R2RH/1	Park Royal H32/25RD	London Transport	RCL2218	R
EOD 524D	1966	AEC Regent V 2D3RA	MCW H34/25F	Devon General	524	R
FEL 751D	1966	Bristol MW6G	ECW C39F	Hants & Dorset Motor Services	904	R
LNN 89E	1967	Albion Lowlander LR3	Northern Counties H41/30F	South Notts Bus Co of Gotham	89	A
KVO 429P	1975	Leyland National 11351/2R	Leyland National B50F	Trent Motor Traction Co	429	A
ORC 545P	1976	Leyland Atlantean AN68/1R	ECW	Northern General Transport Co	3299	R
ARC 666T	1979	Leyland Atlantean AN68A/1R	Northern Counties H47/31D	Nottingham City Transport	666	R

Notes:

APR 167A	Chassis only. Originally registered RAL334
PFN 865	Recovery vehicle
LNN 89E	Last Albion Lowlander delivered Badged Leyland
KVO 429P	Originally B44D
ORC 545P	Originally H45/27D and registered MPT299P; used as promotional vehicle

Note: Please be aware that vehicles on display can vary from time to time as not all museums display their entire 'fleet'. Visitors wishing to see a particular vehicle should make enquiries prior to their visit.

Oxford Bus Museum
Long Hanborough

Contact address: Station Yard, Long Hanborough, Witney, Oxfordshire, OX29 8LA
Phone: 01993 883617 (Answerphone)
Affiliation: NARTM
Brief description: Over 40 buses dating from 1915 to 1994, mainly from City of Oxford Motor Services and other local companies. The collection includes many vehicles of AEC manufacture plus cars, fire engines and support vehicles. New Morris Motors Museum now incorporated.
Events planned: Please see enthusiast press or website for details.
Opening days/times: Wednesdays, Sundays and Bank Holiday Mondays, 10.30 to 16.30. Saturdays open from Easter until the last Saturday in October, 10.30-16.30 (last entries 16.00). Bus rides at 15.00 on the first Sunday of each month from the first Sunday in April to the first Sunday in October inclusive.
Directions by car: The entrance is on the south side of the A4095 (Witney-Bicester), between the villages of Bladon and Long Hanborough.
Directions by public transport: Museum is adjacent to Hanborough railway station on the Oxford-Worcester line, Sunday train services (journey time Oxford 10mins, London Paddington 70mins). Stagecoach bus service from George Street Oxford, weekdays, hourly to Long Hanborough village centre (1 mile)
Charges: Adults £3, Children £1.50, OAP £2.50, Family (2+2) £7.
Facilities: B(e) D P R S T
Other information: School parties welcome by arrangement — please telephone 01865 774233 for booking.

Registration	Date	Chassis	Body	New to	Fleet No	Status
DU 4838	1915	Daimler Y	City of Oxford Electric Tramways B32R	City of Oxford Electric Tramways	39	A
note e	1916	Daimler Y	(chassis only)			A
note f	1916	Daimler Y	(chassis only)			A
note ao	1917	Daimler Y	O18/16RO	City of Oxford Electric Tramways		RP
YL 740	1925	Morris Commercial 1 ton	Ch14			R
JO 5032	1932	AEC Regal 642	(chassis only)	City of Oxford Motor Services	GC41	R
JO 5403	1932	AEC Regent 661	Brush O28/24R	City of Oxford Motor Services	GA16	R
DBW 613	1948	Bedford OB	Duple C29F	Oliver of Long Handborough		A
JVF 528	1949	Bedford OB	Duple C29F	Bensley of Martham		R
NJO 703	1949	AEC Regal III 9621A	Willowbrook DP32F	City of Oxford Motor Services	703	R
OFC 393	1949	AEC Regent III 9612A	Weymann H30/26R	City of Oxford Motor Services	H892	A
OFC 205	1950	AEC Regal III 6821A	Duple C32F	South Midland Motor Services	66	A
PWL 413	1950	AEC Regent III 9613A	Weymann L27/26R	City of Oxford Motor Services	L166	R
GJB 254	1952	Bristol LWL6B	ECW B39R	Thames Valley Traction Co	616	RP
SFC 610	1952	AEC Regal IV 9821S	Willowbrook C37C	City of Oxford Motor Services	610	RP
TWL 928	1953	AEC Regent III 9613S	Park Royal H30/26R	City of Oxford Motor Services	H928	R
956 AJO	1957	AEC Regent V MD3RV	Park Royal H33/28R	City of Oxford Motor Services	H956	R
756 KFC	1960	AEC Reliance 2MU3RV	Park Royal B44F	City of Oxford Motor Services	756	R
14 LFC	1961	Morris FF	Wadham C27F	Morris Motors		RP
304 KFC	1961	Dennis Loline II	East Lancs H35/28F	City of Oxford Motor Services	304	R
305 KFC	1961	Dennis Loline II	East Lancs H35/28F	City of Oxford Motor Services	305	R
850 ABK	1962	AEC Reliance 2MU3RA	Duple C43F	Don Motor Coach Co of Southsea		RP
YWB 494M	1964	International Harvester 1853FC	Superior of Ohio B44F	United States Air Force		RP
FWL 371E	1967	AEC Renown 3B3RA	Northern Counties H38/27F	City of Oxford Motor Services	371	RP
NAC 416F	1967	Leyland Atlantean PDR1A/1	Northern Counties H44/31F	Stratford-upon-Avon Blue Motors	10	A
UFC 430K	1971	Daimler Fleetline CRL6	Northern Counties H43/27D	City of Oxford Motor Services	430	A
EUD 256K	1972	AEC Reliance 6MU4R	Plaxton B47F	Chiltern Queens of Woodcote		RP
VER 262L	1972	AEC Reliance 6U3ZR	Alexander C53F	Premier Travel of Cambridge	262	R
HUD 476S	1977	Bristol VRTSL3/6LXB	ECW H43/27D	City of Oxford Motor Services	476	R
BBW 21V	1980	Leyland Leopard PSU3	Duple C49F	City of Oxford Motor Services	21	R
JUD 597W	1980	Ford R1014	Plaxton C45F	House of Watlington		R
A869 SUL	1983	Leyland Titan TNLXB/2RRSP	Leyland H44/26D	London Transport	T869	R
B106 XJO	1985	Ford Transit 160D	Carlyle B16F	South Midland	SM6	R
C724 JJO	1986	Ford Transit	Carlyle DP20F	City of Oxford Motor Services	724	R
D122 PTT	1987	Ford Transit 190D	Mellor B16F	Thames Transit	122	R
L247 FDV	1994	Iveco 49-10	Mellor B13D	Bayline	2111	R

Notes:

DU 4838	Body new 1920
note e	Chassis only
note f	Chassis only
note ao	Body ex-London built 1906
JO 5032	Passed to Mascot Motors in Jersey and subsequently converted to lorry. Body removed. To be exhibited as chassis.
JO 5403	Originally H28/24R
JVF 528	Restored in Mulleys livery.
OFC 205	Displayed as an unrestored vehicle
305 KFC	Sectioned museum display showing body construction method
14 LFC	Originally used for Morris Motors band
850 ABK	Acquired by Chiltern Queens of Woodcote in 1964
YWB 494M	Original USAF identity 64 B 2428
NAC 416F	Acquired by City of Oxford Motor Services (905) in 1970
A869 SUL	Acquired by City of Oxford Motor Services (975) in 1993
L247 FDV	Bi-mode minibus

Scottish Vintage Bus Museum
Lathalmond

Contact address: M90 Commerce Park, Lathalmond, Fife, KY12 0SJ
Phone: 01383 623380
E-mail: website: www.busweb.co.uk/svbm
Affiliation: NARTM
Brief description: The collection of over 160 buses was, in the main, operated or manufactured in Scotland, from the late 1920s to the early 1980s. Vehicles are generally owned by private individuals or groups. A fully-equipped workshop enables comprehensive restoration to be undertaken. The 42-acre site is a former Royal Navy depot.
Events planned: Please see enthusiast press for details.
Opening days/times: Easter to end of September, Sundays 13.00 to 17.00
Directions by car: Use M90 junction 4. Take B914 Dollar road. Left B915 Dunfermline (2 miles). 2 miles to M90 Commerce Park on right.
Directions by public transport: Nearest bus/train Dunfermline. No public transport to site.
Charges: Sunday opening £3. Other charges apply at special events.
Facilities: B B(e) D E P R S T

Registration	Date	Chassis	Body	New to	Fleet No	Status
CD 7045	1922	Leyland G7	Short O27/24R	Southdown Motor Services	135	R
GE 2446	1928	Leyland Titan TD1	Leyland L27/24RO	Glasgow Corporation	111	R
RU 8678	1929	Leyland Lion PLSC3	Leyland B35F	Hants & Dorset Motor Services	268	RP
SO 3740	1929	Leyland Tiger TS2	Alexander B32F	Scottish General (Northern) Omnibus Co	P63	R
VD 3433	1934	Leyland Lion LT5A	Alexander B36F	Central SMT Co		R
WG 1620	1934	Gilford Hera L176S	no body	Alexander	Y49	R
AAA 756	1935	Albion Victor PK114	Abbott C20C	King Alfred Motor Services		R
WG 3260	1935	Leyland Lion LT5A	Alexander B35F	W Alexander & Sons	P705	A
WS 4522	1935	Leyland Tiger TS7	Cowieson B—R	Scottish Motor Traction Co		RP
CS 3364	1936	Leyland Cheetah LZ2	Alexander B37F	Western SMT Co		A
ASF 365	1937	Leyland Tiger TS7	Duple C33F	W Alexander & Sons	P808	R
ATF 477	1937	Leyland Tiger TS7T	Fowler B39F	Singleton of Leyland		A
AUX 296	1939	Sentinel-HSG	Cowieson B32R	Sentinel of Shrewsbury (demonstrator)		RP
WG 8107	1939	Leyland Tiger TS8	Alexander -	W Alexander & Sons	P528	RP

Note: Please be aware that vehicles on display can vary from time to time as not all museums display their entire 'fleet'. Visitors wishing to see a particular vehicle should make enquiries prior to their visit.

Registration	Date	Chassis	Body	New to	Fleet No	Status
WG 8790	1939	Leyland Tiger TS8	Alexander B39F	W. Alexander & Sons	P573	RP
ETJ 108	1940	Leyland Tiger TS11	Roe -	Leigh Corporation	79	A
HF 9126	1940	Leyland Titan TD7	Metro Cammell	Wallasey Corporation	74	A
WG 9180	1940	Leyland Titan TD7	Leyland L27/26R	W. Alexander & Sons	R266	R
DSG 169	1942	Leyland Titan TD5	Alexander L27/26R	Scottish Motor Traction Co	J66	R
CDR 679	1943	Guy Arab II	Duple UH30/26R	Plymouth Corporation	249	R
JWS 594	1943	Guy Arab II	Duple/Nudd H31/24R	London Transport	G 77	R
BRS 37	1945	Daimler CWD6	Duple H30/26R	Aberdeen Corporation	155	R
AWG 623	1947	AEC Regal I O662	Alexander C31F	W. Alexander & Sons	A36	R
AWG 639	1947	AEC Regal I O662	Alexander C35F	W. Alexander & Sons	A52	R
CUH 859	1947	Leyland Tiger PS1	ECW B-R	Western Welsh Omnibus Co	859	RP
note o	1947	Albion Venturer CX19	Comeng H33/28R	DRTT of Sydney	1877	R
XG 9304	1947	Leyland Titan PD1A	Northern Counties L27/26R	Middlesborough Corporation	52	A
AWG 393	1948	Guy Arab III	Cravens H30/26R	W. Alexander & Sons	RO607	R
BMS 405	1948	Daimler CVD6	Burlingham C33F	W. Alexander & Sons	D10	A
BWG 39	1948	Bedford OB	Scottish Motor Traction C25F	W. Alexander & Sons	W218	RP
CU 4740	1948	Leyland Tiger PS1	Burlingham C33F	Hall Bros of South Shields		A
ESG 652	1948	Guy Arab III	Metro Cammell B35R	Edinburgh Corporation	739	R
FSC 182	1949	Daimler CVG6	Metro Cammell H31/25R	Edinburgh Corporation	135	R
CWG 283	1950	Leyland Tiger PS1	Alexander C35F	W. Alexander & Sons	PA181	R
DCS 616	1950	Daimler CVD6	Massey O32/28RD	Hunter (A1) of Dreghorn	16A	R
EVA 324	1950	Guy Arab III	Guy B33R	Central SMT Co	K24	R
GVD 47	1950	Guy Arab III	Duple H31/26R	Hutchinson's Coaches of Overtown		R
SJ 1340	1950	Bedford OB	Duple C29F	Gordon of Lamlash		RP
SS 7486	1950	Bedford OB	Duple C29F	Stark's Motor Services of Dunbar		A
SS 7501	1950	Bedford OB	Duple C29F	Fairbairn of Haddington		R
AYJ 379	1951	Daimler CVD6	Croft H30/26R	Dundee Corporation	127	R
DGS 536	1951	Leyland Tiger PS1/1	McLennan C39F	A. & C. McLennan of Spittalfield		R
DGS 625	1951	Leyland Tiger PS1/1	McLennan C39F	A. & C. McLennan of Spittalfield		R
DMS 820	1951	Leyland Tiger OPS2/1	Alexander C35F	W. Alexander & Sons	PB7	A
DMS 823	1951	Leyland Tiger OPS2/1	Alexander C35F	W. Alexander & Sons	PB10	A
DWG 526	1951	Leyland Royal Tiger PSU1/15	Leyland C41C	W. Alexander & Sons	PC30	A
MTE 639	1951	AEC Regent III 6812A	Weymann H33/26R	Morecambe & Heysham Corporation	77	R
BMS 222	1952	Leyland Royal Tiger PSU1/15	Alexander C41C	W. Alexander & Sons	PC1	R
JVB 908	1952	Leyland Royal Tiger PSU1/13	Mann Egerton HD24/26F	Homeland of Croydon		RP
CYJ 252	1953	AEC Regent III 9613E	Alexander H32/26R	Dundee Corporation	137	R
FGS 59D	1953	Bedford SB	Mulliner B36F	Royal Navy		RP
CHG 541	1954	Leyland Tiger PS2/14	East Lancs B39F	Burnley Colne & Nelson	41	R
GM 6384	1954	Leyland Titan PD2/10	Leyland L27/28R	Central SMT Co	L484	RP
LFS 480	1954	Leyland Titan PD2/20	Metro-Cammell H34/29R	Edinburgh Corporation	480	R
ETS 964	1955	Daimler CVG6	Metro-Cammell H36/28R	Dundee Corporation	184	RP
FWG 846	1955	Bristol LS6G	ECW B45F	W. Alexander & Sons	E11	RP
HRG 209	1955	AEC Regent V D2RV6G	Crossley H35/29R	Aberdeen Corporation	209	A
TYD 888	1955	AEC Reliance MU3RV	Duple C43F	Wakes of Sparkford		R
UFF 178	1955	AEC Regent V D2RV6G	Crossley H35/29R	Aberdeen Corporation	207	A
OFS 777	1957	Leyland Titan PD2/20	Metro-Cammell H34/29R	Edinburgh Corporation	777	R
OFS 798	1957	Leyland Titan PD2/20	Metro-Cammell H34/29R	Edinburgh Corporation	798	RP
OWS 620	1957	Bristol Lodekka LD6G	ECW H33/27R	Scottish Omnibuses	AA620	RP
TVS 367	1958	Bristol Lodekka LD6G	ECW H33/27R	Central SMT Co	B87	RP
FAS 982	1959	Albion Victor FT39KAN	Reading B35F	Jersey Motor Transport Co	5	R
SWS 671	1959	AEC Reliance 2MU3RV	Alexander C38F	Scottish Omnibuses	B671	R
SWS 715	1959	AEC Reliance 2MU3RV	Park Royal C41F	Scottish Omnibuses	B715	A
EDS 320A	1960	AEC Routemaster R2RH	Park Royal H36/28R	London Transport	RM606	RP
EDS 50A	1960	AEC Routemaster R2RH	Park Royal H36/28R	London Transport	RM560	R
NMS 366	1960	AEC Reliance 2MU3RV	Alexander C41F	W. Alexander & Sons	AC155	RP
RAG 578	1960	Daimler CVG6LX	Northern Counties C25F	T. Hunter (A1) of Kilmarnock		R
VSC 86	1960	Leyland Tiger Cub PSUC1/3	Weymann B47F	Edinburgh Corporation	86	R

Registration	Date	Chassis	Body	New to	Fleet No	Status
WAJ 112	1960	Albion Nimbus NS3N	Plaxton C29F	Watson of Huntingdon		A
XSL 945A	1960	Bristol MW6G	Alexander C41F	Western SMT Co	T1590	A
XSN 25A	1960	Bristol MW6G	Alexander C41F	Western SMT Co	T1591	A
EDS 288A	1961	AEC Routemaster R2RH	Park Royal H36/28R	London Transport	RM 910	R
OSC 711	1961	Leyland Tiger Cub PSUC1/2	Alexander C41F	W. Alexander & Sons (Fife)	FPD225	R
RAG 411	1961	Bristol Lodekka LD6G	ECW H33/27RD	Western SMT Co	1645	R
RCS 382	1961	Leyland Titan PD3A/3	Alexander L35/32RD	Western SMT Co	1684	R
YSG 101	1961	Leyland Leopard PSU3/2R	Alexander B33T	Edinburgh Corporation	101	R
YYJ 914	1961	Leyland Tiger Cub PSUC1/2	Alexander C41F	Stark's Motor Services of Dunbar	H8	A
7424 SP	1962	AEC Reliance 2MU3RV	Alexander C41F	W. Alexander & Sons (Fife)	FAC4	R
LDS 201A	1962	AEC Routemaster R2RH	Park Royal H36/28R	London Transport	RM1607	R
NSJ 502	1962	AEC Reliance 2MU3RV	Alexander C41F	W. Alexander & Sons (Northern)	NAC205	R
UCS 659	1963	Albion Lowlander LR3	Northern Counties H40/31F	Western SMT Co	N1795	R
AFS 91B	1964	AEC Reliance 4MU3RA	Alexander B53F	Scottish Omnibuses	B91	R
ARG 17B	1964	AEC Reliance 2MU3RA	Alexander C41F	W. Alexander & Sons (Northern)	NAC246	RP
ASC 665B	1964	Leyland Titan PD3/6	Alexander H41/29F	Edinburgh Corporation	665	R
AWA 124B	1964	Bedford SB13	Duple C41F	J. O. Andrew of Sheffield		R
BXA 464B	1964	Bristol Lodekka FS6G	ECW H33/27RD	W. Alexander & Sons (Fife)	FRD199	R
CSG 29C	1965	Bristol Lodekka FLF6G	ECW -	Scottish Omnibuses		R
CSG 43C	1965	Bristol Lodekka FLF6G	ECW H38/32F	Scottish Omnibuses	AA43	RP
DMS 325C	1965	Leyland Leopard PSU3/3R	Alexander -	W. Alexander & Sons (Midland)	MPE40	R
DMS 359C	1965	Leyland Leopard PSU3/3R	Alexander -	W. Alexander & Sons (Midland)	MPE73	R
ESF 801C	1965	Leyland Atlantean PDR1/1	Alexander H43/31F	Edinburgh Corporation	801	R
EWS 130D	1966	AEC Reliance 2U3RA	Alexander C—F	Scottish Omnibuses	ZB130	A
EWS 168D	1966	Bristol RELH6G	Alexander C38Ft	Scottish Omnibuses (Eastern Scottish)	XA168	A
EWS 812D	1966	Leyland Atlantean PDR1/1	Alexander H43/31F	Edinburgh City Transport	812	R
FFV 447D	1966	AEC Reliance 2U3RA	Plaxton C45F	J. Abbott & Sons of Blackpool		R
GRS 343E	1967	Albion Viking VK43AL	Alexander DP40F	W. Alexander & Sons (Northern)	NNV43	R
HDV 639E	1967	Bristol MW6G	ECW C39F	Western National Omnibus Co	1434	R
HGM 335E	1967	Bristol Lodekka FLF6G	ECW H44/34F	Central SMT Co	BL335	R
HGM 346E	1967	Bristol Lodekka FLF6G	ECW H44/34F	Central SMT Co	BL346	R
JSC 900E	1967	Leyland Atlantean PDR2/1	Alexander O47/35F	Edinburgh Corporation	900	R
LUS 524E	1967	AEC Reliance 2U3RA	Willowbrook C49F	David MacBrayne of Glasgow	150	R
KGM 664F	1968	Leyland Leopard PSU3/1R	Alexander B53F	Central SMT Co	T64	A
LFS 288F	1968	Bristol VRT/LL/6G	ECW O47/33F	Scottish Omnibuses	AA288	R
LFS 294F	1968	Bristol VRT/LL/6G	ECW H47/36F	Eastern Scottish	AA294	RP
NTY 416F	1968	AEC Reliance 6MU3R	Plaxton C45F	J. Rowell of Prudhoe		RP
VMP 8G	1968	Albion Viking VK43AL	Alexander DP40F	Road Transport Industry Training Board	16	RP
NAG 120G	1969	Bristol REMH6G	Alexander C42Ft	Western SMT Co	T2214	RP
XFM 42G	1969	Guy Arab V	Northern Counties H40/31F	Chester Corporation	42	R
SSF 237H	1970	Bedford VAL 70	Duple C53F	Edinburgh Corporation	237	A
TMS 585H	1970	Leyland Leopard PSU3/1R	Alexander C49F	Road Transport Industry Training Board	84	A
TGM 214J	1971	Daimler Fleetline CRG6LX	ECW H43/34F	Central SMT Co	D14	R
XWS 165K	1971	Bedford J2	Plaxton C20F	Glass of Haddington		R
BFS 1L	1972	Leyland Atlantean AN68/1R	Alexander H45/30D	Edinburgh City Transport	1	R
BWG 833L	1972	Leyland Leopard PSU3/3R	Alexander B53F	W. Alexander & Sons (Midland)	MPE133	A
YSD 350L	1972	Leyland Leopard PSU3/3R	Alexander B41F	Western SMT Co	L2390	R
BFS 463L	1973	Bedford YRQ	Alexander DP45F	Scottish Omnibuses (Eastern Scottish)	C463	A
BWS 105L	1973	Seddon Pennine IV-236	Seddon DP25F	Edinburgh Corporation	105	R
SCS 333M	1974	Leyland Leopard PSU3/3R	Alexander B53F	Western SMT Co	L2464	R
SCS 366M	1974	Leyland Leopard PSU3/3R	Alexander B53F	Western SMT Co	L2497	R
LSX 16P	1975	Volvo Ailsa B57	Alexander H44/35F	W. Alexander & Sons (Fife)	FRA16	A
MSF 750P	1976	Seddon Pennine VII	Alexander C42Ft	Scottish Omnibuses (Eastern Scottish)	XS750	R
NCS 16P	1976	Leyland Fleetline FE30AGR	Alexander H43/31F	Hill (A1) of Stevenston		RP

Note: Please be aware that vehicles on display can vary from time to time as not all museums display their entire 'fleet'. Visitors wishing to see a particular vehicle should make enquiries prior to their visit.

Registration	Date	Chassis	Body	New to	Fleet No	Status
SMS 120P	1976	Daimler Fleetline CRG6LXB	Alexander H44/31F	W. Alexander & Sons (Midland)	MRF120	RP
NDL 656R	1977	Bristol VRTSL3/6LXB	ECW H43/31F	Southern Vectis Omnibus Co	656	RP
ORS 60R	1977	Leyland Leopard PSU4C/4R	Alexander C45F	Grampian Regional Transport	60	R
OSJ 629R	1977	Leyland Leopard PSU3C/3R	Alexander B53F	Western SMT Co	L2629	RP
RRS 46R	1977	Leyland Leopard PSU3E/4R	Duple C49F	W. Alexander & Sons (Northern)	NPE46	R
XMS 252R	1977	Leyland Leopard PSU3C/4R	Alexander B53F	W. Alexander & Sons (Midland)	MPE252	A
CSG 773S	1978	Volvo Ailsa B55-10	Alexander H43/32F	Scottish Omnibuses (Eastern Scottish)	VV773	RP
CSG 792S	1978	Seddon Pennine VII	Plaxton C45F	Scottish Omnibuses (Eastern Scottish)	S792	A
GLS 265S	1978	Leyland Leopard PSU3E/4R	Alexander C49F	Alexander (Midland)	MPE265	R
JSF 928T	1978	Seddon Pennine VII	Alexander DP49F	Scottish Omnibuses	S928	RP
JSX 595T	1979	Leyland Atlantean AN68A/1R	Alexander H45/30D	Lothian Regional Transport	595	R
JTU 588T	1978	Leyland National 10351B/1R	Leyland National B—F	Crosville Motor Services	SNG588	RP
LIL 9929	1979	Bedford VAS	Plaxton C29F	Blood Transfusion Service		RP
RLS 469T	1979	Ford R1014	Alexander B45F	W. Alexander & Sons (Midland)	MT69	RP
WTS 266T	1979	Volvo Ailsa B55-10	Alexander H44/31D	Tayside Regional Council	266	R
XBO 121T	1978	Bristol VRT/SL3/6LXB	ECW O43/31F	National Welsh Omnibus Services		R
DSD 936V	1979	Seddon Pennine VII	Alexander C49F	Western SMT Co	S2936	RP
SSX 602V	1980	Seddon Pennine VII	Alexander B53F	Scottish Omnibuses (Eastern Scottish)	S602	RP
ESF 647W	1980	Guy Victory Mk 2	Alexander H60/24D	China Motor Bus	LV36	R
LMS 374W	1980	Leyland Leopard PSU3F/4R	Alexander B53F	W. Alexander & Sons (Midland)	MPE374	A
RHS 400W	1980	Wales & Edwards	Wales & Edwards B12F	South of Scotland Electricity		R
FES 831W	1981	Volvo B58-61	Duple B59F	Stagecoach of Perth		RP
HSC 173X	1981	Leyland Cub CU435	Duple B31F	Lothian Region Transport	173	RP
GSC 667X	1982	Leyland Olympian ONTL11/1R	Alexander H47/28D	Lothian Region Transport	667	R
KSX 102X	1982	Leyland National Mk 2	Leyland National B40D	Lothian Region Transport	102	R
ULS 716X	1982	Leyland Leopard PSU3G/4R	Alexander C49F	W. Alexander & Sons (Midland)	MPE416	RP
ULS 717X	1982	Leyland Leopard PSU3G/4R	Alexander C49F	W. Alexander & Sons (Midland)	MPE417	RP
NFS 176Y	1982	Leyland Leopard PSU3G/4R	Alexander C49F	W. Alexander & Sons (Fife)	FPE176	RP
B349 LSO	1985	Leyland Olympian ON5LXCT/1R	Alexander H45/32F	W. Alexander & Sons (Northern)	NLO49	A
C777 SFS	1985	Leyland Olympian ONTL11/2R	ECW H51/32D	Lothian Region Transport	777	R

Notes:

CD 7045 — Rebodied 1928. On loan from Southdown Motor Services

SO 3740 — Passed to W. Alexander & Sons in 1930; numbered P63 in 1932 and rebodied in 1934

VD 3433 — Rebodied 1945

WG 3260 — Rebodied 1945

WG 8107 — Breakdown vehicle. Originally C35F.

ETJ 108 — Breakdown vehicle

HF 9126 — Originally H28/26R; acquired by Lancshire County Constabulary in 1952 and converted for use as mobile control post

DSG 169 — Alexander body to Leyland design; converted to open-top in 1959 and restored in 1980/1

JWS 594 — Originally London Transport G77 (GLL577); rebuilt and rebodied 1953

CDR 679 — Original Roe body converted to platform lorry in 1963. Present body from VV9135.

note o — Not registered

SS 7486 — Passed to Scottish Omnibuses (C22) in 1964

DCS 616 — Rebodied in 1958 as H32/28RD

GVD 47 — Acquired by McGill's Bus Services of Barrhead in 1952

AYJ 379 — On loan from Dundee Museums

FGS 59D — Originally registered 51 51 RN

UFF 178 — Originally registered HRG 207

ETS 964 — On loan from Travel Dundee

TVS 367 — Originally registered GM 9287

FAS 982 — Originally registered J 1359

EDS 320A — Originally registered WLT 606; acquired by Kelvin Scottish Omnibuses (1919) in 1986

EDS 50A — Originally registered WLT 560; acquired by Stagecoach at Perth in 1985

XSN 25A — Originally registered OCS 713

XSL 945A — Originally registered OCS 712

EDS 288A — Originally registered WLT 910; acquired by Kelvin Scottish Omnibuses (1929) in 1986

YYJ 914 — Originally registered ESS 989

OSC 711 — Originally registered RMS 714

NSJ 502 — Originally registered SRS117.

LDS 201A — Originally registered 607 DYE; acquired by Stagecoach at Perth in 1986

CSG 29C — Converted to breaddown vehicle

DMS 325C — Converted to Breakdown Vehicle

DMS 359C — Converted to Breakdown Vehicle

HDV 639E — First vehicle operated by Stagecoach

JSC 900E — Originally H47/35F

LFS 288F — Converted to open-top

YSD 350L — Originally C49F; rebuilt and shortened by Western SMT in 1980

XBO 121T — Converted to open-top by SVBM

NDL 656R — Acquired by Lowland Scottish Omnibuses (856) in 1991

LIL 9929 — Originally registered CJU 998T

ESF 647W — Original Hong Kong registration was CH 9399

RHS 400W — Battery-electric bus

FES 831W — First new vehicle delivered to Stagecoach (as C50Ft)

South Yorkshire Transport Museum
Aldwarke

Contact address: 206 London Road, Sheffield S2 4LW
Phone: 0114 255 3010
Website: www.sheffieldbusmuseum.com
Brief description: A collection of over 25 vehicles and many artifacts.
Events planned: Please see enthusiast press and website for details.

Registration	Date	Chassis	Body	New to	Fleet No	Status
GWJ 724	1941	AEC Regent O661	Sheffield Transport Department -	Sheffield Corporation	G54	A
JWB 416	1947	Leyland Tiger PS1	Weymann B34R	Sheffield Corporation	216	A
HD 7905	1948	Leyland Tiger PS1	Brush B34F	Yorkshire Woollen District Transport Co	622	R
KWE 255	1948	AEC Regent III 9612E	Weymann -	Sheffield Corporation	G55	RP
MHY 765	1950	Leyland Comet ECPO/1R	Duple C32F	Orient Coaches of Bristol	-	RP
OWE 116	1952	AEC Regent III 9613A	Roe H33/25R	Sheffield Joint Omnibus Committee	116	RP
KET 220	1954	Daimler CVG6	Weymann H30/26R	Rotherham Corporation	220	R
RWB 87	1954	Leyland Titan PD2/12	Weymann H32/26R	Sheffield Corporation	687	R
WRA 12	1955	AEC Monocoach MC3RV	Park Royal B45F	Booth & Fisher of Halfway	-	R
VDV 760	1958	Bristol Lodekka LD6G	ECW H33/27RD	Western National Omnibus Co	1943	R
TDK 322	1959	AEC Regent V D2RA	Weymann H33/28RD	Rochdale Corporation	322	R
TET 135	1959	Daimler CVG6-30	Roe -	Rotherham Corporation	135	A
6330 WJ	1960	AEC Regent V 2D3RA	Roe H39/30RD	Sheffield Joint Omnibus Committee	1330	A
7874 WJ	1960	AEC Regent V 2D3RA	Alexander H37/32R	Sheffield Corporation	874	R
TUJ 261	1960	Ford Trader	Burlingham C-F			A
1322 WA	1961	AEC Reliance 2MU3RA	Plaxton C36F	Sheffield United Tours	322	A
449 CLT	1963	AEC Routemaster	Park Royal H36/28R	London Transport	RM1449	RP
LJF 30F	1967	Leyland PD3A/12	Metro Cammell H41/33R	Leicester City Transport	30	RP
DWB 54H	1970	AEC Swift 5P2R	Park Royal B50F	Sheffield Transport	54	RP
LWB 388P	1976	Volvo Ailsa B55-10	Van Hool McArdle H44/31D	South Yorkshire PTE	388	RP
PSJ 825R	1976	Volvo Ailsa B55-10	Van Hool McArdle H44/31F	J. Hunter (A1) of Kilmarnock	-	RP
CWG 756V	1979	Leyland Atlantean AN68A/1R	Roe H45/29D	South Yorkshire PTE	1756	R
C53 HDT	1985	Dennis Domino SDA	Optare B33F	South Yorkshire PTE	53	A

Notes:

GWJ 724	Originally bus 462; converted to grit wagon
KWE 255	Originally bus 255; converted to grit wagon
TET 135	Originally H39/31F; converted to breakdown vehicle
PSJ 825R	Originally H44/31D

Note: Please be aware that vehicles on display can vary from time to time as not all museums display their entire 'fleet'. Visitors wishing to see a particular vehicle should make enquiries prior to their visit.

Tameside Transport Collection
Mossley

Contact address: Roaches Industrial Estate, Manchester Road, Mossley, Greater Manchester

Brief description: A working museum comprising a small but varied collection of vehicles ranging from 1929 to the1960s. There is in addition a display of transport-related items.

Opening days/times: Last weekend of each month (except December), 10.00 to 15.00; visits at other times by prior appointment.

Directions by car: From Ashton-under-Lyne take A635 (Huddersfield) through Mossley. Museum is 1 mile on right-hand side, adjacent to Claybank Terrace.

Directions by public transport:
Bus service 355 from Ashton-under-Lyne or Oldham.
By rail to Mossley station (approximately 1 mile walk towards Greenfield).

Charges: No charge but donations welcome.

Facilities: D S R T

Other information: Car parking is limited.

Registration	Date	Chassis	Body	New to	Fleet No	Status
LG 2637	1929	Crossley Arrow	Crossley B32R	S Jackson & Sons of Crewe		RP
DNF 204	1937	Crossley Mancunian	Metro-Cammell/Crossley B32R	Manchester Corporation	129	RP
DBN 978	1949	Crossley SD42/7	Crossley B32R	Bolton Corporation	8	R
JND 728	1950	Daimler CVG6	Metro-Cammell H32/26R	Manchester Corporation	4127	RP
CRC 911	1951	Crossley DD42/8A	Brush H30/26R	Derby Corporation	111	R
FRJ 511	1951	Daimler CVG6	Metro-Cammell H30/24R	Salford City Transport	511	R
422 CAX	1961	AEC Regent V MD3RV	Massey L31/28R	Bedwas & Machen UDC	5	R
105 UTU	1962	Leyland Titan PD2/37	Northern Counties H36/28F	SHMD Board	5	RP
7209 PW	1962	Bedford J2SZ2	Plaxton C20F	H. & I. Jarvis of Downham Market	4	R
BWO 585B	1964	AEC Regent V 2MD3RA	Massey L31/28R	Bedwas & Machen UDC	8	A
NMA 328D	1966	Daimler Fleetline CRG6LX	Northern Counties H-/-F	SHMD Board	28	RP

Notes:

LG 2637	Passed to Crosville Motor Services (U2) in 1934
DNF 204	Open rear platform
422 CAX	Converted to trainer by Rhumney Valley UDC 1976
BWO 585B	Last AEC to receive lowbridge body
NMA 328D	Used as exhibition bus 1983-92

Transport Museum Society of Ireland
Howth

Contact address: Howth Castle Demesne, Howth, Dublin 13, Ireland

Phone: (00) 353 1 832 0427

Affiliation: NARTM

Brief description: The museum is run by a group of volunteers dedicated to the preservation and restoration of valuable road transport heritage. Exhibits include buses, trams and commercial, public utility, military, fire-appliance, electric and horse-drawn vehicles. Other displays include transport-associated memorabilia. The museum is a registered charity.

Opening days/times:
June to August: Monday to Saturday 10.00 to 17.00; Sunday 14.00 to 17.00.
September to May: Saturdays, Sundays and Bank Holidays 14.00 to 17.00.

Directions by car: Howth is 9 miles north of Dublin City Centre or 7 miles from the M1/M50 junction at Dublin Airport. Museum is located in grounds of Howth Castle Demesne.

Directions by public transport: Bus 31 from Dublin City Centre; Local DART rail service to Howth station, then short walk.

Charges: Please telephone for charges.
Facilities: E G P T
Other information: Limited access for disabled.
Note: No recent vehicle data received from this museum.

Registration	Date	Chassis	Body	New to	Fleet No	Status
TE 5110	1928	Leyland Lion PLSC3	(chassis only)	Colne Corporation	22	A
note i	1933	AEC Regal I	(chassis only)	(unknown)		A
ZI 9708	1933	Dennis Lancet I	Dublin United Tramways Co B32R	Dublin United Tramways Co	F21	A
ZC 714	1937	Leyland Titan TD4	Leyland H32/26R	Dublin United Tramways Co	R1	R
FRU 305	1945	Bristol K6A	Hants & Dorset FO31/28R	Hants & Dorset Motor Services	1108	A
GZ 7638	1947	Leyland Tiger PS1	Northern Ireland Road Transport Board B34R	Northern Ireland Road Transport Board	A8570	A
IY 1940	1948	AEC Regent III 9621E	Park Royal O33/26R	Morecambe & Heysham Corporation	58	A
ZD 7163	1948	Leyland Tiger OPS3	(chassis only)	CIE	P23	A
ZH 3926	1948	AEC Regal III O962	Park Royal C35R	Great Northern Railway (Ireland)	427	A
ZH 3937	1948	AEC Regent III 9612E	Park Royal H30/26RD	Great Northern Railway (Ireland)	438	R
ZH 4538	1948	Leyland Titan PD2/3	Leyland H33/27R	CIE	R389	R
LTU 869	1949	Commer Avenger I	Plaxton C33F	Thornley of Woodley		A
MZ 7396	1950	Guy Arab III	Harkness B31F	Belfast Corporation	298	A
ZL 2718	1950	GNR Gardner	Park Royal/GNR	Great Northern Railway (Ireland)	387	A
GUX 188	1951	Bedford OB	Duple B31F	Lloyd of Oswestry		A
IY 7384	1951	GNR Gardner	Park Royal/GNR DP33R	Great Northern Railway (Ireland)	390	RP
ZJ 5933	1951	Leyland Tiger OPS3	CIE	CIE	P193	A
OZ 6686	1953	Daimler CVG6	Harkness H30/26R	Belfast Corporation	432	A
ZL 6816	1953	Leyland Titan OPD2/1	CIE H37/31R	CIE	R506	A
ZO 6819	1953	Leyland Tiger PS2/14	CIE B39R	CIE	P309	A
ZO 6857	1953	Leyland Tiger PS2/14	CIE B39R	CIE	P347	R
ZO 6881	1954	Leyland Royal Tiger PSU1/15	CIE C34C	CIE	U10	A
ZO 6949	1954	Leyland Royal Tiger PSU1/15	CIE B39D	CIE	U78	A
ZY 79	1954	AEC Regal IV 9822E	Park Royal/GNR B45R	Great Northern Railway (Ireland)	274	A
ZU 9241	1955	Leyland Titan OPD2/1	CIE H37/31RD	CIE	R567	A
CYI 621	1958	Leyland Titan OPD2/2	CIE	CIE	R819	A
HZA 230	1960	Leyland Titan PD3/2	CIE H41/33R	CIE	RA105	RP
HZA 279	1961	AEC Regent V 2D2RA	CIE H41/28RD	CIE	AA2	A
404 RIU	1963	Albion Lowlander LR1	Alexander H41/31F	W Alexander & Sons (Midland) Ltd	MRE38	A
HZD 593	1963	Leyland Worldmaster ERT2/1	Van Hool DP53F	CIE	WVH13	A
NZE 598	1964	Leyland Leopard L2	CIE B45F	CIE	E170	A
NZE 620	1964	Leyland Titan PD3A/6	Dundalk (Park Royal frame) H41/33R	CIE	R911	A
EZH 17	1965	Leyland Leopard PSU3/4R	CIE B45F	CIE	C17	A
EZH 64	1965	Leyland Leopard PSU3/4R	CIE/North East Health Board	CIE	C64	A
NZE 629	1965	Leyland Titan PD3A/3	Dundalk (Park Royal frame) O41/33R	CIE	R920	A
EZH 231	1966	Leyland Leopard PSU3/4R	CIE B53F	CIE	C231	A
VZL 179	1966	Bedford VAL 14	Plaxton C53F	Wallace Arnold Tours of Leeds		A
EZL 1	1967	Bedford VAS 5	CIE B33F	CIE	SS1	RP
VZI 44	1967	Leyland Atlantean PDR1/1	CIE H43/35F	CIE	D44	A
WZJ 724	1967	Bedford VAM 14	Duffy C45F	P O'Grady of Santry		A
DIV 83	1971	Daimler Fleetline CRG6LX	Alexander H45/32F	Trent Motor Traction Co	550	A
AIT 934	1972	Mercedes 406D	Asco Clubman	Flagline of Athlone		A
note j	1972	Bedford VAL 70	Duffy B40D	Aer Lingus	301	A
694 ZO	1975	Leyland Atlantean AN68/1R	Van Hool H45/29D	CIE	D694	A
GSI 353	1983	Bombardier	Bombardier H45/29D	CIE	KD353	A
UZG 100	1984	Bombardier GAC	Bombardier B44D	CIE	KC100	A

Note: Please be aware that vehicles on display can vary from time to time as not all museums display their entire 'fleet'. Visitors wishing to see a particular vehicle should make enquiries prior to their visit.

Notes:

note i	Not registered	404 RIU	Originally registered VWG 376
FRU 305	Originally numbered TD774; renumbered in 1950 and rebodied 1952	EZH 64	Originally B45F; converted to mobile hospital
		NZE 629	Originally H41/33R
IY 1940	Originally H38/26R; registered KTF 587	VZL 179	Originally registered EUG 907D
ZL 2718	Ambulance conversion	DIV 83	Originally registered DRC 550J
ZJ 5933	Breakdown vehicle	note j	Not registered
CYI 621	Breakdown vehicle		

The Transport Museum — Wythall

Contact address: The Transport Museum, Chapel Lane, Wythall, Worcestershire, B47 6JX
Phone: 01564 826471
E-mail: enquiries@bammot.org.uk
Web site: www.bammot.org.uk
Affiliations: AIM, NARTM, Transport Trust, MLA West Midlands
Brief description: The collection is based on buses built and/or operated locally, plus others of significant PSV history. In addition, there is a unique collection of battery-operated road vehicles and a miniature passenger-carrying steam railway on site. Museum developed and run by volunteers. A third display hall should open in May 2007, thanks to a Heritage Lottery Fund project
Events planned:
Major operating days 8/9 April 2007; 6/7, 27/28 May 2007
24 June 2007 — Two Museums Day, half hourly buses to Aston Manor Transport Museum; 26/27 August 2007; 14 October 2007 — Midlands Enthusiasts' Day
Opening days/times: Saturdays, Sundays and Bank Holidays 11.00 to 16.30 (10.30 to 17.00 on event days), Easter Sunday to end November. Also Wednesdays in July 13.00-16.30. Last admission 30min before closing time
Directions by car: Wythall is on the main A435 Birmingham-Evesham road. The museum is next to Wythall old church. From M42 use junction 3 and head towards Birmingham.
Directions by public transport: Museum services operate on event days (including ex-Hill St, Birmingham 11.00 and 12.00 on 9 April; 7, 28 May, 24 June, 27 August, 14 October.
Bus services serve Wythall from Birmingham and Solihull. Neither operates on Sundays
Wythall rail station is 25min walk from museum.
Charges: £3.00 (£4 on major operating days). Admission ticket can be upgraded to all-day riding ticket at additional charge of £3 — £4 on 24 June when it includes admission to Aston Manor Transport Museum
Facilities: B(e) E P S T
Other information: Refreshments available on event days

Registration	Date	Chassis	Body	New to	Fleet No	Status
O 9926	1913	Tilling Stevens TTA2	Thomas Tilling O18/16RO	BMMO ('Midland Red')	26	RP
HA 3501	1925	SOS Standard	Ransomes Sims & Jefferies B32F	BMMO ('Midland Red')	501	A
CN 2870	1927	SOS Q	Brush B37F	Northern General Transport Co	321	RP
CC 7745	1928	SOS QL	Brush B37F	Royal Blue of Llandudno		A
OV 4090	1931	Morris Commercial Dictator	Metro Cammell B34F	Birmingham Corporation Tramways	90	A
OV 4486	1931	AEC Regent 661	Metro Cammell H27/21R	Birmingham Corporation Tramways	486	A
OC 527	1933	Morris Commercial Imperial	Metro Cammell H50R	Birmingham Corporation Tramways	527	A
AHA 582	1935	SOS DON	Brush B36F	BMMO ('Midland Red')	1703	A
CVP 207	1937	Daimler COG5	Metro Cammell H30/24R	Birmingham City Transport	1107	R
RC 4615	1937	AEC Regal O662	Willowbrook B34F	Trent Motor Traction Co	714	R
GHA 333	1940	SOS SON	(chassis only)	BMMO ('Midland Red')	2414	RP
GHA 337	1940	SOS SON	Brush B38F	BMMO ('Midland Red')	2418	RP
HHA 637	1946	BMMO S6	Metro Cammell B40F	BMMO ('Midland Red')	3036	A
FFY 402	1947	Leyland Titan PD2/3	Leyland O30/26R	Southport Corporation	85	RP
GUE 247	1948	Leyland Tiger PS1	Northern Coachbuilders B34F	Stratford-upon-Avon Blue Motors	41	A
HOV 685	1948	Leyland Titan PD2/1	Brush H30/24R	Birmingham City Transport	1685	R

Registration	Date	Chassis	Body	New to	Fleet No	Status
JRR 404	1948	Leyland Titan PD1	Duple L29/26F	Barton Transport of Chilwell	473	RP
KAL 579	1948	Daimler CVD6	Massey H33/28RD	W Gash & Sons of Newark	DD2	R
FDM 724	1949	Foden PVD6	Massey H30/26R	E H Phillips Motor Services of Holywell		A
FJW 616+	1949	Sunbeam F4	Park Royal H28/26R	Wolverhampton Corporation	616	RP
HDG 448	1949	Albion Venturer CX19	Metro Cammell H30/26R	Cheltenham District Traction Co	72	R
HWO 334	1949	Guy Arab III	Duple L27/26R	Red & White Services	34	R
JOJ 245	1950	Leyland Tiger PS2/1	Weymann B34F	Birmingham City Transport	2245	R
JOJ 533	1950	Guy Arab III special	Metro Cammell H30/24R	Birmingham City Transport	2533	R
JUE 349	1950	Leyland Tiger PS2/3	Northern Counties H35/28F	Stratford-upon-Avon Blue Motors	33	RP
KFM 775	1950	Bristol L5G	ECW B35R	Crosville Motor Services	KG126	R
NHA 744	1950	BMMO S12	Brush B44F	BMMO ('Midland Red')	3744	RP
NHA 795	1950	BMMO D5B	Brush H30/26RD	BMMO ('Midland Red')	3795	A
ORB 277	1950	Daimler CVD6	Duple C35F	Tailby & George ('Blue Bus Services') Willington		R
MXX 23	1952	AEC Regal IV 9821LT RF	Metro Cammell B41F	London Transport	RF381	R
JOJ 976	1953	Guy Arab IV	Metro Cammell H30/25R	Birmingham City Transport	2976	R
PDH 808	1953	Leyland Royal Tiger PSU1	Park Royal DP40F	Walsall Corporation	808	R
RDH 505	1953	Leyland Titan PD2/12	Roe FH33/23RD	Walsall Corporation	815	A
SHA 431	1953	Leyland Titan PD2/12 Special	Leyland H30/26RD	BMMO ('Midland Red')	4031	RP
FRC 956	1954	Leyland Titan PD2/12	Leyland H32/26RD	Trent Motor Traction Co	1256	R
UHA 255	1955	BMMO S14	BMMO B44F	BMMO ('Midland Red')	4255	R
XHA 482	1956	BMMO D7	Metro Cammell H37/26RD	BMMO ('Midland Red')	4482	R
XHA 496	1956	BMMO D7	Metro Cammell	BMMO ('Midland Red')	4496	A
SUK 3	1957	Guy Arab IV	Metro Cammell H33/27R	Wolverhampton Corporation	3	RP
UTU 596J	1957	Guy Otter NLLODP	Mulliner B26F	Douglas Corporation	9	A
VVP 911	1958	Bedford SB3	Duple C41F	Sandwell Motor Co of Birmingham		R
WDF 569	1959	Leyland Tiger Cub PSUC1	Willowbrook DP41F	Soudley Valley Coaches of Cinderford		R
871 KHA	1960	BMMO D9	BMMO H40/32RD	BMMO ('Midland Red')	4871	R
943 KHA	1960	BMMO D10	BMMO H43/35F	BMMO ('Midland Red')	4943	R
802 MHW	1961	Bristol Lodekka FSF6G	ECW H34/26F	Cheltenham District Traction Co	6037	R
3016 HA	1962	BMMO D9	BMMO/LPC O40/32RD	BMMO ('Midland Red')	5016	R
5073 HA	1962	BMMO S15	BMMO B40F	BMMO ('Midland Red')	5073	R
5212 HA	1962	Leyland Leopard PSU3/4R	Willowbrook B53F	BMMO ('Midland Red')	5212	A
SBF 233	1962	Leyland Titan PD2/28	Northern Counties -	Harper Bros of Heath Hayes	25	R
248 NEA	1963	Daimler CVG6-30	Metro Cammell H41/33R	West Bromwich Corporation	248	R
6545 HA	1964	BMMO S16	BMMO B52F	BMMO ('Midland Red')	5545	R
BHA 399C	1965	BMMO D9	BMMO H40/32RD	BMMO ('Midland Red')	5399	R
BHA 656C	1965	BMMO CM6T	BMMO C44Ft	BMMO ('Midland Red')	5656	R
BON 474C	1965	Daimler Fleetline CRG6LX	Marshall B37F	Birmingham City Transport	3474	R
CUV 219C	1965	AEC Routemaster R2RH/1	Park Royal CH36/29RD	London Transport	RCL2219	R
EHA 767D	1966	BMMO S17	BMMO/Plaxton B52F	BMMO ('Midland Red')	5767	R
GHA 415D	1966	Daimler Fleetline CRG6LX	Alexander H44/33F	BMMO ('Midland Red')	6015	RP
GRY 60D	1966	Leyland Titan PD3A/1	Park Royal H41/33R	Leicester City Transport	60	R
HBF 679D	1966	Leyland Titan PD2A/27	Metro Cammell H36/28RD	Harper Bros of Heath Hayes	27	R
Q124 VOE	1966	Leyland Leopard PSU4/4R	Plaxton -	Midland Red Omnibus Co	5826	A
JHA 868E	1967	BMMO S21	BMMO DP49F	BMMO ('Midland Red')	5868	R
KHW 306E	1967	Bristol RELL6L	ECW B53F	Cheltenham District Traction Co	1000	R
NJW 719E	1967	Daimler Roadliner SRC6	Strachan B54D	Wolverhampton Corporation	719	R
KOX 780F	1968	Daimler Fleetline CRG6LX	Park Royal H43/33F	Birmingham City Transport	3780	R
NEA 101F	1968	Daimler Fleetline CRG6LX	Metro Cammell H42/31F	West Bromwich Corporation	101	R
NOV 796G	1968	Daimler Fleetline CRG6LX	Park Royal H43/29D	Birmingham City Transport	3796	R
XDH 56G	1968	Daimler CRC6-36	Northern Counties H51/34D	Walsall Corporation	56	R
SHA 645G	1969	Leyland Leopard PSU4A/4R	Plaxton C36F	BMMO ('Midland Red')	6145	R
SOE 913H	1969	Daimler Fleetline CRG6LX-33	Park Royal H47/33D	West Midlands PTE	3913	RP
UHA 956H	1969	BMMO S23	BMMO/Plaxton B51F	BMMO ('Midland Red')	5956	R
XDH 516G	1969	Daimler Fleetline CRG6LX	Northern Counties H41/27D	Walsall Corporation	116	R

Note: Please be aware that vehicles on display can vary from time to time as not all museums display their entire 'fleet'. Visitors wishing to see a particular vehicle should make enquiries prior to their visit.

Registration	Date	Chassis	Body	New to	Fleet No	Status
FRB 211H	1970	Bristol VRTSL6LX	ECW H39/31F	Midland General Omnibus Co	322	R
UHA 941H	1970	BMMO S23	BMMO B51F	BMMO ('Midland Red')	5941	A
UHA 981H	1970	BMMO S23	BMMO/Plaxton B51F	BMMO ('Midland Red')	5981	R
WNG 864H	1970	Bristol RELL6G	ECW DP50F	Eastern Counties Omnibus Co	RLE 864	R
AHA 451J	1971	Leyland Leopard PSU4B/4R	Plaxton C36F	BMMO ('Midland Red')	6451	R
OWE 271K	1972	Bristol VRTSL6LX	East Lancs H43/30F	Sheffield Transport	271	RP
PDU 135M	1973	Daimler Fleetline CRG6LX	East Lancs H44/30F	Coventry City Transport	135	RP
NOB 413M	1974	Bristol VRTSL6LX	MCW H43/33F	West Midlands PTE	4413	R
PHA 370M	1974	Ford R1014	Plaxton/Midland Red DP23F	Midland Red Omnibus Co	370	R
JOV 613P	1975	Daimler Fleetline CRG6LX	Park Royal H43/33F	West Midlands PTE	4613	R
99-64-HB	1976	Den Oudsten LOK	Den Oudsten B35D	VAD of Ermele (Netherlands)	5656	A
KON 311P	1976	Leyland Fleetline FE30ALR	Metro-Cammell H43/33F	West Midlands PTE	6311	R
NOE 544R	1976	Leyland National 11351A/1R	Leyland National B49F	Midland Red Omnibus Co	544	R
SDA 757S	1977	Leyland Fleetline FE30AGR	East Lancs H43/33F	West Midlands PTE	6757	R
WDA 835T	1978	MCW Metrobus DR102/1	MCW H43/30F	West Midlands PTE	6835	RP

Notes:

RC 4615	Rebodied 1950
GHA 333	Converted to works tug with AEC engine by Midland Red c1960.
FFY 402	Originally H30/26R
KAL 579	Rebodied 1958
JUE 349	Rebodied 1963
PDH 808	Originally B42F
XHA 496	Converted to Breakdown Vehicle 1972
UTU 596J	Originally registered WMN 485
943 KHA	Entered service 1961
3016 HA	Originally H40/32RD; converted to open-top by Marshall ('Obsolete Fleet') London (OM5)

5073 HA	Reseated from DP40F in 1969
SBF 233	Rebuilt as towing tender 1981
Q124 VOE	Rebuilt as towing tender 1977
PHA 370M	Shortened to B27F by Midland Red in 1979. Reseated to DP23F in 1983.
99-64-HB	Netherlands registration
KON 311P	Gardner engine fitted in 1981. Reverted to Leyland O680 Oct 2005.
WDA 835T	Exhibited at 1978 Commercial Motor Show

Trolleybus Museum at Sandtoft

Contact address: Belton Road, Sandtoft, Doncaster DN8 5SX
Phone: 01724 711391
E-mail: enquiries@sandtoft.org.uk
Web site: www.sandtoft.org.uk
Affiliation: NARTM
Brief description: Home of the nation's trolleybuses
Events planned: 7-9 April 2007 — Easter Trolleydays; 5-7 May 2007 — European Weekend; 26-28 May 2007 — Spring Trolley Weekend featuring trolleybuses from the south of England; 10 June 2007 — Trolleyday; 24 June 2007 — Trolleyday; 8 July 2007 — Trolleyday featuring Vintage Bicycle Rally; 28/29 July 2007 — The Gathering; 11/12 August 2007 — Trolley Weekend with 1940s/50s theme: 25-27 August 2007 — East Midlands Weekend; 8 September 2007 — Trolleyday; 9 September 2007 — Trolleyday; 22/23 September 2007 — Trolley Weekend featuring 6-wheel trolleybuses; 14 October 2007 — St Leger Rally; 11 November 2007 — Twilight Trolleybuses; 8/9 December 2007 — Santa Weekend
Opening days/times: 11.00 to 17.00 on the above dates.
Directions by car: From M180 junction 2, take A161 southbound to Belton. Turn right and museum is 2 miles on right-hand side.
Directions by public transport: Free bus from Doncaster station at 13.30 on 9 April, 7, 28 May, 28,29 July, 27 August, 23 September and 14 October
(please telephone to check operation)
Charges: Adult £4.50, Child/Senior Citizen £2.50, Family £12.
Except: 29/30 July — Adult £6.00, Child/Senior Citizen £4.00.
Facilities: A B(e) D E F G H L P R S T
Other information: Coach tours and private party visits can be accommodated at other times by prior arrangement

Registration	Date	Chassis	Body	New to	Fleet No	Status
note h	1902	Rob Blackwell & Co	Horse-drawn tower wagon	Reading Corporation	'William'	A
WW 4688+	1927	Garrett O type	Garrett B32C	Mexborough & Swinton Traction Co	34	A
KW 6052+	1929	English Electric A	English Electric B32F	Bradford Corporation	562	A
note t+	1929	Guy BTX	Ransomes B—C	Hastings Tramways Co		RP
TV 4484+	1931	Ransomes Sims & Jefferies D6	(chassis only)	Nottingham City Transport	346	R
1425 P+	1932	Fabrique Nationale	Fabrique Nationale B26SD	Liege (Belgium)	425	R
TV 9333+	1934	Karrier E6	Brush H64R	Nottingham City Transport	367	A
ALJ 973+	1935	Sunbeam MS2	Park Royal H31/25D	Bournemouth Corporation	99	R
CU 3593+	1937	Karrier E4	Weymann H29/26R	South Shields Corporation	204	R
FW 8990+	1937	AEC 661T	Park Royal H30/26R	Cleethorpes Corporation	54	RP
ARD 676+	1939	AEC 661T	Park Royal H30/26R	Reading Corporation	113	R
FTO 614	1939	AEC Regent O661		Nottingham City Transport	802	R
CKG 193+	1942	AEC 664T	Northern Counties H38/32R	Cardiff Corporation	203	R
964 H87+	1943	Vetra CB60	CTL B17D	Limoges (France)	5	R
GHN 574+	1944	Karrier W	East Lancs H39/31F	Bradford Corporation	792	R
GKP 511+	1944	Sunbeam W	Roe H34/28R	Maidstone Corporation	56	R
RC 8472+	1944	Sunbeam W	Weymann UH30/26R	Derby Corporation	172	R
CDT 636+	1945	Karrier W	Roe H34/28R	Doncaster Corporation	375	RP
DKY 706+	1945	Karrier W	East Lancs H37/29F	Bradford Corporation	706	R
GTV 666+	1945	Karrier W	Brush UH30/26R	Nottingham City Transport	466	RP
RC 8575+	1945	Sunbeam W	Park Royal UH30/26R	Derby Corporation	175	RP
SVS 281	1945	Daimler CWA6	Duple UH30/26R	Douglas Corporation	52	R
CVH 741+	1947	Karrier MS2	Park Royal H40/30R	Huddersfield Corporation	541	RP
EDT 703	1947	Leyland Titan PD2/1	Roe H34/28R	Doncaster Corporation	94	RP
HKR 11+	1947	Sunbeam W	Northern Coachbuilders H30/26R	Maidstone Corporation	72	R
JV 9901	1947	AEC Regent III O961 RT	Roe H31/25R	Grimsby Corporation	81	RP
HYM 812+	1948	BUT 9641T	Metro Cammell H40/30R	London Transport	1812	R
JMN 727	1948	AEC Regent III O961 RT	Northern Counties H30/26R	Douglas Corporation	63	R
KTV 493+	1948	BUT 9611T	Roe H31/25R	Nottingham City Transport	493	RP
BCK 939	1949	Leyland Titan PD1		Preston Corporation	6	RP
DRD 130+	1949	BUT 9611T	Park Royal H33/26RD	Reading Corporation	144	R
EKU 743+	1949	BUT 9611T	Roe H33/25R	Bradford Corporation	743	A
EKU 746+	1949	BUT 9611T	Roe H33/25R	Bradford Corporation	746	R
EKY 558	1949	Leyland Titan PD2/3	Leyland H33/26R	Bradford Corporation	558	RP
GDT 421	1949	Daimler CVD6	Roe L27/26R	Doncaster Corporation	112	A
LHN 784+	1949	BUT 9611T	East Lancs H37/29F	Bradford Corporation	834	R
ERD 145+	1950	Sunbeam S7	Park Royal H38/30RD	Reading Corporation	174	R
ERD 152+	1950	Sunbeam S7	Park Royal H38/30RD	Reading Corporation	181	R
FET 618+	1950	Daimler CTE6	Roe H40/30R	Rotherham Corporation	44	R
GAJ 12+	1950	Sunbeam F4	Roe H35/26R	Tees-side Railless Traction Board	2	RP
GFU 692+	1950	BUT 9611T	Northern Coachbuilders H30/26R	Cleethorpes Corporation	59	A
JWW 375+	1950	Sunbeam F4	East Lancs H37/29F	Bradford Corporation	845	RP
JWW 376+	1950	Sunbeam F4	East Lancs H37/29F	Bradford Corporation	846	A
JWW 377+	1950	Sunbeam F4	East Lancs H37/29F	Bradford Corporation	847	A
KTV 506+	1950	BUT 9641T	Brush H38/32R	Nottingham City Transport	506	R
BDJ 87+	1951	BUT 9611T	East Lancs H30/26R	St Helens Corporation	387	RP
FKU 758+	1951	BUT 9611T	Weymann H33/26R	Bradford Corporation	758	RP
NDH 959+	1951	Sunbeam F4	Brush H34/31R	Walsall Corporation	342	R
LYR 542	1952	AEC Regent III O961 RT	Park Royal H30/26R	London Transport	RT3323	RP
MDT 222	1953	AEC Regal III 9621A	Roe B39F	Doncaster Corporation	22	R
OTV 137	1953	AEC Regent III 9613E	Park Royal H30/26R	Nottingham City Transport	137	RP
AC-L 379+	1956	Henschel 562E	Ludewig RB17/44T	Aachen (Germany)	22	R
KVH 219+	1956	BUT 9641T	East Lancs H40/32R	Huddersfield Corporation	619	R
FYS 839+	1958	BUT 9613T	Crossley H37/34R	Glasgow Corporation	TB78	R

Note: Please be aware that vehicles on display can vary from time to time as not all museums display their entire 'fleet'. Visitors wishing to see a particular vehicle should make enquiries prior to their visit.

Registration	Date	Chassis	Body	New to	Fleet No	Status
PVH 931+	1959	Sunbeam S7A	East Lancs H40/32R	Huddersfield Corporation	631	R
XWX 795	1959	AEC Reliance 2MU3RV	Roe C—F	Felix Motors of Doncaster	40	RP
9629 WU	1960	AEC Reliance 2MU3RV	Roe DP41F	Felix Motors of Doncaster	41	R
WLT 529	1960	AEC Routemaster R2RH	Park Royal H36/28R	London Transport	RM 529	R
VRD 193+	1961	Sunbeam F4A	Burlingham H38/30F	Reading Corporation	193	RP
657 BWB	1962	Leyland Atlantean PDR1/1	Park Royal H44/33F	Sheffield Joint Omnibus Committee	1357	R
433 MDT	1963	Leyland Tiger Cub PSUC1/11	Roe B45F	Doncaster Corporation	33	R
7830 LG 69+	1964	Vetra EH87	B22T	Lyon (France)	1704	A
JTF 920B	1964	AEC Reliance 2MU3RV	East Lancs B—D	Reading Corporation	48	A
KDT 206D	1966	Daimler CVG6LX	Roe H34/28F	Doncaster Corporation	206	A
66+	1967	Lancia	Dalfa H43/25D	Oporto (Portugal)	140	R
UDT 455F	1968	Leyland Royal Tiger Cub RTC1/2	Roe B45D	Doncaster Corporation	55	R
WWJ 754M	1973	Daimler Fleetline CRG6LXB	Park Royal H43/27D	Sheffield Transport	754	R
8319 JD 13+	1980	Renault ER100	B—T	Marseilles (France)	202	RP
C45 HDT+	1985	Dennis Dominator DTA1401	Alexander H47/33F	South Yorkshire PTE	2450	R
D472 OWE	1986	Dennis Dominator DDA	Alexander DPH45/33F	South Yorkshire PTE	2472	A

+ Trolleybus

Notes:

note h	note h. Unregistered wooden bodied tower wagon. Owned by British Trolleybus Society
WW 4688	Owned by British Trolleybus Society
KW 6052	Caravan conversion to be restored
note t	Possibly Hastings 57 - not yet proven
ALJ 973	Owned by British Trolleybus Society
CU 3593	Owned by British Trolleybus Society
ARD 676	Owned by British Trolleybus Society
FTO 614	Converted to tower wagon
CKG 193	Owned by British Trolleybus Society
964 H 87	French registration
GHN 574	Originally single-decker; rebodied 1958
GKP 511	Rebodied 1960
SVS 281	Originally registered FMN 955
DKY 706	Rebodied 1960
CDT 636	Rebodied 1955
EDT 703	Originally Leyland body. Roe body 1955 ex-Trolleybus
HKR 11	On loan from Maidstone Borough Council
HYM 812	Owned by British Trolleybus Society
LHN 784	Rebodied 1962; chassis new to Darlington
BCK 939	Converted to breakdown vehicle
FET 618	Rebodied 1957 (formerly single-decker)
JWW 375	Rebodied 1962; chassis ex-Mexborough & Swinton
JWW 376	Rebodied 1962; chassis ex-Mexborough & Swinton
JWW 377	Rebodied 1962; chassis ex-Mexborough & Swinton
GAJ 12	Rebodied 1964
NDH 959	Rebuilt/lengthened 1965. Owned by Bristish Trolleybus Society
AC-L 379	German registration. Owned by British Trolleybus Society
FYS 839	Owned by British Trolleybus Society
PVH 931	Owned by British Trolleybus Society
657 BWB	Rebodied 1968; renumbered 227 in 1970 following dissolution of JOC
JTF 920B	Caravan conversion; originally registered 5148 DP
66	Portuguese registration
8319 JD 13	French registration
C45 HDT	Experimental vehicle; originally registered B450 CKW

Ulster Folk & Transport Museum
Cultra

Contact address: Cultra, Holywood, Co Down, BT18 OEU

Phone: 028 9042 8428

Brief description: A unique collection of wheeled vehicles from cycles to trams, railways, buses and cars. Interpretive exhibitions show the development of road transport. Not all the vehicles listed are always on display. Please enquire before your visit.

Opening days/times: All the year round but closing for a few days at Christmas time. From 10.00 on weekdays and 11.00 on Sundays (please 'phone for details)

Directions by car: On A2 Belfast-Bangor road

Directions by public transport: On main Belfast-Bangor railway and bus routes

Charges: £7 (discounts for groups)

Facilities: A D E F G L P R T

Registration	Date	Chassis	Body	New to	Fleet No	Status
CZ 7013	1935	Dennis Lancet I	Harkness B31F	Belfast Corporation	102	R
FZ 7897+	1948	Guy BTX	Harkness H36/32R	Belfast Corporation	112	R

Registration	Date	Chassis	Body	New to	Fleet No	Status
EOI 4857	1948	Guy BTX	Harkness H36/32R	Belfast Corporation	112	R
+ Trolleybus						

Notes:
EOI 4857   Passed to Citybus (2857) in 1973; rebodied 1976

Western Isles Transport Preservation Group
Isle of Lewis

Contact address: 43b Lower Barvas, Isle of Lewis, HS2 0QY
Phone: 01851 840294
Web site: www.witpg.org.uk
Affiliation: NARTM
Brief description: The collection of vehicles can be visited at any time by prior arrangement. At present stored at a variety of locations, the group is planning to bring the collection to a common site incorporating a working museum
Events planned:
Motoring fun day at Stornoway Airport, 11th August 2007
Opening days/times: Viewing at any time by arrangement
Directions: By air from Glasgow, Inverness or Aberdeen or by Ferry via Ullapool or Uig or Oban

Registration	Date	Chassis	Body	New to	Fleet No	Status
DSE 980T	1979	Bedford YRQ	Plaxton C33F	Low of Tonintoul		A
A913 ERM	1984	Bedford YNT	Plaxton B54F	George T. Irving of Dalston		A
F649 FGE	1988	Mercedes	Steedrive 16			A

Notes:
DSE 980T   Originally 45 seats

Wirral Transport Museum
Birkenhead

Contact address: 1 Taylor Street, Birkenhead, Merseyside, L41 5HN
Phone: 0151 666 2756
Web site: www.wirraltransportmuseum.org
Affiliation: NARTM
Brief description: The museum houses a collection of buses, tramcars, motor cycles, cars and a model railway. Local enthusiast groups are restoring some of the trams and buses. Trams operate during weekends and some school holidays.
Opening days/times: Weekends 13.00-17.00. Please see web site for further details
Directions by car: Adjacent to Woodside ferry terminal
Directions by public transport: Bus or ferry to Woodside, or train to Hamilton Square station

Registration	Date	Chassis	Body	New to	Fleet No	Status
BG 8557	1944	Guy Arab II	Massey H31/26R	Birkenhead Corporation	242	RP
BG 9225	1946	Leyland Titan PD1A	Massey H30/26R	Birkenhead Corporation	105	RP
HKF 820	1949	AEC Regent III 9612E	Weymann/LCPT H30/26R	Liverpool Corporation	A344	RP
AHF 850	1951	Leyland Titan PD2/1	Metro Cammell H30/26R	Wallasey Corporation	54	R
CHF 565	1956	Leyland Titan PD2/10	Burlingham H30/26R	Wallasey Corporation	106	RP
FBG 910	1958	Leyland Titan PD2/40	Massey H31/28R	Birkenhead Corporation	10	R
FHF 451	1958	Leyland Atlantean PDR1/1	Metro Cammell H44/33F	Wallasey Corporation	1	R
101 CLT	1962	AEC Routemaster R2RH	Park Royal H36/28R	London Transport	RM1101	R
RCM 493	1964	Leyland Leopard L1	Massey B42D	Birkenhead Corporation	93	R
GCM 152E	1967	Leyland Titan PD2/37	Massey H36/30R	Birkenhead Corporation	152	R
UFM 52F	1968	Bristol RELL6G	ECW DP50F	Crosville Motor Services	ERG52	R

Registration	Date	Chassis	Body	New to	Fleet No	Status
OFM 957K	1972	Daimler Fleetline CRG6LX-30	Northern Counties O43/29F	Chester Corporation	57	R
THM 692M	1973	Daimler Fleetline CRL6-30	MCW H34/10Dt	London Transport	DMS 1692	R
CWU 146T	1979	Leyland Fleetline FE30AGR	Roe H43/33F	West Yorkshire PTE	7146	R
B926 KWM	1984	Leyland Atlantean AN68D/1R	Alexander H43/32F	Merseyside PTE	1070	R

Notes:

BG 8557	Rebodied in 1953. Original body was Park Royal utility
HKF 820	Private ownership. On display at Wirral Transport Museum 6/05
CHF 565	Carries 1949 body
FHF 451	First production Atlantean
FBG 910	Driver trainer 1974-81
RCM 493	Former road safety unit
OFM 957K	Originally H43/29F; rebodied 1984 and converted to open-top (renumbered 75) in 1998
THM 692M	Mobile classroom
CWU 146T	Promotional vehicle for The Hamilton Quarter. Currently H6/2FL
B926 KWM	Last production Atlantean

Below: The Midland Transport Group has United Automobile Services 6080 (SHN 80L), an ECW-bodied Bristol RE restored to the poppy red variant of NBC dual-purpose livery. *Andrew Bagshaw*

Right: Eastbourne Corporation No 12 (JK 8418), a 1939 Leyland Lion with Leyland bodywork, is affiliated with the British Bus Preservation Group.

Part 2

Other Collections of Preserved Buses & Coaches

Aldershot & District Bus Interest Group

Contact address: 111 Park Barn Drive, Guildford, Surrey, GU2 6ER
Web site: www.geocities.com/adbigweb
Affiliation: NARTM, FBHVC.
Brief description: The group was formed in 1994 to consolidate the collection of ex-Aldershot & District preserved vehicles and other artefacts which had been saved over the years. The vehicles range from 1920s Dennis E types to Dennis, AEC and Bristol buses which entered service in the 1960s and 1970s at the very end of the company's existence. The group works closely with the Dennis Bus Owners Association.
Other information: Regular working parties; new members welcome.

Registration	Date	Chassis	Body	New to	Fleet No	Status
OT 8283	1928	Dennis E	(chassis only)	Aldershot & District Traction Co	D210	A
OT 8592	1928	Dennis E	Strachan & Brown	Aldershot & District Traction Co	D217	A
OT 8898	1928	Dennis E	Strachan & Brown	Aldershot & District Traction Co	D226	A
OT 8902	1928	Dennis E	Dennis B32R	Aldershot & District Traction Co	D235	A
BOT 303	1937	Dennis Lancet II	(chassis only)	Aldershot & District Traction Co	709	A
GAA 580	1948	Dennis Lancet III	Strachans B32R	Aldershot & District Traction Co	944	A
GAA 616	1948	Dennis Lancet III	Strachans C32R	Aldershot & District Traction Co	980	RP
GOU 845	1950	Dennis Lance K3	East Lancs L25/26R	Aldershot & District Traction Co	145	R
HOU 904	1950	Dennis Lancet J10	Strachans B38R	Aldershot & District Traction Co	178	R
LAA 231	1953	Dennis Lancet J10C	Strachans FC38R	Aldershot & District Traction Co	196	RP
LOU 48	1954	Dennis Lance K4	East Lancs L28/28R	Aldershot & District Traction Co	220	R
MOR 581	1954	AEC Reliance MU3RV	Metro Cammell B40F	Aldershot & District Traction Co	543	R
POR 428	1956	Dennis Falcon P5	Strachans B30F	Aldershot & District Traction Co	282	R
SOU 456	1958	Dennis Loline	East Lancs H37/31RD	Aldershot & District Traction Co	348	RP
SOU 465	1958	Dennis Loline	East Lancs H37/31RD	Aldershot & District Traction Co	357	R
XHO 370	1960	AEC Reliance 2MU3RV	Weymann DP40F	Aldershot & District Traction Co	370	R
462 EOT	1962	Dennis Loline III	Alexander H39/29F	Aldershot & District Traction Co	462	RP
488 KOT	1964	Dennis Loline III	Weymann H39/29F	Aldershot & District Traction Co	488	R
AAA 503C	1965	Dennis Loline III	Weymann H39/29F	Aldershot & District Traction Co	503	R
AAA 506C	1965	Dennis Loline III	Weymann H39/29F	Aldershot & District Traction Co	506	R
AAA 508C	1965	Dennis Loline III	Weymann H39/29F	Aldershot & District Traction Co	508	RP
CCG 296K	1971	Bristol RESL6G	ECW B40D	Aldershot & District Traction Co	651	RP
KCG 627L	1973	Leyland National 1151/1R/0402	Leyland National B49F	Thames Valley & Aldershot Omnibus Co	127	R

Notes:

OT 8283	Originally Dennis F converted to E type
MOR 581	Rebodied 1967

Aycliffe & District Bus Preservation Society

Contact address: 35 Lowther Drive, Newton Aycliffe, Co Durham, DL5 4UL
Affiliation: NARTM
Brief description: A collection of Darlington area service buses, the majority fully restored and in running order.
Opening days/times: Viewing by prior appointment only.

Registration	Date	Chassis	Body	New to	Fleet No	Status
FHN 923	1940	Bristol K5G	-	United Automobile Services	BDO23	A
GHN 189	1942	Bristol K5G	ECW L27/26R	United Automobile Services	BGL29	R
LHN 860	1950	Bristol L5G	ECW B35F	United Automobile Services	BG413	R

304 GHN	1958	Bristol LS6B	ECW C39F	United Automobile Services	BUC4	RP
AHN 451B	1964	Daimler CCG5	Roe H33/28R	Darlington Corporation	7	R
NDL 769G	1969	Bristol LHS6L	Marshall B35F	Southern Vectis Omnibus Co	833	R

Notes:

FHN 923	Breakdown Vehicle
GHN 189	1949 body fitted in 1954
LHN 860	Converted to OMO c1957
304 GHN	Now fitted with Gardner engine. Was C34F when new.
NDL 769G	Acquired by United Automobile Services (1452) in 1977

Barrow Transport Group

Phone: 01229 870336
Web site: http://website.lineone.net/~barrow_transport
Brief Description: A brief collection of ex-Barrow in Furness vehicles. Restored examples can be seen at rallies. The group plans a museum in the future.

Registration	Date	Chassis	Body	New to	Fleet No	Status
EO 9051	1949	Leyland Titan PD2/3	Park Royal	Barrow in Furness Corporation	124	
EO 9177	1950	Leyland Titan PD2/3	Roe H31/28RD	Barrow in Furness Corporation	147	A
CEO 956	1958	Leyland Titan PD2/40	Park Royal H33/28R	Barrow in Furness Corporation	169	R
CEO 957	1958	Leyland Titan PD2/40	Park Royal H33/28R	Barrow in Furness Corporation	170	R
SEO 209M	1974	Leyland National 11351/1R	Leyland National B48F	Barrow in Furness Corporation	9	R
UEO 478T	1974	Leyland National 11351A/1R	Leyland National B49F	Barrow in Furness Corporation	16	R
CEO 720W	1981	Leyland National NL116L11/1R	Leyland National B45F	Barrow in Furness Corporation	20	A
CEO 723W	1981	Leyland National NL116L11/1R	Leyland National B49F	Barrow in Furness Corporation	23	A
LEO 734Y	1983	Leyland Atlantean AN68	Northern Counties H43/32F	Barrow in Furness Corporation	104	RP
LEO 735Y	1983	Leyland Atlantean AN68	Northern Counties H43/32F	Barrow in Furness Corporation	105	A
E570 MAC	1988	Talbot Pullman	Talbot B20F	Barrow Borough Transport	99	RP

Notes:

EO 9051	Converted to recovery vehicle

Bohemia-Buses Transport Museum

Contact address: Zamek Borec, 41002 Borec, Near Lovosice, Czech Republic
Phone: 00420 6062 89770
Brief description: The Heritage Park is currently closed for development. Vehicles in the collection may be viewed by arrangement. Please contact the address given
E-mail: heritage.collection@bohemiabuses.com
Web site: www.bohemiabuses.com
Opening days/times: Daily 10.00-18.00. Please phone to confirm
Directions by car: Two miles from end of D8 motorway/E55 direction Teplice
Directions by public transport: 550010 Lovosice–Borec–Velemin–Milesov
Facilities: B, D, E, L, P, R, S, T

Registration	Date	Chassis	Body	New to	Fleet No	Status
NRH 802A	1961	AEC Routemaster	Park Royal H36/28R	London Transport	RM798	R
AED 31B	1964	Leyland Titan PD2/40	East Lancs H37/28R	Warrington Corporation	149	A
LJF 31F	1968	Leyland Titan PD3A/12	MCW H41/31R	Leicester City Transport	31	RP
LHC 919P	1976	Bedford YLQ	Duple C45F	"Warrens Coaches, Ticehurst"	-	A
SDX 33R	1977	Leyland Atlantean AN68A/1R	Roe H43/29D	Ipswich Borough Transport	33	R
WYW 82T	1979	MCW Metrobus DR101/9	MCW H43/26D	London Transport	M82	R
OTB 26W	1981	Leyland Atlantean AN68C/1R	East Lancs H45/33F	Warrington Borough Transport	26	R
C386 XFD	1986	Bedford CF250	Bedford -12-	Birmingham City Council		
D176 NON	1987	Freight Rover Sherpa 350	Carlyle B18F	Bee Line Buzz Company		

Notes:

NRH 802A   Originally registered WLT 798

Bolton Bus Group

Contact address: 12 Arundale, Westhoughton, Bolton BL5 3YB
Brief description: A small group of enthusiasts formed to preserve examples of Bolton's buses. Some of the vehicles are displayed at Bury Transport Museum, which can be visited by prior arrangement.
Opening days/times: Please write to the above address to arrange a visit

Registration	Date	Chassis	Body	New to	Fleet No	Status
NBN 436	1959	Leyland Titan PD3/4	East Lancs H41/32F	Bolton Corporation	128	RP
UBN 902	1962	Leyland Titan PD3A/2	East Lancs FH41/32F	Bolton Corporation	169	R
UWH 185	1963	Leyland Atlantean PDR1/1	East Lancs H45/33F	Bolton Corporation	185	RP
FBN 232C	1965	Leyland Atlantean PDR1/1	East Lancs H45/33F	Bolton Corporation	232	R
KUS 607E	1967	Leyland Atlantean PDR1/1	Alexander H44/34F	Glasgow Corporation	LA352	RP
TWH 809K	1971	Leyland Atlantean PDR2/1	East Lancs H49/37F	SELNEC PTE	6809	R

Bounty Country Buses

Contact e-mail: gerald@emerton-roof.fsbusiness.co.uk
Affiliation: NARTM, HCVS and Leyland Society
Brief description: A carefully assembled and unique collection of country buses, representing the great number of independent operators who established a network of country bus services from the 1920s through to the most profitable years of the 40s and 50s and beyond, a tribute to their pioneering spirit of taking the country to the town and the town to the countryside, put together by the Emerton family of Nantwich, Cheshire
Opening days/times: Viewing by prior arrangements only

Registration	Date	Chassis	Body	New to	Fleet No	Status
EC 8852	1929	Vulcan Duchess	Vulcan B26D	Fawcett of Milnthorpe	7	R
WX 2658	1929	Dennis 30cwt	Short B16F	Jackson of Westgate on Sea		R
AG 6470	1931	Reo FB	Economy B20F	Liddell of Auchinleck		R
ABH 358	1933	Leyland Cub KP3	Duple C20F	Oborne of Aylesbury		RP
WP 6114	1934	Commer Centaur B40	Carmichael B20F	Burnhams of Worcester		R
J 9567	1935	Morris Commercial CS11/40	Willowbrook B18F	Safety of Jersey	10	A

Registration	Date	Chassis	Body	New to	Fleet No	Status
HL 7538	1936	Leyland Cub KPZ2/1	Roe B24F	West Riding Automobile Co	464	R
ETA 280	1937	Dennis Ace	Dennis HB16F	Hydro Hotel Torquay		R
DDM 652	1947	Maudslay Marathon II	Duple C33F	Rhyl United Coachways	4	R
GDL 33	1949	Crossley SD42/7	Whitson C33F	Nash of Ventnor		RP
JP 7538	1949	Crossley SD42/7	Duple FC35F	Liptrot of Bamfurlong		R
KTB 672	1949	Crossley SD42/7	Burlingham C33F	Warburton of Bury		RP
HUY 655	1950	Bedford OB	Duple C29F	Ketley of Stourport		RP
NKR 529	1950	Crossley SD42/7	Brockhouse FC33F	Molins Saunderton		R
SVA 438	1958	Bedford C5Z1	Duple Midland B30F	Hutchison of Overtown		RP
TEC 599N	1974	AEC Reliance 6MU4R	Plaxton C45F	Jackson of Kirkby Stephen		R

Notes:

WX 2658	Originally registered KR 66
J 9567	Body new 1929, previously on Bean chassis.
ETA 280	Hotel bus with rear luggage compartment.
DDM 652	Rebodied 1956. Previously Santus half cab.
JP 7538	Rebodied 1955. Previously Bellhouse Hartwell half cab.

Bournemouth Heritage Transport Collection

Phone: 01202 658333

Brief description: The collection comprises vehicles, mainly from Bournemouth Corporation or the Bournemouth area, built between the years 1928 and 1980. Most are owned by the Bournemouth Passenger Transport Association Ltd, which is a registered charity.

Events planned: Please see the enthusiast press for details

Opening days/times: Owing to storage relocation, the collection is not currently open to the public.

Registration	Date	Chassis	Body	New to	Fleet No	Status
RU 2266	1925	Shelvoke & Drewery Tramocar	(chassis only)	Bournemouth Corporation	9	A
LJ 500	1929	Karrier WL6/1	Hall Lewis B40D	Bournemouth Corporation	33	RP
VH 6217	1934	AEC Regent 661	Lee Motors -	Huddersfield Corporation	120	R
BOW 162	1938	Bristol L5G	Hants & Dorset -	Hants & Dorset Motor Services	9081	R
DKY 712+	1944	Karrier W	East Lancs H37/29F	Bradford Corporation	712	A
FRU 224	1944	Guy Arab		Bournemouth Corporation	40	A
JLJ 403	1949	Leyland Tiger PS2/3	Burlingham FDP35F	Bournemouth Corporation	46	R
KEL 110	1949	Leyland Titan PD2/3	Weymann FH33/25D	Bournemouth Corporation	110	R
NNU 234+	1949	BUT 9611T	Weymann H32/26R	Nottinghamshire & Derbyshire Traction Co	353	RP
KEL 133	1950	Leyland Titan PD2/3	Weymann FH27/21D	Bournemouth Corporation	247	R
KLJ 346+	1950	BUT 9641T	Weymann H31/25D	Bournemouth Corporation	212	R
NLJ 268	1953	Leyland Royal Tiger PSU1/13	Burlingham B42F	Bournemouth Corporation	258	R
NLJ 272	1953	Leyland Royal Tiger PSU1/13	Burlingham B42F	Bournemouth Corporation	262	R
RRU 903	1955	Leyland Tiger Cub PSUC1/1	Park Royal B40F	Bournemouth Corporation	266	R
RRU 904	1955	Leyland Tiger Cub PSUC1/1	Park Royal B42F	Bournemouth Corporation	267	R
LJ 147	1959	Leyland Titan PD3/1	Weymann H37/25D	Bournemouth Corporation	147	R
8154 EL	1960	Leyland Titan PD3/1	Weymann H37/25D	Bournemouth Corporation	154	R
297 LJ+	1962	Sunbeam MF2B	Weymann H37/28D	Bournemouth Corporation	297	R
6167 RU	1963	Leyland Titan PD3A/1	Weymann H39/30F	Bournemouth Corporation	167	R
AEL 170B	1964	Leyland Atlantean PDR1/1	Weymann H43/31F	Bournemouth Corporation	170	R
ALJ 340B	1964	Daimler Fleetline CRG6LX	M. H. Cars H44/33F	Bournemouth Corporation	40	R
CRU 103C	1965	Leyland Leopard PSU3/2R	Weymann DP45F	Bournemouth Corporation	103	R
CRU 180C	1965	Daimler Fleetline CRG6LX	Weymann CO43/31F	Bournemouth Corporation	180	R
CRU 187C	1965	Daimler Fleetline CRG6LX	Weymann CO43/31F	Bournemouth Corporation	187	R
CRU 197C	1965	Daimler Fleetline CRG6LX	Weymann H43/31F	Bournemouth Corporation	197	R

Registration	Date	Chassis	Body	New to	Fleet No	Status
KRU 55F	1967	Daimler Roadliner SRC6	Willowbrook B49F	Bournemouth Corporation	55	R
ORU 230G	1969	Leyland Atlantean PDR1A/1	Alexander H43/31F	Bournemouth Corporation	230	R
VRU 124J	1971	Daimler Fleetline CRG6LXB	Roe H43/31F	Hants & Dorset Motor Services	1901	R
XRU 277K	1972	Leyland Atlantean PDR1A/1	Alexander H43/31F	Bournemouth Corporation	277	RP
DLJ 111L	1972	Daimler Fleetline CRL6	Alexander O43/31F	Bournemouth Corporation	111	R
FEL 105L	1973	Leyland Leopard PSU3B/4R	Plaxton C47F	Bournemouth Corporation	105	RP
+ Trolleybus						

Notes:

RU 2266	Believed only chassis & axles are from RU 2266
VH 6217	Converted to tower wagon in 1948
BOW 162	New with Beadle body; converted to breakdown vehicle
FRU 224	Converted to mobile crane for traction poles.
DKY 712	Rebodied 1960

NLJ 268	Originally B42F; used as canteen at Chesterfield 1970-81. Now mobile museum display vehicle.
RRU 903	Converted for OMO and rear door removed in 1957
DLJ 111L	Originally H43/31F

Bristol Omnibus Vehicle Collection

Contact address: 'Combe Barton', High Street, Dinder, Wells BA5 3PL
e-mail: drmichaelwalker@hotmail.com
Brief description: A collection of former of Bristol Omnibus Company vehicles.
Events planned: The vehicles will be attending rallies during the season

Registration	Date	Chassis	Body	New to	Fleet No	Status
JHT 802	1946	Bristol K6A	ECW H31/28R	Bristol Tramways	C3386	A
KHW 630	1948	Leyland Titan PD1	ECW H30/26R	Bristol Tramways	C4019	A
LHY 976	1949	Bristol L5G	ECW B33D	Bristol Tramways	C2736	R
NHU 2	1950	Bristol LSX5G	ECW B42D	Bristol Tramways	2800	R
OHY 938	1952	Bristol KSW6B	ECW L27/28RD	Bristol Tramways	L8089	R
UHY 360	1955	Bristol KSW6B	ECW H32/28R	Bristol Tramways	C8320	R
UHY 384	1955	Bristol KSW6G	ECW H32/28RD	Bristol Tramways	8336	R
924 AHY	1958	Bristol MW5G	ECW B45F	Bristol Omnibus Co	2934	R
969 EHW	1959	Bristol Lodekka LD6G	ECW H33/25RD	Bristol Omnibus Co	L8515	R
972 EHW	1959	Bristol Lodekka LD6B	ECW H33/25R	Bristol Omnibus Co	LC8518	RP
869 NHT	1961	Bristol Lodekka FS6G	ECW CO33/27R	Bristol Omnibus Co	L8579	RP
BHU 92C	1965	Bristol MW6G	ECW C39F	Bristol Omnibus Co	2138	R
FHU 59D	1966	Bristol Lodekka FLF6B	ECW H38/32F	Bristol Omnibus Co	C7246	RP
AFB 592V	1980	Bristol LH6L	ECW B43F	Bristol Omnibus Co	461	R
A954 SAE	1983	Leyland Olympian ONLXB1/R	Roe H76F	Bristol Omnibus Co	9554	RP

Notes:

JHT 802	1949 body fitted in 1957
NHU 2	Prototype Bristol LS

Bristol Road Transport Collection

Contact address: 'The Nook', Water Lane, Walls Quarry, Brinscombe, Stroud GL5 2SS
E-mail: william.staniforth@virgin.net
Brief Description: Collection not currently on public display. For enquiries or an appointment to view a particular vehicle, please write to the address shown, enclosing a stamped self-addressed envelope.

Registration	Date	Chassis	Body	New to	Fleet No	Status
FAE 60	1938	Bristol L5G	-	Bristol Tramways & Carriage Co	W75	A
KHU 28	1948	Bedford OB	Duple C29F	Wessex Coaches of Bristol		A
HPW 108	1949	Bristol K5G	ECW H30/26R	Eastern Counties Omnibus Co	LKH108	A
JEL 257	1949	Bristol K5G	ECW L27/28R	Hants & Dorset Motor Services	1238	A
LHW 918	1949	Bristol L5G	ECW B35R	Bristol Tramways & Carriage Co	2410	RP
MHU 49	1949	Bedford OB	Duple B30F	Bristol Tramways & Carriage Co	207	R
GAM 216	1950	Bristol L6B	Portsmouth Aviation C32R	Wilts & Dorset Motor Services	297	A
LFM 753	1950	Bristol L6B	ECW DP31R	Crosville Motor Services	KW172	R
CNH 699	1952	Bristol KSW6B	ECW L27/28R	United Counties Omnibus Co	860	A
NFM 67	1952	Bristol KSW6B	ECW H32/28R	Crosville Motor Services	MW435	A
UHY 359	1955	Bristol KSW6B	ECW H32/28R	Bristol Tramways & Carriage Co	C8319	A
YHT 958	1958	Bristol Lodekka LD6B	ECW O33/25RD	Bristol Omnibus Co	L8462	RP
980 DAE	1959	Bristol MW5G	ECW B45F	Bristol Omnibus Co	2960	A
904 OFM	1960	Bristol SC4LK	ECW C33F	Crosville Motor Services	CSG655	R
57 GUO	1961	Bristol MW6G	ECW C39F	Western National Omnibus Co (Royal Blue)	2268	A
Q507 OHR	1961	Bristol MW6G	ECW	Bristol Omnibus Co	W151	RP
507 OHU	1962	Bristol Lodekka FLF6G	ECW H38/32F	Bristol Omnibus Co	7062	RP
862 RAE	1962	Bristol SUS4A	ECW B30F	Bristol Omnibus Co	301	R
RDB 872	1964	Dennis Loline III	Alexander H39/32F	North Western Road Car Co	872	RP
DFE 963D	1966	Bristol Lodekka FS5G	ECW H33/27RD	Lincolnshire Road Car Co	2537	R
OHU 770F	1968	Bristol RELL6L	ECW B50F	Bristol Omnibus Co	1071	R
LRN 60J	1970	Bristol VRL/LH/6L	ECW CH42/18Ct	W. C. Standerwick	60S	R
GYC 160K	1971	Bristol LH6L	ECW B45F	Hutchings & Cornelius Services of South Petherton		RP
HAX 399N	1975	Bristol LHS6L	Duple C35F	R. I. Davies & Son of Tredegar		RP
KHU 326P	1976	Bristol LH6L	ECW B43F	Bristol Omnibus Co	376	RP
KOU 791P	1976	Bristol VRTSL3/6LXB	ECW H39/31F	Bristol Omnibus Co	5505	A
C416 AHT	1986	Ford Transit 190D	Carlyle B16F	Bristol Omnibus Co	7416	A

Notes:

FAE 60	Originally bus 2086, converted to lorry in 1952 and tower wagon in 1956.
NFM 67	To Chelveston Group
YHT 958	Originally H33/25RD
Q507 OHR	Originally coach 2111 registered 404 LHT; converted to breakdown vehicle in 1974

Bristol Vintage Bus Group

Contact address: 74 Ridgeway Lane, Whitchurch, Bristol BS14 9PJ
Location: Unit G, Flowers Hill Road, Brislington, Bristol
Affiliation: NARTM
Brief description: A small group of enthusiasts formed to preserve examples of Bristol's buses.
Events planned: Please see enthusiast press for details
Opening days/times: At any time by prior arrangement if someone is available
Directions by car: Flowers Hill Road is off the A4 Bath road, right on the City boundary near the Park & Ride
Directions by public transport: Main bus service to Bath from the Bus Station and Temple Meads railway station stops near Flowers Hill
Charges: No admission charge for viewing or special events

Registration	Date	Chassis	Body	New to	Fleet No	Status
AHU 803	1934	Bristol J5G	BBW B35R	Bristol Tramways & Carriage Co	2355	R
GHT 154	1940	Bristol K5G	BBW H30/26R	Bristol Tramways & Carriage Co	C3336	R
GHT 127	1941	Bristol K5G	ECW O30/26R	Bristol Tramways & Carriage Co	C3315	R
FTT 704	1945	Bristol K6A	ECW L27/28R	Western National Omnibus Co	353	R
LAE 13	1948	Leyland Titan PD1A	ECW H30/26R	Bristol Tramways & Carriage Co	C4044	R

Registration	Date	Chassis	Body	New to	Fleet No	Status
EMW 284	1949	Bristol L6B	Beadle C32R	Wilts & Dorset Motor Services	279	R
JXC 323	1949	Leyland Tiger PS1	Mann Egerton B30F	London Transport	TD130	A
KLB 721	1950	AEC Regent III O961 RT	Park Royal H30/26R	London Transport	RT1599	R
YHY 80	1957	Bristol LS6G	ECW B43F	Bristol Omnibus Co	3004	RP
63 CLT	1962	AEC Routemaster	Park Royal H36/28R	London Transport	RM1363	RP
CWN 629C	1965	Bristol MW6G	ECW B45F	United Welsh Services	134	A

Notes:

AHU 803	Rebodied 1947. Originally a petrol-engined coach; rebodied 1947
GHT 127	Restored in Brighton Hove & District livery
FTT 704	Original Strachans body replaced in 1955
YHY 80	Rebodied 1972.

British Trolleybus Society

Contact address: 8 Riding Lane, Hildenborough, Tonbridge, Kent, TN11 9HX
Affiliation: NARTM
Brief description: The British Trolleybus Society is a contributor society to the Trolleybus Museum at Sandtoft. Vehicles from the collection of trolleybuses can be seen from time to time at Sandtoft on display, and are included in the Sandtoft listing.
Events planned: Details given in the section on Sandtoft Transport Centre

Registration	Date	Chassis	Body	New to	Fleet No	Status
RD 7127	1935	AEC Regent O661	Park Royal L26/26R	Reading Corporation	47	R

Cardiff & South Wales Trolleybus Project

Contact address: 211 Hillrise, Llanedeyrn, Cardiff CF23 6UQ
Affiliation: NARTM
Brief description: The only trolleybus preservation group in the principality of Wales. A regular newsletter is issued, and new members are always welcome, presently £10/annum.

Registration	Date	Chassis	Body	New to	Fleet No	Status
DKY 704+	1945	Karrier W	East Lancs H37/29F	Bradford Corporation	704	A
EBO 919+	1949	BUT 9641T	Bruce H38/29D	Cardiff Corporation	262	RP
KBO 961+	1955	BUT 9641T	East Lancs B40R	Cardiff Corporation	243	RP
DHW 293K	1972	Bristol LH6L	ECW B42F	Bristol Omnibus Co	353	R
+ Trolleybus						

Notes:

DKY 704	Rebodied 1959
EBO 919	Body built on East Lancs frames
DHW 293K	Support vehicle

Chelveston Preservation Society

Contact address: 36 Moor Road, Rushden, Northants, NN10 9SP
Affiliation: NARTM
Brief description: A private collection owned by a few members has evolved to represent most types of Bristol chassis from a range of former Tilling group companies.

Registration	Date	Chassis	Body	New to	Fleet No	Status
MPU 21	1948	Bristol K6B	ECW L27/28R	Eastern National Omnibus Co	3960	RP
FRP 692	1950	Bristol KS5G	ECW L27/28R	United Counties Omnibus Co	692	R
FRP 828	1950	Bristol LL5G	ECW B39R	United Counties Omnibus Co	828	A
NAE 3	1950	Bristol L6B	ECW FC31F	Bristol Tramways	2467	RP
CNH 860	1952	Bristol LWL6B	ECW B39R	United Counties Omnibus Co	426	R
CNH 862	1952	Bristol LWL6B	ECW DP33R	United Counties Omnibus Co	428	R
HWV 294	1952	Bristol KSW5G	ECW L27/28R	Wilts & Dorset Motor Services	365	A
JBD 975	1953	Bristol KSW6B	ECW L27/28R	United Counties Omnibus Co	938	A
KNV 337	1954	Bristol KSW6B	ECW L27/28R	United Counties Omnibus Co	964	R
ONU 425	1957	Bristol SC4LK	ECW B35F	United Counties Omnibus Co	125	RP
RFU 689	1958	Bristol SC4LK	ECW DP33F	Lincolnshire Road Car Co	2611	R
TFF 251	1958	Bristol MW6G	ECW -	Crosville Motor Services	G341	A
675 COD	1960	Bristol SUS4A	ECW B30F	Western National Omnibus Co	603	A
264 KTA	1962	Bristol MW6G	ECW C39F	Western National Omnibus Co	1395	A
268 KTA	1962	Bristol SUL4A	ECW C37F	Western National Omnibus Co	434	A
271 KTA	1962	Bristol SUL4A	ECW C33F	Southern National Omnibus Co	421	R
675 AAM	1962	Bristol MW6G	ECW C34F	Wilts & Dorset Motor Services		A
815 XFM	1962	Bristol MW6G	ECW C39F	Crosville Motor Services	CMG434	A
ABD 252B	1964	Bristol RELH6G	ECW C47F	United Counties Omnibus Co	253	A
EDV 555D	1966	Bristol SUL4A	ECW B36F	Southern National Omnibus Co	692	RP
HFM 561D	1966	Bristol MW6G	ECW C39F	Crosville Motor Services	CMG561	R
TBD 279G	1969	Bristol RELH6G	ECW DP49F	United Counties Omnibus Co	279	A
HAH 537L	1972	Bristol LH6P	ECW B45F	Eastern Counties Omnibus Co	LH537	R
YFM 283L	1973	Bristol RELL6G	ECW DP50F	Crosville Motor Services	ERG283	R
JFJ 506N	1975	Bristol LH6L	Plaxton C43F	Greenslades Tours	326	R
HBD 919T	1977	Bristol VRTSL3/6LXB	ECW DPH41/25F	United Counties Omnibus Co	919	R

Notes:

VV 5696	Rebodied 1949
CNH 860	Renumbered 426 in 1952; Gardner 5LW engine fitted 1956
CNH 862	Gardner 5LW engine fitted in 1956; reverted to Bristol AVW in 1996
TFF 251	Converted to towing vehicle

Cherwell Bus Preservation Group

Contact address: 32 Mill Street, Kidlington OX5 2EF
Brief description: A collection of mainly ex-City of Oxford vehicles housed under cover.
Events planned: The operational vehicles will attend a few events during the rally season.

Registration	Date	Chassis	Body	New to	Fleet No	Status
OJO 727	1950	AEC Regal III 9621A	Willowbrook B32F	City of Oxford Motor Services	727	R
191 AWL	1956	AEC Regent V MD3RV	Weymann L30/26R	City of Oxford Motor Services	L191	R
975 CWL	1958	AEC Regent V LD3RA	Park Royal H37/28R	City of Oxford Motor Services	H975	RP

Registration	Date	Chassis	Body	New to	Fleet No	Status
12 MFC	1961	AEC Bridgemaster 2B3RA	Park Royal H43/29F	City of Oxford Motor Services	312	R
332 RJO	1963	AEC Renown 3B3RA	Park Royal H38/27F	City of Oxford Motor Services	332	R
OFC 902H	1970	Bristol VRTSL6LX	ECW H39/31F	City of Oxford Motor Services	902	RP
AUD 310J	1971	Leyland Leopard PSU3B/4R	Plaxton C51F	O. A. Slatter & Sons of Long Hanborough	40	A
TJO 56K	1971	AEC Reliance 6MU4R	Marshall DP49F	City of Oxford Motor Services	56	A
YWL 134K	1972	Leyland Leopard PSU3B/4R	Plaxton C53F	R. Jarvis & Sons of Middle Barton		A
NUD 105L	1973	Bristol VRTSL6LX	ECW CH41/27F	City of Oxford Motor Services	105	A
RBW 87M	1974	Bristol RELH6L	ECW DP49F	City of Oxford Motor Services	87	A
PWL 999W	1980	Leyland Olympian ONTL11/2R	Alexander H50/32D	Leyland (prototype)	OBC999	A
VJO 201X	1982	Leyland Olympian ONLXB/1R	ECW H47/28D	City of Oxford Motor Services	201	A
VUD 30X	1982	Leyland Leopard PSU3G/4R	ECW C49F	City of Oxford Motor Services	30	R
C729 JJO	1986	Ford Transit 190D	Carlyle DP20F	City of Oxford Motor Services	729	RP

Notes:

PWL 999W   Prototype operated by Singapore Bus Service as SBS 5396B; acquired by COMS in 1987

City of Portsmouth Preserved Transport Depot

Contact address: Friends of CPPTD, 58 South View Gardens, Andover, Hampshire SP10 2AQ
Affiliation: NARTM
Brief description: A collection comprising a range of veteran and vintage buses, most of which spent their working lives in the South of England. Suitable premises in the Portsmouth area are being sought for the Museum following closure of the Broad Street site, but the collection's vehicles (currently in storage at two locations) still operate free bus services and attend rallies, carnivals and other events. Please see the enthusiast press for the latest developments.

Registration	Date	Chassis	Body	New to	Fleet No	Status
note a	1876	Horse bus		G. Wheeler of Fawley		RP
BK 2986	1919	Thornycroft J	Dodson O18/16R	Portsmouth Corporation	10	R
RV 3411	1933	Leyland Titan TD2	English Electric/ Portsmouth Corporation	Portsmouth Corporation	17	R
RV 4649+	1934	AEC 661T	English Electric H26/24R	Portsmouth Corporation	201	RP
RV 6368	1935	Leyland Titan TD4	English Electric O26/24R	Portsmouth Corporation	8	R
CTP 200	1944	Bedford OWB	Duple (replica) UB32F	Portsmouth Corporation	170	R
DTP 823	1947	Leyland Titan PD1	Weymann H30/26R	Portsmouth Corporation	189	RP
AHC 442	1951	AEC Regent III 9613A	Bruce H30/26R	Eastbourne Corporation	42	R
EHV 65	1951	Bedford OB	Duple B29F	East Ham Borough Council		R
LRV 996	1956	Leyland Titan PD2/12	Metro-Cammell O33/26R	Portsmouth Corporation	4	R
ORV 989	1958	Leyland Titan PD2/40	Metro-Cammell H30/26R	Portsmouth Corporation	112	RP
BBK 236B	1964	Leyland Atlantean PDR1/1	Metro-Cammell H43/33F	Portsmouth Corporation	236	R
BTR 361B	1964	AEC Regent V 2D3RA	East Lancs/Neepsend H37/29R	Southampton Corporation	361	R
GTP 175F	1967	Leyland Panther Cub PSURC1	MCW B42D	Portsmouth Corporation	175	R
TBK 190K	1971	Leyland Atlantean PDR2/1	Seddon Pennine B40D	Portsmouth Corporation	190	R
XTP 287L	1973	Leyland Atlantean AN68/1R	Alexander H45/30D	Portsmouth Corporation	287	RP
+ Trolleybus						

Notes:

note a	Not registered
BK 2986	Body is c1910 ex-LGOC B-type. Currently loaned by Portsmouth City Museum to Milestones Museum Basingstoke
RV 3411	Converted to Tower Wagon in 1955. Currently loaned by Portsmouth City Museum to Milestones Museum Basingstoke
RV 4649	Currently loaned by Portsmouth City Museum to Milestones Museum Basingstoke
RV 6368	Originally H26/24R. Currently loaned by Portsmouth City Museum to Milestones Museum Basingstoke
CTP 200	Replica body; wartime livery
EHV 65	Preserved in Hants & Sussex livery
LRV 996	Originally H33/26R

Classic Southdown Omnibuses

Contact address: Dormy Cottage, 2 Alan Road, Wimbledon Village, London SW19 7PT
Affiliation: NARTM
Brief description: One of the largest single privately owned collections of Southdown Vehicles in the country, ranging from 1939 Leyland Titan TD4 to the last Bristol VR delivered new to Southdown.
Events planned: The operational vehicles will attend events in the south of England during the rally season as well as being used for private hire work.

Registration	Date	Chassis	Body	New to	Fleet No	Status
GCD 48	1939	Leyland Titan TD5	Park Royal H28/26R	Southdown Motor Services	248	R
RUF 186	1956	Leyland Titan PD2/12	Beadle H33/26R	Southdown Motor Services	786	R
410 DCD	1964	Leyland Titan PD3/4	Northern Counties FCO39/30F	Southdown Motor Services	410	R
422 DCD	1964	Leyland Titan PD3/4	Northern Counties FCO39/30F	Southdown Motor Services	422	R
HCD 347E	1967	Leyland Titan PD3/4	Northern Counties FH39/30F	Southdown Motor Services	347	R
UUF 110J	1971	Bristol VRTSL6LX	ECW H39/31F	Southdown Motor Services	510	RP
JWV 976W	1981	Bristol VRTSL3/680	ECW H43/31F	Southdown Motor Services	276	R

Notes:

GCD 48	Rebodied 1950
RUF 186	Body built on Park Royal frames
JWV 976W	Fitted with Gardner 6LXB engine

Colin Billington Collection

Contact Phone: 07990 505373
E-mail: royal_blue@lineone.net
Affiliation: NARTM, WHOTT
Brief Description: A private collection of vehicles, formerly operated by the Western & Southern National Omnibus Companies and their successors, spanning the years 1927 to 1985 many of which have undergone extensive restoration. A particular feature is a collection of Royal Blue coaches which can be seen regularly recreating bygone coach travel to the West Country along the old coach routes. Vehicles also regularly attend rallies and running days.
Opening days/times: Viewing by prior arrangements only

Registration	Date	Chassis	Body	New to	Fleet No	Status
VW 203	1927	Leyland Lion PLSC3	Mumford B—R	National Omnibus & Transport Co	2407	A
YF 714	1927	Guy FBB	Vickers B32R	Great Western Railway	1268	RP
RU 8805	1929	AEC Reliance	Beadle C28R	Elliot Bros Royal Blue		A
FJ 8967	1933	Bristol H	Brislington Body Works	Western National Omnibus Co (Royal Blue)	137	RP
BTA 59	1934	Dennis Mace	Eastern Counties B26F	Southern National Omnibus Co	668	R
FTA 634	1941	Bristol K5G	ECW L27/28R	Western National Omnibus Co	345	RP
JUO 983	1948	Bristol LL6B	ECW FB39F	Southern National Omnibus Co	1218	R
LTA 748	1950	Bedford OB	Duple C27F	Southern National Omnibus Co (Royal Blue)	1409	RP
LTA 946	1950	Bristol KS6B	ECW L27/28R	Southern National Omnibus Co	1836	RP
LTA 729	1951	Bristol LL6B	Duple C37F	Western National Omnibus Co (Royal Blue)	1250	R
MOD 973	1952	Bristol LS6G	ECW C39F	Southern National Omnibus Co (Royal Blue)	1286	RP

Registration	Date	Chassis	Body	New to	Fleet No	Status
RTT 996	1954	Bristol Lodekka LD6B	ECW H33/27RD	Southern National Omnibus Co	1876	A
519 BTA	1960	Bristol Lodekka FS6G	ECW H33/27RD	Western National Omnibus Co	1967	A
468 FTT	1960	Bristol Lodekka FLF6G	ECW H38/30F	Western National Omnibus Co	1969	R
672 COD	1960	Bristol SUS4A	ECW B30F	Western National Omnibus Co	600	R
JVS 293	1961	Bristol MW6G	ECW C39F	Western National Omnibus Co	2266	A
286 KTA	1962	Bristol SUL4A	ECW C37F	Southern National Omnibus Co	1234	R
BOD 25C	1965	Bristol Lodekka FLF6B	ECW H38/32F	Southern National Omnibus Co	2065	RP
HDV 624E	1967	Bristol RELH6G	ECW C45F	Western National Omnibus Co (Royal Blue)	2365	R
MOD 823P	1976	Leyland National 11351A/1R	Leyland National B50F	Western National Omnibus Co	2820	R
AFJ 708T	1978	Leyland National 11351A/1R	Leyland National B50F	Western National Omnibus Co	2869	R
AFJ 729T	1979	Bristol LH6L	Plaxton C43F	Western National Omnibus Co	3309	A
FDV 790V	1979	Bristol LHS6L	ECW B35F	Western National Omnibus Co	1560	R
FDV 803V	1980	Leyland Leopard PSU3E/4R	Plaxton C45FT	Western National Omnibus Co	3547	R
LFJ 847W	1980	Bristol VRTSL3/6LXB	ECW H43/31F	Western National Omnibus Co	1203	RP
A686 KDV	1983	Bristol Olympian ONLXB/1R	ECW H45/32F	Devon General Ltd	1814	R
C862 DYD	1985	Ford Transit 190D	Dormobile B16F	Southern National Ltd	300	R
C869 DYD	1985	Ford Transit 190D	Dormobile B16F	Southern National Ltd	307	A

Notes:

VW 203	Body new 1936; original body was Strachan & Brown B32R	JUO 983	Rebodied 1958
		LTA 946	Returned from USA 2002
RU 8805	Rebodied 1935	JVS 293	Originally registered 55GUO
FJ 8967	Re-engined 1939; rebodied 1942	AFJ 708T	Converted to B21D + cycles in 1994
FTA 634	Major rebuild by ECW in 1941 following bomb damage	A686 KDV	Last bus chassis built by Bristol

County Durham Bus Preservation Group

Contact address: 38 Lambton Drive, Hetton-le-Hole, Houghton-le-Spring, Tyne & Wear DH5 0EW
E-mail: enquiries.cdbpg@hotmail.co.uk
Affiliation: NARTM
Brief description: The group comprises individuals who own a number of restored vehicles and are in the process of restoring others. The collection is not normally open to the public but may be viewed by prior arrangement

Registration	Date	Chassis	Body	New to	Fleet No	Status
BTN 113	1934	Daimler COS4	Northern Coachbuilders B34R	Newcastle Corporation	173	A
HHN 202	1947	Bristol L5G	ECW B35R	United Automobile Services	DB216	R
HUP 236	1948	Albion Valiant CX39N	ACB C33F	Economic Bus Services of Whitburn	W7	R
LVK 123	1948	Leyland Titan PD2/1	Leyland H30/26R	Newcastle Corporation	123	A
NVK 341	1950	AEC Regent III 9612A	Northern Coachbuilders H30/26R	Newcastle Corporation	341	R
TUG 20	1954	AEC Reliance MU3RV	Roe C41C	Roe demonstrator		RP
TUP 859	1956	AEC Regent V MD3RV	Roe H35/28R	Hartlepool Corporation	4	RP
VUP 328	1957	Leyland Tiger Cub PSUC1/1	Crossley B44F	Economic Bus Services of Whitburn	A2	A
YPT 796	1958	AEC Reliance MU3RV	Roe C41C	Economic Bus Services of Whitburn	W3	R
221 JVK	1962	Leyland Atlantean PDR1/1	Alexander H44/34F	Newcastle Corporation	221	R
EUP 405B	1964	AEC Routemaster 3R2RH	Park Royal H41/31F	Northern General Transport Co	2105	R
GGR 103N	1974	Leyland Atlantean AN68/2R	Northern Counties H47/36F	OK Motor Services		RP
VPT 598R	1977	Leyland National 11351A/1R	Leyland National B49F	Northern General Transport Co	4598	RP
JPT 906T	1979	Bristol VRTSL3/501	ECW DPH41/29F	Northern General Transport Co	3406	RP
SGR 935V	1979	Bristol VRTSL3/501	ECW H43/31F	Northern General Transport Co	3435	RP

Registration	Date	Chassis	Body	New to	Fleet No	Status
SPT 963V	1980	Leyland Leopard PSU3E/4R	Plaxton C53F	OK Motor Services		RP
AUP 369W	1980	Leyland Atlantean AN68B/1R	Roe H43/30F	Northern General Transport Co	3469	RP
UTN 501Y	1983	MCW Metrobus DR102/37	MCW H46/31F	Northern General Transport Co	3501	RP

Notes:

HHN 202	Rebodied 1957 with 1946 body; passed to Durham District Services (DB216) in 1959
JPT 906T	Originally H43/31F. Has been re-registered twice and now retains original number.

Dennis Bus Owners Association

Contact web site: www.dennisbusowners.co.uk
E-mail: secretary@dennisbusowners.co.uk
Affiliation: NARTM
Brief Description: The Association is the focal point for owners and enthusiasts, offering advice and information to assist in the preservation and restoration of buses built by Dennis Bros of Guildford. The vehicles listed are some of those which are preserved. Other Dennis vehicles are listed in the collections of the Aldershot & District Bus Interest Group, Amberley Working Museum, Bounty Country Buses, Buckland Omnibus Co, Cobham Bus Museum, Dover Transport Museum, East Kent Road Car Heritage Trust, Leicester Corporation Bus Preservation Group, Oxford Bus Museum, SELNEC collection, the TH Collection, the Trolleybus Museum at Sandtoft and others. Membership is open to all Dennis Bus Owners and others interested in the make, details being published on the web site.

Registration	Date	Chassis	Body	New to	Fleet No	Status
KE 4771	1921	Dennis 4-ton	(chassis only) Ch 27	Cooperabancs in Kent		RP
CC 8671	1929	Dennis GL	Roberts T19	Llandudno UDC	2	R
CC 9424	1930	Dennis GL	Roberts T20	Llandudno UDC	3	A
MJ 4549	1932	Dennis Lancet I	Short B32F	Smith of Westoning		R
DL 9015	1934	Dennis Ace	Harrington B20F	Southern Vectis Omnibus Co	405	RP
YD 9533	1934	Dennis Ace	Dennis B20F	Southern National Omnibus Co	3560	RP
JA 5506	1935	Dennis Lancet I	Eastern Counties B31R	North Western Road Car Co	706	RP
JG 8720	1937	Dennis Lancet II	Park Royal B35R	East Kent Road Car Co		RP
FUF 181	1939	Dennis Falcon	Harrington B30C	Southdown Motor Services	81	A
CFN 136	1947	Dennis Lancet III	Park Royal B35R	East Kent Road Car Co		A
CFN 154	1948	Dennis Lancet III	Park Royal B35R	East Kent Road Car Co		R
EFN 568	1950	Dennis Falcon P3	Dennis B20F	East Kent Road Car Co		R
EFN 584	1950	Dennis Lancet III	Park Royal C32F	East Kent Road Car Co		A
HJG 17	1954	Dennis Lancet UF	Duple C41C	East Kent Road Car Co		A
JDC 599	1958	Dennis Loline	Northern Counties H36/31RD	Middlesborough Corporation	99	R
GRD 576D	1966	Dennis Loline III	East Lancs H38/30F	Reading Corporation	76	R
EBB 846W	1980	Dennis Dominator	Angloco Fire Incident Unit			R
C113 CAT	1986	Dennis Dominator DDA	East Lancs CH43/28F	Kingston-upon-Hull Corporation	113	RP

Notes:

JG 8720	Rebodied 1949

The Devon General Society

Contact address: Membership Secretary, Greenfields, The Rowe, Stableford, Newcastle-under-Lyme, Staffs ST5 4EN
Web site: www.devongeneral.org.uk
Brief description: The Devon General Society was formed in 1982 to promote interest in the former Devon General company and its successors, also to stimulate the preservation of all aspects of the company's past for the benefit of future generations. Approximately 35 former Devon General vehicles are currently preserved privately by society members, The society actively assists them and regularly stages events in Devon whereby these vehicles can be enjoyed.
Events planned: Please see web site

Registration	Date	Chassis	Body	New to	Fleet No	Status
NTT 661	1952	AEC Regent III 9613A	Weymann H30/26R	Devon General	DR661	R
VDV 798	1957	AEC Reliance MU3RA	Weymann B41F	Devon General	SR798	A
VDV 817	1957	AEC Regent V MD3RV	Metro Cammell H33/26R	Devon General	DR817	R
XTA 839	1958	Albion Nimbus NS3N	Willowbrook B31F	Devon General	SN839	R
XUO 721	1958	Bristol MW6G	ECW B41F	Western National Omnibus Co (Royal Blue)	2238	R
872 ATA	1959	Leyland Atlantean PDR1/1	Metro Cammell H44/32F	Devon General	DL872	RP
913 DTT	1960	Leyland Atlantean PDR1/1	Roe H43/31F	Devon General	DL913	R
928 GTA	1961	Leyland Atlantean PDR1/1	Metro Cammell CO44/31F	Devon General	DL928	RP
931 GTA	1961	Leyland Atlantean PDR1/1	Metro Cammell CO44/31F	Devon General	DL931	R
932 GTA	1961	Leyland Atlantean PDR1/1	Metro Cammell CO44/31F	Devon General	DL932	R
935 GTA	1961	AEC Reliance 2MU3RV	Willowbrook C41F	Devon General (Grey Cars)	TCR935	R
960 HTT	1962	AEC Reliance 2MU3RV	Willowbrook C41F	Devon General (Grey Cars)	TCR960	R
1 RDV	1964	AEC Reliance 2MU3RA	Harrington C41F	Devon General (Grey Cars)	1	R
9 RDV	1964	AEC Reliance 2U3RA	Marshall B49F	Devon General	9	R
CTT 23C	1965	AEC Reliance 2MU3RA	Park Royal B39F	Devon General	23	R
CTT 513C	1965	AEC Regent V 2D3RA	Park Royal H40/29F	Devon General	513	R
NDV 537G	1968	Leyland Atlantean PDR1/1	MCW H44/31F	Devon General	537	R
TUO 74J	1970	AEC Reliance 6MU3R	Willowbrook B41F	Devon General	74	R
VOD 545K	1971	Bristol VRTSL6LX	ECW H39/31F	Western National (Devon General)	545	RP
VOD 550K	1971	Bristol VRTSL6LX	ECW H39/31F	Western National (Devon General)	550	RP
VOD 88K	1972	Bristol LHS6L	Marshall B33F	Western National (Devon General)	88	RP
ATA 563L	1973	Bristol VRTSL6LX	ECW H43/31F	Western National (Devon General)	563	R
KTT 42P	1975	Bristol LH6L	ECW B43F	Western National (Devon General)	112	R
VDV 123S	1978	Bristol VRTSL3/6LXB	ECW H43/31F	Western National Omnibus Co (Devon General)	584	A
FDV 829V	1979	Leyland National 2 NL116L/1R	Leyland National B50F	Western National (Devon General)	2883	R
LFJ 862W	1980	Bristol VRTSL3/6LXB	ECW H43/31F	Western National (Devon General)	1215	R
A680 KDV	1983	Leyland Olympian ONLXB/1R	ECW H45/32F	Devon General Ltd	1804	R
C526 FFJ	1986	Ford Transit 160D	Carlyle B16F	Devon General Ltd	526	R

Notes:

XUO 721	Originally C39F Royal Blue coach. Rebuilt 1973 as bus numbered 2902 in Devon General fleet.
1 RDV	7ft 6in wide
CTT 513C	Restored by the Oxford Bus Museum Trust
FDV 829V	First production National 2 to enter service in UK

Left: Part of the Bolton Bus group and currently under restoration, former Glasgow Corporation LA352 (KUS 607E) is a 1967 Leyland Atlantean with Alexander bodywork.

Below: Great Yarmouth Corporation 85 (WEX 685M) is an ECW-bodied AEC Swift dating from 1973 and now housed at Dewsbury Bus Museum.

Dewsbury Bus Museum

Contact address: 5 Oakenshaw Street, Agbrigg, Wakefield WF1 5BT
Phone: 01924 258314
Affiliation: NARTM
Brief description: The group was formed in the early 1970s and concentrated on ex-West Riding vehicles. By 1989 the collection had grown and, to provide covered accommodation, a new, 14-vehicle shed was erected. Vehicles can be seen at local events, or on site by appointment.
Opening days/times: Open only on rally days and when work is being done on vehicles (please enquire before visiting).
Transport Collectors Fairs 11 March and 11 November 2007.
Plus museum open day in association with West Yorkshire Transport Society spring rally in Dewsbury town centre (date to be confirmed).
Other information: Other events are being planned — please see enthusiast press for details.

Registration	Date	Chassis	Body	New to	Fleet No	Status
CCX 801	1945	Guy Arab II	Roe L27/26R	County Motors of Lepton	70	A
BHL 682	1948	Leyland Titan PD2/1	Leyland L27/26R	West Riding Automobile Co	640	RP
TWY 8	1950	Albion CX39N	Roe L27/26RD	South Yorkshire Motors	81	RP
EHL 344	1952	Leyland Tiger PS2/12A	Roe B39F	West Riding Automobile Co	733	R
JHL 708	1956	AEC Reliance MU3RV	Roe B44F	West Riding Automobile Co	808	RP
LEN 101	1960	Guy Wulfrunian	(chassis only)	Bury Corporation	101	A
PJX 35	1962	Leyland Leopard L1	Weymann B44F	Halifax Corporation	35	R
WHL 970	1963	Guy Wulfrunian	Roe H43/32F	West Riding Automobile Co	970	RP
CUV 208C	1965	AEC Routemaster R2RH	Park Royal H36/28R	London Transport	RM2208	R
JJD 524D	1966	AEC Routemaster R2RH1	Park Royal H40/32R	London Transport	RML2524	RP
LHL 164F	1967	Leyland Panther PSUR1/1	Roe B51F	West Riding Automobile Co	164	R
NWW 89E	1967	Leyland Leopard L1	Willowbrook B45F	Todmorden Joint Omnibus Committee	9	R
MCK 229J	1971	Leyland Panther PSUR1B/1R	Pennine B47D	Preston Corporation	229	RP
WEX 685M	1973	AEC Swift 3MP2R	ECW B43D	Great Yarmouth Corporation	85	R
XUA 73X	1982	Leyland National 2 NL116AL11/1R	Leyland National B49F	West Riding Automobile Co	73	RP

Notes:

CCX 801	Rebodied 1953
TWY 8	New in 1950 registered JWT 112; rebodied and reregistered in 1958
XUA 73X	Gardner engine fitted c12/87

East Kent Road Car Heritage Trust

Contact address: 33 Alfred Road, Dover, Kent, CT16 2AD
Phone/Fax: 01304 204612
Brief Description: Between the trust and Friends of the East Kent members have around 18 former East Kent vehicles, based at various locations. A museum is planned but until then, the vehicles are taken to the public at various locations and some are available for stage carriage and hire work.

Registration	Date	Chassis	Body	New to	Fleet No	Status
CJG 959	1947	Leyland Titan PD1A	Leyland L27/26R	East Kent Road Car Co		A
EFN 592	1950	Dennis Lancet III	Park Royal C32F	East Kent Road Car Co		R
FFN 399	1951	Guy Arab III	Park Royal H32/26R	East Kent Road Car Co		R
MLL 570	1951	AEC Regal IV 9821LT	Metro-Cammell B39F	London Transport	RF183	RP
GFN 273	1952	Leyland Titan TD5	Beadle C35F	East Kent Road Car Co		R
KFN 239	1955	AEC Reliance MU3RV	Weymann DP41F	East Kent Road Car Co		RP
MFN 898	1956	Guy Arab IV	Park Royal H33/28RD	East Kent Road Car Co		RP

Registration	Date	Chassis	Body	New to	Fleet No	Status
PFN 867	1959	AEC Regent V 2LD3RA	Park Royal FH40/32F	East Kent Road Car Co		R
6801 FN	1961	AEC Regent V 2D3RA	Park Royal H40/32F	East Kent Road Car Co		R
YJG 807	1962	AEC Bridgemaster 2B3RA	Park Royal H43/29F	East Kent Road Car Co		R
AFN 780B	1963	AEC Regent V 2D3RA	Park Royal H40/30F	East Kent Road Car Co		R
AFN 488B	1964	AEC Reliance 2MU4RA	Duple C34F	East Kent Road Car Co		RP
DJG 619C	1965	AEC Reliance 2U3RA	Park Royal C49F	East Kent Road Car Co		A
OFN 721F	1968	AEC Reliance 6U3ZR	Marshall B53F	East Kent Road Car Co		RP
VJG 187J	1970	AEC Swift 5P2R	Marshall B51F	East Kent Road Car Co		R
EFN 178L	1973	Leyland National	Leyland National B49F	East Kent Road Car Co		R
NFN 84R	1977	Leyland National 11351A/1R	Leyland National DP48F	East Kent Road Car Co	1084	RP
TFN 980T	1978	Bristol VRTSL3	Willowbrook H43/31F	East Kent Road Car Co	7980	RP
SKL 681X	1981	Bristol VRTSL3/6LXB	ECW H41/31F	East Kent Road Car Co	7681	RP

Notes:

GFN 273	Running units are ex-AJG30 1939 Leyland TD5
PFN 867	Driver training vehicle from 1976
EFN 178L	Fitted with a wheelchair lift

Eastern Transport Collection Society
Attleborough

Phone: 01603 891284
Affiliation: NARTM
Brief description: The collection includes a number of vehicles owned by the society and members, together with a range of bus memorabilia bequeathed by the late Tony Powell together with other items added by the society. Viewing is by appointment only.
Events planned: Norwich Bus Rally - please see enthusiast press for date.
Opening days/times: By appointment only.
Charges: Free admission but donations welcome.

Registration	Date	Chassis	Body	New to	Fleet No	Status
KNG 718	1950	Bristol LL5G	ECW B39F	Eastern Counties Omnibus Co	LL718	R
NAH 941	1952	Bristol KSW5G	ECW H32/28R	Eastern Counties Omnibus Co	LKH341	RP
MXX 481	1953	AEC Regal IV 9821LT	Metro-Cammell B41F	London Transport	RF504	R
OVF 229	1954	Bristol Lodekka LD5G	ECW H33/25RD	Eastern Counties Omnibus Co	LKD229	R
KDB 696	1957	Leyland Tiger Cub PSUC1/1	Weymann B44F	North Western Road Car Co	696	RP
5789 AH	1959	Bristol MW5G	ECW C39F	Eastern Counties Omnibus Co	LS789	R
675 OCV	1962	Bedford SB3	Duple C41F	Crimson Tours		R
MOO 177	1962	Bristol MW6G	ECW B45F	Eastern National Omnibus Co	556	RP
KVF 658E	1967	Bristol RESL6G	ECW B46F	Eastern Counties Omnibus Co	RS658	R
PBJ 2F	1967	Leyland Titan PD2/47	Massey H34/28R	Lowestoft Corporation	12	RP
EPW 516K	1972	Bristol RELL6G	ECW B53F	Eastern Counties Omnibus Co	RL516	RP
OCK 988K	1972	Bristol VRTSL6LX	ECW H39/31F	Ribble Motor Services	BT988	RP
WNO 556L	1972	Leyland National 1151/1R/0401	Leyland National B50F	Eastern National Omnibus Co	1707	RP
RRM 148M	1974	Leyland National 1151/1R/2308	Leyland National DP51F	Leyland demonstrator		R
NAH 135P	1976	Bristol VRTSL3/501	ECW H43/31F	Eastern Counties Omnibus Co	VR172	RP
RGS 598R	1976	Bedford YMT	Duple C57F	Eagre Coaches		RP
H74 ANG	1990	Dennis Condor DDA1810	Duple Metsec H69/41D	China Motor Bus	DM17	R

Notes

RRM 148M	Suburban Express demonstrator

Ensign Transport Museum

Contact address: Ensignbus, Jubilee Close, Purfleet, RM15 4YF
Telephone: 01708 865656
Affiliation: NARTM
Brief description: The collection is based on ex-London types, the emphasis being to keep vehicles to Class 6 condition, enabling regular operation on heritage services. A number of buses have been successfully repatriated from overseas and Ensign continue to seek rare or unusual ex-London types.

Registration	Date	Chassis	Body	New to	Fleet No	Status
ELP 223	1938	AEC Regal O662	LPTB C33F	London Transport	T499	RP
FXT 183	1940	AEC Regent III O661 RT	LPTB H30/26R	London Transport	RT8	RP
CSL 498	1948	AEC Regent III O961 RT	H30/26R	London Transport	RT981	A
HLJ 44	1948	Bristol K6A	ECW L27/28R	Hants & Dorset Motor Services	TD895	R
JXC 432	1948	AEC Regent III O961 RT	Weymann H30/26R	London Transport	RT624	R
JXC 194	1949	AEC Regent III O961 RT	Cravens H30/26R	London Transport	RT1431	R
KGK 758	1949	AEC Regent III O961 RT	Cravens H30/26R	London Transport	RT1499	R
KYY 961	1950	AEC Regent III O961 RT	Weymann H30/26R	London Transport	RT3232	R
MLL 952	1952	AEC Regal IV 9821LT RF	Metro Cammell B39F	London Transport	RF315	A
MXX 261	1952	AEC Regent III 9613E	Weymann L27/26R	London Transport	RLH61	R
NLE 603	1953	AEC Regal IV 9821LT RF	Metro Cammell B39F	London Transport	RF603	A
NLE 882	1953	AEC Regent III O961 RT	Park Royal H30/26R	London Transport	RT3775	R
NXP 775	1954	AEC Regent III O961 RT	Weymann H30/26R	London Transport	RT4421	R
5280 NW	1959	Leyland Titan PD3/5	Roe H38/32R	Leeds City Transport	280	R
LDS 279A	1959	AEC Routemaster	Park Royal H36/28R	London Transport	RM54	R
VLT 25	1959	AEC Routemaster	Park Royal H36/28R	London Transport	RM25	R
348 CLT	1962	AEC Routemaster	Park Royal H36/28R	London Transport	RM1348	R
799 DYE	1963	AEC Routemaster	Park Royal H36/28R	London Transport	RM1799	R
BCJ 710B	1964	Leyland Tiger Cub PSUC1/12	Harkness C45F	Wye Valley of Hereford		R
CRU 184C	1965	Daimler Fleetline CRG6LX	Weymann O43/31F	Bournemouth Corporation	184	A
CUV 220C	1965	AEC Routemaster	Park Royal H36/29RD	London Country Bus Services	RCL2220	R
JJD 405D	1966	AEC Routemaster	Park Royal H36/28R	London Transport	RML2405	R
NMY 655E	1967	AEC Routemaster R2RH	Park Royal H32/24F	British European Airways		R
SMM 90F	1968	AEC Merlin	MCW B45D	London Transport	MB90	A
EGP 33J	1970	Daimler Fleetline CRG6LXB	Park Royal O45/23F	London Transport	DMS33	R
THX 646S	1978	Leyland Fleetline FE30ALR	Park Royal H44/27D	London Transport	DM2646	A
A250 SVW	1983	Leyland Tiger TRCTL11/3R	Duple C57F	Southend Transport	250	A
B115 ORU	1984	MCW Metroliner	MCW O—F	Shamrock & Rambler	3115	A

Notes:

CSL 498	Originally registered JXN 9
LDS 279A	Originally registered VLT 54
CRU 184C	Originally CO43/31F
EGP 33J	Originally H44/24D
THX 646S	Fitted with Iveco engine 1988 to 1996

Friends of King Alfred Buses

Contact address: 27 White Dirt Lane, Catherington, Waterlooville, Hampshire, PO8 ONB
E-mail: info@fokab.org.uk
Web site: www.fokab.org.uk
Affiliation: NARTM
Brief description: The collection includes 12 former King Alfred Motor Services vehicles that have been rescued from around the world and restored. A charitable trust, FoKAB aims eventually to establish a museum. In the meantime, the vehicles can be viewed at the annual running day and other events.
Events planned:
1 Jan 2008 — Annual running day at Winchester.

Registration	Date	Chassis	Body	New to	Fleet No	Status
OU 9286	1931	Dennis 30cwt	Short B18F	King Alfred Motor Services		R
JAA 708	1950	Leyland Olympic HR40	Weymann B40F	King Alfred Motor Services		RP
POU 494	1956	Leyland Titan PD2/24	East Lancs L27/28R	King Alfred Motor Services		R
WCG 104	1959	Leyland Tiger Cub PSUC1/1	Weymann B45F	King Alfred Motor Services		R
326 CAA	1961	Bedford SB3	Harrington C41F	King Alfred Motor Services		R
595 LCG	1964	AEC Renown 3B2RA	Park Royal H43/31F	King Alfred Motor Services		R
596 LCG	1964	AEC Renown 3B2RA	Park Royal H43/31F	King Alfred Motor Services		R
BHO 543C	1965	Bedford CAL230	Martyn Walker B11	Richmond of Epsom		A
CCG 704C	1965	Bedford VAL 14	Plaxton C49F	King Alfred Motor Services		R
HOR 590E	1967	Leyland Atlantean PDR1/2	Roe O43/31F	King Alfred Motor Services		R
HOR 592E	1967	Leyland Atlantean PDR1/2	Roe H43/33F	King Alfred Motor Services		R
UOU 417H	1970	Leyland Panther PSUR1A/1R	Plaxton B52F	King Alfred Motor Services		RP
UOU 419H	1970	Leyland Panther PSUR1A/1R	Plaxton B52F	King Alfred Motor Services		R
NKJ 849P	1976	Commer Karrier KC6055	Rootes B22F	Enham Village Disabled Transport		R

Notes:

POU 494	Repatriated from the USA in 1993
596 LCG	Repatriated from the USA in 1988
BHO 543C	To be restored to King Alfred condition
CCG 704C	Restoration involved body-swap
HOR 590E	Originally H43/33F; acquired by Bristol Omnibus Co (8602) and converted to open-top in 1979
HOR 592E	Acquired by Bristol Omnibus Co (8600) and converted to open-top in 1979; restored using roof from sister vehicle HOR 591E
NKJ 849P	Mobile display vehicle

Glasgow Vintage Vehicle Trust

Museum address: Fordneuk Street, Glasgow G40 3AH
Phone: 0141 554 0544
E-mail: info@gvvt.org
Affiliation: NARTM
Brief description: Established in a former Glasgow Corporation bus depot.
Opening days/times: Telephone for access information. Prior arrangement only.
Directions by car: From City centre follow London Road eastbound.
Directions by public transport: First Glasgow 43 or 64 from City centre. SPT rail network to Bridgeton station
Events planned: 14 October 2007 — Open Day. Please see enthusiast press or telephone for details
Facilities: B(e), D, T

Registration	Date	Chassis	Body	New to	Fleet No	Status
DBY 001	1932	Fordson ET7	Barbara B31F	Malta		RP
WG 2373	1934	Leyland Lion LT5B	Burlingham B35F	W. Alexander & Sons	P169	R
WG 4445	1937	Leyland Tiger TS7	Alexander C35F	W. Alexander & Sons	P331	A
BUS 181	1938	AEC Regent O661	Scottish Commercial	Glasgow Corporation	AR292	R
CRG 811	1947	Daimler CVD6	Alexander C35F	Aberdeen Corporation	11	A
CRS 834	1948	Daimler CVD6	Walker / Aberdeen CT C31F	Aberdeen Corporation	14	A
GUS 926	1949	Maudslay Marathon III	Park Royal C35F	MacBrayne	136	R
CHL 772	1950	Daimler CVD6	Willowbrook DP35F	Bullock of Featherstone		R
FVA 854	1950	Albion Valiant CX39N	Duple C33F	Hutchisons of Overtown		R
HGG 359	1950	Thornycroft HF/ER4	Croft B20F	MacBrayne	149	R
6769	1955	Albion Victor FT39AN	Heaver B35F	Guernsey Railway Co	55	RP
NSF 757	1956	Leyland Titan PD2/20	Metro Cammell H34/29R	Edinburgh Corporation	757	A
JPA 82V	1957	Albion Victor FT39KAN	Heaver B35F	Guernsey Motor Co	72	RP
KAG 856	1957	Leyland Titan PD2/20	Alexander L31/28R	Western SMT Co	D1375	RP
FYS 999	1958	Daimler CVD6-30	Alexander H41/32R	Glasgow Corporation	D217	R
SGD 65	1958	Leyland Titan PD2/24	Alexander H33/28R	Glasgow Corporation	L163	R
FYS 8	1959	Leyland Titan PD2/24	Glasgow Corporation O29/28R	Glasgow Corporation	L108	R
MSD 407	1959	Leyland Titan PD3/3	Alexander L35/32RD	Western SMT Co	D1543	RP
MSD 408	1959	Leyland Titan PD3/3	Alexander L35/32RD	Western SMT Co	D1544	R
NMS 358	1960	AEC Reliance 2MU3RV	Alexander C41F	W. Alexander & Sons	AC147	R
YYS 174	1960	Bedford C5Z1	Duple C21FM	David MacBrayne of Glasgow	54	R
198 CUS	1961	AEC Reliance 2MU3RA	Duple (Midland) C41F	MacBrayne	63	RP
RAG 400	1961	Bristol Lodekka LD6G	ECW H33/27RD	Western SMT Co	B1634	A
SGD 448	1961	Leyland Titan PD3/2	Alexander H41/31F	Glasgow Corporation	L446	R
SGD 500	1961	AEC Regent V D2RA	Alexander H41/31F	Glasgow Corporation	A350	RP
TCK 821	1963	Leyland Titan PD3/5	Metro Cammell FH41/31F	Ribble Motor Services	1821	R
NGE 172P	1964	AEC Reliance 2U3RA	Plaxton C46F	World Wide of Lanark		A
BJX 848C	1965	Bedford VAS 1	Duple C29F	Abbeyways of Halifax		A
CUV 121C	1965	AEC Routemaster	Park Royal H36/28R	London Transport	RM2121	R
DMS 348C	1965	Leyland Leopard PSU3/3R	Alexander	Alexander (Midland)	MPE62	R
GYS 896D	1966	Leyland Atlantean PDR1/1	Alexander H44/34F	Glasgow Corporation	LA320	R
HGA 983D	1966	Bedford VAS 1	Willowbrook B24FM	David MacBrayne of Glasgow	210	R
GRS 334E	1967	Albion Viking VK43AL	Alexander DP40F	Alexander (Northern)	NNV34	A
HFR 501E	1967	Leyland Titan PD3A/1	MCW H41/30R	Blackpool Corporation	501	A
JMS 452E	1967	Albion Viking VK43AL	Alexander DP40F	Alexander (Midland)	MNV37	RP
NDL 375G	1969	Bedford VAM 70	Duple C45F	Paul of Ryde	12	R
NRG 26H	1969	AEC Swift 2MP2R	Alexander B43D	Aberdeen Corporation	26	A
VMP 10G	1969	AEC Reliance 6U3ZR	Alexander DP57F	Road Transport Industry Training Board		R
XTC 530H	1970	Bedford VAL 70	Plaxton			RP
WSD 756K	1972	Leyland Leopard PSU3/3R	Alexander -	Western SMT Co	L2366	R
XGM 450L	1972	Leyland Leopard PSU3/3R	Alexander B53F	Central SMT Co	T150	R
VSB 164M	1974	Bedford YRT	Plaxton B60F	Craig West Coast Motors of Campbeltown		A
VSS 158M	1974	Ford R1014	Plaxton C45F	Wiles of Port Seton		RP
JGA 189N	1975	Leyland Atlantean AN68/1R	Alexander H45/31F	Greater Glasgow PTE	LA907	R
JUS 774N	1975	Leyland Atlantean PDR1/1	Alexander H45/31F	Greater Glasgow PTE	LA927	RP
MSF 122P	1975	Leyland Leopard PSU3C/4R	Alexander C49F	Lothian Region Transport	122	A
MSF 465P	1976	Leyland Atlantean AN68A/1R	Alexander H-/-/D	Lothian Region Transport	465	RP
OJD 903R	1977	Leyland National 10351A/1R	Leyland National B36D	London Transport	LS103	R
PAU 204R	1977	Daimler Fleetline CRG6LX	Northern Counties H-/-/D	Nottingham City Transport	204	A
RSD 973R	1977	Seddon Pennine VII	Alexander C49F	Western SMT Co	S2670	RP
SSN 248S	1977	Volvo Ailsa B55-10	Alexander H44/35F	Tayside Regional Council	248	RP
XUS 575S	1977	Leyland Atlantean AN68A/1R	Alexander H-/-/F	Greater Glasgow PTE	LA1204	A
TSJ 47S	1978	Leyland Leopard PSU3D/4R	Alexander B53F	Western SMT Co	L2747	RP
VHB 678S	1978	Bristol VRT/SL3/501	ECW O43/31F	National Welsh Omnibus Services	HR4378	A
SAS 859T	1978	Leyland Fleetline FE30AGR	ECW H43/32F	Highland Omnibuses	D17	RP
WTS 270T	1979	Volvo Ailsa B55-10	Alexander H44/31D	Tayside Regional Council	270	RP
EMS 362V	1980	Leyland Leopard PSU3E/4R	Alexander C49F	Alexander (Midland)	MPE362	A
GSO 80V	1980	Leyland Leopard PSU3E/4R	Alexander B53F	Alexander (Northern)	NPE80	R
HSD 73V	1980	Leyland Fleetline FE30AGR	Alexander H44/31F	Western SMT Co	R73	RP
HSD 86V	1980	Leyland Fleetline FE30AGR	Alexander H44/31F	Western SMT Co	R86	R

Registration	Date	Chassis	Body	New to	Fleet No	Status
RSG 825V	1980	Leyland National II NL116L11/1R	Leyland National B52F	Alexander (Fife)	FPN25	A
UHG 141V	1980	Leyland Atlantean AN68A/2R	Alexander H49/36F	Preston Bus	141	R
FSL 615W	1980	Bedford YMQ	Plaxton C45F	Henderson Coaltown of Markinch		R
LMS 168W	1980	Leyland Fleetline FE30AGR	Alexander H44/31F	Alexander (Midland)	MRF168	R
RMS 400W	1981	Leyland Leopard PSU3F/4R	Alexander C49F	Alexander (Midland)	MPE400	R
RRM 386X	1981	Leyland National NL116AL11/1R	Leyland National B52F	Cumberland Motor Services	386	RP
SSA 5X	1981	Leyland Olympian ONLXB/1R	Alexander H45/32F	Alexander (Northern)	NL05	R
UGB 196W	1981	Leyland Atlantean AN68A/1R	Alexander H45/33F	Strathclyde Transport	LA1443	RP
YFS 310W	1981	Leyland National II NL116L11/1R	Leyland National B48F	Scottish Omnibuses	N310	A
KYV 781X	1982	MCW Metrobus DR101/14	MCW H43/28D	London Transport	M781	R
TMS 403X	1982	Leyland Leopard PSU3G/4R	Alexander DP49F	Alexander (Midland)	MPE403	RP
TSO 16X	1982	Leyland Olympian ONLXB/1R	ECW H45/32F	Alexander (Northern)	NL016	R
FLD 447Y	1982	Bedford YMP	Plaxton C35F	Bonas of Coventry		RP
RSC 194Y	1982	Leyland Leopard PSU3G/4R	Alexander C49F	Alexander (Fife)	FPE194	R
ALS 102Y	1983	Leyland Tiger TRBTL11/2R	Alexander C49F	Alexander (Midland)	MPT102	RP
MNS 10Y	1983	Leyland Tiger TRBTL11/2R	Alexander C49F	Central SMT Co	LT10	RP
XMS 422Y	1983	Leyland Leopard PSU3G/4R	Alexander B53F	Alexander (Midland)	MPE422	A
A735 PSU	1983	Volvo Ailsa B55-10 Mk III	Alexander H44/35F	Strathclyde PTE	A109	A
47638	1984	Ford R1015	Wadham Stringer B45F	Jersey Motor Transport Co	23	RP
B177 FFS	1985	Volvo Citybus B10M-50	Alexander H47/37F	Alexander (Fife)	FRA77	A
B100 PKS	1985	MCW Metrobus DR132/6	Alexander H45/33F	Alexander (Midland)	MRM100	A
E186 BNS	1988	MCW Metrorider MF154/12	MCW B33F	Strathclyde Buses	M89	RP
F300 SSX	1989	Renault G10	Wadham Stringer DP29F	Blood Transfusion Service		A

Notes:

WG 2373	Rebodied 1947
WG 4445	Rebodied 1949
BUS 181	Converted to Breakdown Vehicle by J. Hunter A1 buses
CRG 811	Rebodied 1958
CRS 834	Body rebuilt 1962
6769	Guernsey registration
FYS 999	Current Gardner engine replaced original Daimler unit
FYS 8	Originally registered SGD 10
NGE 172P	Chassis originally registered AAG 651B. Rebodied and reregistered 1976
DMS 348C	Converted to recovery vehicle 1982
VMP 10G	Restored in Baxters livery
WSD 756K	Converted to recovery vehicle 1982
VHB 678S	Converted to open top
XUS 575S	Exhibition unit
FLD 447Y	Originally registered BAC 551Y
47638	Original registration Jersey J43063. Currently carries Guernsey registration

Golcar Transport Collection

Contact address: 45 Cowlersley Lane, Cowlersley, Huddersfield HD4 5TZ
Affiliation: NARTM
Brief description: A unique collection of Karrier vehicles, most of which are long-term restoration projects. The collection includes two WL6 six-wheeled saloons.
Opening days/times: Collection opens to coincide with craft weekends at the Colne Valley Museum; can be opened at other times by prior arrangement.

Registration	Date	Chassis	Body	New to	Fleet No	Status
note v	1922	Karrier	(unknown) B20F	(unknown)		A
WT 9156	1925	Karrier JH	Strachan & Brown B26F	Premier Transport of Keighley		RP
DY 5029	1928	Karrier JKL	London Lorries C26D	A Timpson & Son of Catford	117	A
KD 3185	1928	Karrier WL6	Liverpool Corporation B38R	Liverpool Corporation		A
TE 5780	1928	Karrier WL6	English Electric B32F	Ashton-under-Lyne Corporation	8	RP
VH 2088	1929	Karrier ZA	(unknown) B14F			RP
RB 4757	1932	Commer Centaur	Reeve & Kenning B14D	H G Fox of Alfreton		R
JC 5313	1938	Guy Wolf	Waveney C20F	Llandudno UDC		R
14 PKR	1961	Karrier BFD	Plaxton C14F	W Davis & Sons of Sevenoaks		A

Notes:

note v	Unregistered solid-tyred disc-wheeled chassis
WT 9156	Body originally on EH 4960
VH 2088	Period body acquired from Anglesey
RB 4757	Carries 1929 body from Ford AA chassis

Halifax Bus Museum

Contact address: 1 Vicar Park Road, Norton Tower, Halifax HX2 ONL
Brief description: A collection of privately-owned vehicles, most of which operated originally in West Yorkshire.
Events planned: Please see enthusiast press for details.
Opening days/times: The collection is not normally open to the
public, but an appointment to view can be arranged by contacting the above address.

Registration	Date	Chassis	Body	New to	Fleet No	Status
JUB 29	1932	Leyland Titan TD2	Eastern Counties L27/26R	Keighley / West Yorkshire Services	K451	A
JX 7046	1939	AEC Regent O661	Park Royal H30/26R	Halifax Corporation	80	A
JX 9106	1946	AEC Regal O662	Weymann	Hebble Motor Services	181	A
GTJ 694	1947	AEC Regent II O661	Park Royal	Morecambe & Heysham Corporation	10	RP
HHP 755	1948	Maudslay Regal III	Duple FC33F	Greenslades Tours of Exeter		A
AJX 369	1949	AEC Regent III 9612E	Park Royal H33/26R	Halifax Joint Omnibus Committee	243	A
ECX 425	1949	AEC Regent III 9612E	Northern Coachbuilders L29/26R	Huddersfield Joint Omnibus Committee	225	RP
BCP 671	1950	AEC Regent III 9612E	Park Royal H33/26R	Halifax Joint Omnibus Committee	277	R
LTF 254	1950	AEC Regent III 9612E	Park Royal H33/26R	Morecambe & Heysham Corporation	69	R
ODK 705	1956	AEC Regent V D2RA6G	Weymann H3328R	Rochdale Corporation	305	
ROD 765	1956	AEC Regent V MD3RV	Metro Cammell H33/26RD	Devon General	DRD765	R
TTT 781	1956	AEC Regent V MD3RV	Metro Cammell H33/26RD	Devon General	DRD781	RP
UTV 229	1956	AEC Regent V D3RV	Park Royal H33/28R	Nottingham City Transport	229	RP
3916 UB	1959	AEC Regent V 2D3RA	Metro Cammell H38/32R	Leeds City Transport	916	R
LJX 198	1959	AEC Regent V 2D3RA	Metro Cammell H39/32F	Hebble Motor Services	307	R
LJX 215	1960	AEC Regent V 2D3RA	Metro Cammell H40/32F	Halifax Joint Omnibus Committee	215	RP
1925 WA	1961	AEC Bridgemaster 2B3RA	Park Royal H43/29F	Sheffield Corporation	525	R
214 CLT	1962	AEC Routemaster	Park Royal H36/28R	London Transport	RM1214	R
TSJ 272	1962	AEC Bridgemaster 2B3RA	Park Royal	East Yorkshire Motor Services		RP
CTT 518C	1965	AEC Regent V 2MD3RA	Willowbrook H33/28F	Devon General	518	RP

Notes:

JUB 29	Rebodied in 1951 using 1932 body
JX 9106	Converted to tow lorry in 1956 and renumbered L4
GTJ 694	Breakdown Vehicle
HHP 755	Exhibited at the 1948 Commercial Motor Show
TSJ 272	Originally registered 9725 AT
214 CLT	In Halifax Joint Omnibus livery.

Huddersfield Transport Preservation Group

Contact address: 127 Edale Avenue, Newsome, Huddersfield HD4 6LW
Affiliation: NARTM
Brief description: The collection is based in Huddersfield and comprises nearly 20 vehicles, including commercial vehicles and trams.
Opening days/times: Please contact the above address for an appointment to view.

Registration	Date	Chassis	Body	New to	Fleet No	Status
LHN 785+	1949	BUT 9611T	East Lancs H37/29F	Bradford Corporation	835	R
JVH 373	1955	AEC Regent III 9613E	East Lancs L30/28R	Huddersfield Corporation	243	R
JVH 378	1955	AEC Regent III	East Lancs H33/28R	Huddersfield Joint Omnibus Committee	178	R
GHD 215	1961	Ford 570E	Duple C41F	Yorkshire Woollen District Transport Co	871	R
RWU 534R	1977	Leyland Leopard PSU4D/4R	Plaxton DP43F	West Yorkshire PTE	8534	R
+ Trolleybus						

Notes:
LHN 785   Rebodied 1962. Chassis originally Darlington

Irish Transport Trust

Contact address: 14 Mayfields, Lisburn, Co Antrim, Northern Ireland BT28 3RP
Affiliation: NARTM
Website: www.irishtransporttrust.freeserve.co.uk
Brief description: Formed in 1969, the Trust provides for the preservation, recording and information exchange on all aspects pertaining to road transport history, current and future matters. A number of vehicles both pre- and postwar have been restored by Trust members and the Trust itself has seven vehicles from more recent times which are under-represented in preservation. It is planned to obtain limited company status ithis year, and ultimately charitable status with a view to establishing a museum dedicated to road passenger transport in Northern Ireland.
Events planned: 28 April 2007. Annual bus and coach rally at Cultra, Co Down, at the site of the Ulster Folk & Transport Museum. For other events, please refer to the enthusiast press.

Registration	Date	Chassis	Body	New to	Fleet No	Status
FOI 1629	1973	Bristol LH6L	Alexander (Belfast) B45F	Ulsterbus	1629	R
OSJ 620R	1977	Leyland Leopard PSU3C/3R	Alexander (Falkirk) B53F	Western SMT Co	1886	R
SOI 3591	1978	Leyland Leopard PSU3A/4R	Alexander (Belfast) B53F	Ulsterbus	1591	R
VOI 8415	1980	Bristol RELL6G	Alexander (Belfast) B43D	Citybus	2415	R
AXI 2259	1982	Leyland Leopard PSU3E/4R	Wright C49F	Ulsterbus	259	R
BXI 2583	1982	Bristol RELL6G	Alexander (Belfast) B51F	Ulsterbus	2583	R
BXI 339	1984	Leyland Leopard PSU3F/4R	Alexander (Belfast) DP49F	Ulsterbus	339	A

Notes
FOI 1629   First of batch of 100 LH
SOI 3591   Chassis originally AOI 1347 of 1969. Rebuilt 1974-8
VOI 8415   B32D+47 standing when new
AXI 2259   Wright Royale body

John Shearman Collection
Tunbridge Wells

Phone: 01892 534067

Brief description: A private collection which includes vehicles representing traditional British double deckers designed for export markets.

Opening days/times: Vehicles attend rallies every summer.

Registration	Date	Chassis	Body	New to	Fleet No	Status
LEV 917	1946	Leyland Titan PD1/1	Alexander O33/26R	City Coach Company of Brentwood	LD1	R
KSV 102	1954	AEC Regent III 9631E	Weymann H37/28R	Carris of Lisbon	255	R
AD 7156	1966	AEC Regent V 2D2RA	Metal Sections H51/39D	Kowloon Motor Bus	A165	RP

Notes:

LEV 917 — Converted to open-top by Eastern National in 1958. Originally H30/26R. Restored as Eastern National 2102 with the support of the Springhill Vehicle Preservation Group

KSV 102 — Left-hand drive. Portugese registration GB-21-07. Originally H32/26R. Restored with support of Carris AEC Preservation Group

AD 7156 — Hong Kong registration. Originally H50/28D. On display at the Oxford Bus Museum. Restored with support from KMB.

Kelvin Amos Collection

Contact address: 30 Blandford Close, Nailsea, Bristol BS48 2QQ

Brief description: The vehicles in the collection are regularly shown and run on free bus services.

Registration	Date	Chassis	Body	New to	Fleet No	Status
LHT 911	1948	Bristol L5G	Brislington Body Works B35R	Bristol Tramways	2388	R
KED 546F	1968	Leyland Panther Cub PSURC1	East Lancs B41D	Warrington Corporation	92	R
PWS 492S	1977	Leyland Leopard PSU3E/4R	Plaxton C49F	Bristol Omnibus Co	2098	R

Notes:

LHT 911 — Rebodied 1958 with 1950 body

PWS 492S — Rebodied 1983 with Paramount body after a fire

Kent Heritage Bus Collection

Contact: 6 Chelsfield House, Queen's Avenue, Maidstone, ME16 0EP

Brief Description: From its beginnings in 1967 the main emphasis has been to secure for preservation a good cross section of the important passenger models constructed by Tilling-Stevens of Maidstone backed by a general archive of their activities. Local body builders, Short Bros of Rochester and Beadle of Dartford are also represented. The early years of Maidstone & District Motor Services are another special interest. To this end, rare examples operated by the company during its first 50 years 1911-61 have been secured.

Opening days/times: Viewing by prior arrangements only.

Registration	Date	Chassis	Body	New to	Fleet No	Status
KL 7796	1925	Tilling Stevens TS6 Petrol Electric	Short O51RO	Maidstone & District Motor Services	73	RP
KO 117	1927	Tilling Stevens B9A Express	(chassis only)	Maidstone & District Motor Services	425	A
KO 54	1927	Albion PM28	Beadle B30R	Redcar Services of Tunbridge Wells	A54	A
DX 7657	1928	Tilling Stevens B10B2 Express	(chassis only)	Eastern Counties Roadcar Co	P113	R
KO 7311	1928	Tilling Stevens B9A Express	Short B31R	Maidstone & District Motor Services	461	RP
JG 669	1930	Tilling Stevens B10C2 Express	Brush B37R	East Kent Road Car Co	669	R
JG 691	1930	Tilling Stevens B10C2 Express	Brush B37R	East Kent Road Car Co	691	A
KR 8385	1931	Leyland Tiger TS2	Burlingham B34F	Maidstone & District Motor Services	665	RP
OU 7951	1931	Tilling Stevens B10A2 Express	(chassis only)	Aldershot & District Traction Co	TS15	A
LKT 991	1950	Bristol L6A	ECW B35R	Maidstone & District Motor Services	SO43	R

Notes:

KL 7796	Petrol Electric transmission.
KO 54	Exhibited at Amberley as example of pre-war holiday home
KO 117	"Recovered Wormley nr Godalming 6/2001, woodcutter's hut? Beadle body rotted away. Possibly Army HL27, sold off 1942."
DX 7657	Forward control conv and body by ECOC 1935. Restored as normal control chassis.
KO 7311	Body reconstructed from original using original parts
JG 691	One of 35 requisitioned by military 1940
KR 8385	Fitted with utility body 1943

Lancastrian Transport Trust

Contact address: Apt. 11, Admiral Heights, 164 Queens Promenade, Blackpool FY2 9GJ
E-mail: philip@ltt.org.uk
Web site: www.ltt.org.uk
Brief description: The Trust is dedicated to preserving historic buses from Fylde Coast. Vehicles can often be seen at local rallies and other events. Open days held at Blackpool based vehicle restoration workshops. The Lancashire Transport trust also has a growing tramcar collection
Membership details: Support organisation is TransSupport with a £12 annual membership fee. Quarterly magazine published *In Trust*.

Registration	Date	Chassis	Body	New to	Fleet No	Status
GTB 903	1946	Leyland Titan PD1	Leyland H30/26R	Lytham St Annes Corporation	19	R
CCK 663	1949	Leyland Titan PD2/3	Brush L27/26R	Ribble Motor Services	2687	A
DFV 146	1949	Leyland Titan PD2/5	Burlingham FH31/23C	Blackpool Corporation	246	A
JCK 530	1956	Leyland Titan PD2/12	Burlingham H33/28RD	Ribble Motor Services	1455	RP
760 CTD	1957	Leyland Titan PD2/20	Northern Counties H30/28R	Lytham St Annes Corporation	61	A
PFR 346	1959	Leyland Titan PD2/27	Metro Cammell FH35/28RD	Blackpool Corporation	346	A
534 RTB	1961	Guy Arab IV	Metro Cammell H41/32R	Lancashire United Transport	43	R
561 TD	1962	Daimler Fleetline CRG6LX	Northern Counties H43/33F	Lancashire United Transport	97	R
583 CLT	1962	AEC Routemaster 2R2RH	Park Royal H36/28R	London Transport	RM1583	R
RRN 405	1962	Leyland Atlantean PDR1/1	Metro-Cammell L38/33F	Ribble Motor Services	1805	RP
YFR 351	1962	Leyland Titan PD3/1	Metro Cammell FH41/32R	Blackpool Corporation	351	A
CTF 627B	1964	Leyland Titan PD2A/27	Massey H37/27F	Lytham St Annes Corporation	70	R
DTJ 139B	1964	Leyland Titan PD2/40	Roe H37/28R	Ashton-under-Lyne Corporation	39	RP
CUV 290C	1965	AEC Routemaster	Park Royal H40/32R	London Transport	RML2290	R
HFR 512E	1967	Leyland Titan PD3A/1	MCW H41/30R	Blackpool Corporation	512	R
HFR 516E	1967	Leyland Titan PD3A/1	MCW H41/30R	Blackpool Corporation	516	R
SMK 734F	1967	AEC Routemaster	Park Royal H40/32R	London Transport	RML2734	R
LFR 529F	1968	Leyland Titan PD3/11	MCW H41/30R	Blackpool Corporation	529	R
LFR 540G	1968	Leyland Titan PD3/11	MCW H41/30R	Blackpool Corporation	540	A
PFR 554H	1970	AEC Swift MP2R	Marshall B47D	Blackpool Corporation	554	R
ATD 281J	1971	Leyland Atlantean PDR1A/1	Northern Counties H44/33F	Lytham St Annes Corporation	77	R
OCK 995K	1972	Bristol VRTSL6LX	ECW O39/31F	Ribble Motor Services	1995	RP

Registration	Date	Chassis	Body	New to	Fleet No	Status
OCK 997K	1972	Bristol VRTSL6G	ECW H43/31F	Ribble Motor Services	1997	RP
STJ 847L	1972	Seddon RU	Pennine B51F	Lytham St Annes Corporation	47	A
OFR 970M	1974	AEC Swift 3MP2R	Marshall B47D	Blackpool Corporation	570	R
SCS 335M	1974	Leyland Leopard PSU3/3R	Alexander DP49F	Western SMT Co	L2466	R
HRN 99N	1975	Leyland Atlantean AN68/1R	Northern Counties H43/31F	Fylde Borough Transport	79	RP
NRN 397P	1976	Leyland Atlantean AN68/1R	Park Royal H43/30F	Ribble Motor Services	1397	RP
OJI 4371	1977	Leyland Atlantean	Northern Counties H74F	Fylde Borough Transport	71	R
AHG 334V	1980	Leyland Atlantean AN68	East Lancs H50/36F	Blackpool Transport	331	RP
NKU 214X	1982	Dennis Dominator DDA	Alexander H47/33F	South Yorkshire PTE	2214	
F575 RCW	1988	Volkswagen LT55	Optare B21F	Blackpool Transport	575	R

Notes:

583 CLT	Restored to Blackpool livery
CTF 627B	On loan from North West Museum of Road Transport
HFR 516E	Preserved as driver training bus
OCK 995K	Open top conversion 1985
SCS 335M	On display at Glasgow Vintage Vehicle Trust
OJI 4371	Orginally registered EBV 85S

Legionnaire Group

Contact address: 66 Montfort Road, Strood, Rochester, Kent ME2 3EX
E-mail: bob.wingrove@btinternet.com
Brief description: The group aims to restore at least one of each combination of chassis/Legionnaire so that Harrington's last body style is represented in preservation.

Registration	Date	Chassis	Body	New to	Fleet No	Status
SPU 985	1951	Leyland Olympic HR44	Weymann DP44F	Jennings Coaches of Ashen		RP
72 MMJ	1964	Bedford VAL14	Harrington C52F	Reliance Coaches of Meppershall	72	RP
CDK 409C	1965	Bedford VAL14	Harrington C52F	Yelloway Motor Services of Rochdale		A
JNK 681C	1965	Ford Thames 36 676E	Harrington C52F	SP Coaches of Sutton		RP

Notes:

SPU 985	Engine is O600 horizontal No 2
JNK 681C	Used as Harrington demonstrator when new

Leicester Corporation Bus Preservation Group

Contact address: 13 Warren Road, Enderby, Leicester LE19 2DR
Phone: 0116 2751642
Affiliation: NARTM
Brief description: Formed in 2002, the group has been set up to bring together those owning buses formerly operated by 'The Corpo'. Vehicles are mostly stored in the Leicester area and may be viewed by appointment.
Opening days/times: By appointment only.
Charges: Free admission but donations welcome.

Registration	Date	Chassis	Body	New to	Fleet No	Status
OJF 191	1956	Leyland Tiger Cub PSUC1/1	Weymann B44F	Leicester City Transport	191	RP
217 AJF	1961	AEC Bridgemaster B3RA	Park Royal H76R	Leicester City Transport	217	RP
90 HBC	1964	Leyland Titan PD3A/1	East Lancs H41/33R	Leicester City Transport	90	RP
DBC 190C	1965	AEC Renown 3B3RA	East Lancs H44/31F	Leicester City Transport	190	R
FJF 40D	1966	AEC Renown 3B3RA	East Lancs H43/31R	Leicester City Transport	40	RP
GRY 48D	1966	Leyland Titan PD3A/1	MCW H41/33R	Leicester City Transport	48	A
PBC 98G	1968	Leyland Atlantean PDR1A/1	ECW H43/31F	Leicester City Transport	98	RP
PBC 113G	1969	Leyland Atlantean PDR1A/1	Park Royal H43/31F	Leicester City Transport	113	RP
TRY 122H	1969	Bristol RELL6L	ECW B47D	Leicester City Transport	122	RP
ARY 225K	1972	Scania BR111MH	MCW B46D	Leicester City Transport	225	R
GJF 301N	1975	Scania BR111DH	MCW H45/28D	Leicester City Transport	301	R
UFP 233S	1977	Dennis Dominator DD	East Lancs H43/31F	Leicester City Transport	233	RP
MUT 253W	1980	Dennis Dominator DD	East Lancs H43/31F	Leicester City Transport	253	RP
TBC 50X	1982	Dennis Dominator DDA	East Lancs H76F	Leicester City Transport	50	RP

Notes:
ARY 225K   Exhibited Earl's Court 1972

London's Transport Museum Depot
Acton

Contact address: London's Transport Museum, 39 Wellington Street, London WC2E 7BB.
Phone: 020 7565 7299 — 24hr recorded information; 020 7379 6344 — Admin etc
Fax: 020 7565 7250
E-mail: resourcedesk@ltmuseum.co.uk
Web site: www.ltmuseum.co.uk
Affiliation: HRA, NARTM, TT
Brief description: The museum at Covent Garden, London, is now closed for major refurbishment until autumn 2007.
The Depot is a working museum store and treasure trove of over 370,000 objects. Attractions include rare road and rail vehicles, station models, signs, ticket machines, posters and original artworkk.
Depot location: 118-120 Gunnersbury Lane, Acton, London W3 8BQ
Opening days/times: Open for pre-booked guided tours for individuals on the last Friday and Saturday of the month until end of June 2007.
Access by public transport: Tube: Acton Town
Bus: to Acton Town
Car parking: On site parking is reserved for Blue Badge holders and must be requested in advance. Parking available for groups booking a private view.
Facilities for the disabled: Full disabled access including toilets
Charges: Guided Tours — Adult £10, Concession £8.50
Facilities: L S (weekends only)

Registration	Date	Chassis	Body	New to	Fleet No	Status
XC 8059	1921	AEC K	LGOC O24/22RO	London General Omnibus Co	K424	R
MN 2615	1923	Tilling Stevens TS3A Petrol Electric	(chassis only)	Douglas Corporation	10	R
XM 7399	1923	AEC S	LGOC O28/26RO	London General Omnibus Co	S742	R
YR 3844	1926	AEC NS	LGOC H28/24RO	London General Omnibus Co	NS1995	R
GK 3192	1931	AEC Regent 661	LGOC H28/20R	London General Omnibus Co	ST821	R
GK 5323	1931	AEC Renown 663	LGOC H33/23R	London General Omnibus Co	LT165	R
GK 5486	1931	AEC Regal 662	Duple C30F	London General Omnibus Co	T219	R
GO 5198	1931	AEC Renown 664	LGOC B35F	London General Omnibus Co	LT1076	R
HX 2756+	1931	AEC 663T	UCC H32/24R	London United Tramways	1	R
AXM 649	1934	AEC Regent 661	Chalmers -	London Transport	830J	R
AYV 651	1934	AEC Regent 661	LPTB H30/26R	London Transport	STL469	R
BXD 576	1935	AEC Q O762	Birmingham R C & W B35C	London Transport	Q55	R

Registration	Date	Chassis	Body	New to	Fleet No	Status
CLE 122	1936	Leyland Cub KP03	Weymann B20F	London Transport	C94	R
EXV 253+	1939	Leyland LPTB70	Leyland H40/30R	London Transport	1253	R
HYM 768+	1948	BUT 9641T	Metro Cammell H40/30R	London Transport	1768	R
MXX 364	1953	Guy Special NLLVP	ECW B26F	London Transport	GS64	R
NLE 537†	1953	AEC Regal IV 9821LT RF	Metro Cammell B39F	London Transport	RF537	R
NXP 997†	1954	AEC Regent III O961 RT	Park Royal H30/26R	London Transport	RT4712	R
OLD 589†	1954	AEC Regent III O961 RT	Park Royal H30/26R	London Transport	RT4825	R
SLT 56	1956	AEC Routemaster	Park Royal/LTE H36/28R	London Transport	RM1	R
SLT 57	1957	AEC Routemaster	Park Royal/LTE H36/28R	London Transport	RM2	RP
CUV 229C	1965	AEC Routemaster R2RH/1	Park Royal H36/29RD	London Transport	RCL2229	R
KGY 4D	1966	AEC Routemaster FR2R	Park Royal H41/31F	London Transport	FRM1	R
AML 582H†	1969	AEC Merlin 4P2R	MCW B25D	London Transport	MBA582	R
KJD 401P†	1976	Bristol LH6L	ECW B39F	London Transport	BL1	A
TPJ 61S	1977	Bristol LHS6L	ECW B35F	London Country Bus Services	BN61	R
NUW 567Y†	1982	Leyland Titan TNLXB/2RR	Leyland H44/24D	London Transport	T567	R
C526 DYT†	1986	Volkswagen LT55	Optare B25F	London Transport	OV2	R
F115 PHM†	1988	Volvo B10M	Alexander H75D	Grey Green	115	R
note r	1993	Optare MetroRider	Optare B26F	London Transport	MRL242	R

+ Trolleybus

† stored off site, no public access

Notes:

note p	Unregistered; Garden Seat type
AXM 649	Rebuilt with Breakdown Vehicle body in 1950
SLT 56	Prototype new 1954. First Registered 1956.
SLT 57	Prototype new 1955. First Registered 1957.
TPJ 61S	Support collection vehicle
F115 PHM	On loan from Arriva London
note r	Unregistered sectioned exhibit built especially for LT Museum

Medstead Depot Omnibus Group

Contact Address: Hon Secretary, Medstead Depot Omnibus Group, c/o InterPower House, Windsor Way, Aldershot, Hants GU11 1JG.
Affiliation: NARTM, WOMP, Aldershot & District Bus Interest Group, Aldershot & District Omnibuses Rescue & Restoration Society, Southampton & District Transport Heritage Trust. MDOG is a part of the Working Omnibus Museum Project (WOMP), which is a registered charity.
Brief Description: Vehicles from the Medstead Depot Omnibus Group are regularly to be seen at shows and rallies throughout the season. In addition to the vehicles listed, others belonging to members of the Aldershot & District Bus Interest Groups and the Southampton & District Transport Heritage Trust are associated with the Group and stored on site from time to time. There is an open day once per year, associated with the Mid-Hants Railway Alton Bus Rally, usually held in July.
Events Planned: Free bus services between Alton station and Chawton or Selborne and Medstead & Four Marks station and Petersfield station usually operated on the first Sunday of each month between April and September, in association with the City of Portsmouth Preserved Transport organisation, another part of WOMP.

Registration	Date	Chassis	Body	New to	Fleet No	Status
JRX 823	1955	Bristol KSW6B	ECW L27/28R	Thames Valley Traction Co	748	R
TDL 998	1960	Bristol Lodekka FS6G	ECW H33/27R	Southern Vectis Omnibus Co	565	R
RCP 237	1962	AEC Regent V 2D3RA	Northern Counties H39/32F	Hebble Motor Services	619	A
YDL 315	1962	Bristol Lodekka FS6G	ECW H33/27RD	Southern Vectis Omnibus Co	570	R
KHC 367	1963	AEC Regent V 2D3RV	East Lancs H32/28R	Eastbourne Corporation	67	R

Merseyside Transport Trust

Contact address: The Secretary, Merseyside Transport Trust, Carlton House, 17-19 Carlton Street, Liverpool L3 7ED
E-mail: info@mttrust,co,uk
Web site: www.mttrust.co.uk
Affiliation: AEC Society; Leyland Society
Brief description: A collection of around 35 vehicles, mostly from the Merseyside area but including others of special interest.

Registration	Date	Chassis	Body	New to	Fleet No	Status
GKD 434	1946	AEC Regent II O661	Weymann/LCPT H30/26R	Liverpool Corporation	A233	RP
JKC 178	1949	Daimler CVA6	Northern Counties H30/26R	Liverpool Corporation	D553	A
KMN 501	1949	Leyland Titan PD2/1	Leyland H30/26R	Isle of Man Road Services	71	A
KMN 519	1950	Leyland Comet CP01	Park Royal B30F	Douglas Corporation	21	R
MKB 994	1952	AEC Regent III 9613A	Crossley H30/26R	Liverpool Corporation	A801	A
NKD 536	1953	AEC Regent III 9613S	Crossley H30/26R	Liverpool Corporation	A36	RP
NKD 540	1954	AEC Regent III 9613S	Saunders Roe H32/26R	Liverpool Corporation	A40	RP
RKC 262	1955	Leyland Titan PD2/20	Alexander H32/26R	Liverpool Corporation	L161	RP
SKB 168	1956	Leyland Royal Tiger PSU1/13	Crossley/MCW RC23/21F	Liverpool Corporation	XL171	A
SKB 224	1956	Leyland Titan PD2/20	Crossley/LCPT H32/26R	Liverpool Corporation	L227	RP
VKB 711	1956	Leyland Titan PD2/20	Crossley H33/29R	Liverpool Corporation	L255	RP
VKB 841	1957	Leyland Titan PD2/20	Crossley H33/29R	Liverpool Corporation	L320	A
VKB 900	1957	AEC Regent V D3RV	Metro Cammell H33/29R	Liverpool Corporation	A267	R
116 TMD	1958	AEC Bridgemaster B3RA	Park Royal H43/33R	Liverpool Corporation	E3	A
371 BKA	1959	AEC Regent V LD3RA	Park Royal FH40/32F	Liverpool Corporation	E1	R
372 BKA	1959	Leyland Atlantean PDR1/1	Metro Cammell H43/35F	Liverpool Corporation	E2	RP
BHT 677A	1960	Leyland Atlantean PDR1/1	MCW	Wallasey Corporation	15	RP
256 SFM	1961	Bristol Lodekka FLF6B	ECW H38/22F	Crosville Motor Services	DFB43	A
875 VFM	1961	Bristol Lodekka FSF6G	ECW H34/26F	Crosville Motor Services	DFG65	A
501 KD	1962	Leyland Atlantean PDR1/1	Metro Cammell H43/35F	Liverpool Corporation	L501	R
FKF 801D	1966	Leyland Atlantean PDR1/1	MCW H43/35F	Liverpool City Transport	L801	A
FKF 835E	1967	Leyland Atlantean PDR1/1	MCW H43/28D	Liverpool City Transport	L835	RP
FKF 933G	1968	Leyland Panther PSUR1A/1R	MCW B47D	Liverpool City Transport	1054	RP
SKB 695G	1969	Bristol RELL6G	Park Royal B45D	Liverpool City Transport	2025	R
UKA 562H	1969	Leyland Atlantean PDR2/1	Alexander H47/32D	Liverpool City Transport	1111	R
BKC 236K	1972	Leyland Atlantean PDR1A/1	Alexander H43/32F	Merseyside PTE	1236	R
BKC 276K	1972	Leyland Atlantean PDR1A/1	Alexander H43/32F	Merseyside PTE	1276	RP
CKC 308L	1972	Daimler Fleetline CRG6LXB	MCCW H43/32F	Merseyside PTE	3008	A
DKC 330L	1972	Leyland Atlantean AN68/1R	Alexander H43/32F	Merseyside PTE	1330	A
VWM 83L	1973	Leyland Atlantean AN68/1R	Alexander H45/29D	Southport Corporation	83	R
OLV 551M	1974	Leyland Atlantean AN68/1R	Alexander O43/32F	Merseyside PTE	1551	A
GKA 74N	1975	Bristol VRTSL6LX	East Lancs H43/32F	Merseyside PTE	2122	A
MTJ 771S	1977	Leyland National 11351A/1R	Leyland National B49F	Merseyside PTE	1771	RP
OEM 788S	1978	Leyland Atlantean AN68A/1R	MCW H43/32F	Merseyside PTE	1788	RP
TWM 220V	1979	Leyland Atlantean AN68A/1R	East Lancs H45/33F	Merseyside PTE	1836	R
UKA 23V	1980	MCW Metrobus DR103/2	MCW H43/30F	Merseyside PTE	0023	RP
VHF 57V	1980	Bedford YMT	Plaxton C49F	Toppings Coaches		A
WWM 904W	1980	Dennis Dominator DD	Willowbrook H45/33F	Merseyside PTE	0027	RP
EKA 220Y	1982	Leyland Tiger TRCTL11/1R	Duple C49F	Merseyside PTE	7020	RP
A112 HLV	1984	Leyland Atlantean AN68D/1R	Alexander H43/32F	Merseyside PTE	1032	R
A135 HLV	1984	Leyland Atlantean AN68D/1R	Alexander H43/32F	Merseyside PTE	1055	R
D685 SEM	1986	Dodge S56	Alexander B23F	Merseyside Transport	7685	A
F261 YTJ	1989	Leyland Olympian ONCL10/1/R2	Northern Counties H47/30F	Merseyside Transport	0261	RP

Notes

KMN 519	On loan to British Commercial Vehicle Museum at Leyland ? 6/05 parked Burscough Privately owned
SKB 168	Originally B40D numbered SL171; rebuilt by Metro Cammell in 1961

116 TMD	Former AEC demonstrator; acquired by Liverpool Corporation (E3) in 1959
BHT 677A	Originally registered HHF15
FKF 835E	Originally H43/35F. Rebuilt by Pennine Coachcraft 1969.
OEM 788S	Private ownership - on loan to MTT
A112 HLV	Private ownership - on loan to MTT

The Mike Sutcliffe Collection

Phone: 01525 221676
E-mail: sutcliffes@leylandman.co.uk
Affiliation: NARTM; Leyland Society member; HCVS member
Brief description: A collection of 15 vehicles, mainly buses of Leyland manufacture from the period 1908 to 1934, this is the most significant collection of early motorbuses in the world, and includes the oldest British-built motorbus. Mike Sutcliffe was recently awarded the MBE 'for his services to Motor Heritage'
Opening days/times: Viewing can be arranged by prior appointment only. There is no charge, but donations are welcome.

Registration	Date	Chassis	Body	New to	Fleet No	Status
LN 7270	1908	Leyland X2	Thomas Tilling O18/16RO	London Central Motor Omnibus Co	14	R
HE 12	1913	Leyland S3.30.T	Brush B27F	Barnsley & District Electric Traction Co	5	R
LF 9967	1913	Leyland S3.30.T	Birch O20/16RO	Wellingborough Motor Omnibus Co	H	R
CC 1087	1914	Leyland S4.36.T3	Leyland Ch32	London & North Western Railway	59	R
BD 209	1921	Leyland G7	Dodson Ch/B32D	United Counties Omnibus Co	B15	R
C 2367	1921	Leyland G	Phoenix O23/20RO	Todmorden Corporation	14	R
DM 2583	1923	Leyland SG7	Leyland FB40D	Brookes Bros ('White Rose') of Rhyl	27	R
XU 7498	1924	Leyland LB5	Dodson O26/22RO	Chocolate Express Omnibus Co	B6	R
PW 8605	1926	ADC 415	United B35F	United Automobile Services	E61	A
YG 7831	1934	Leyland Tiger TS6	Northern Counties B36R	Todmorden Joint Omnibus Committee	15	RP

Notes:

LN 7270	Body new 1906 Bought by LCMOC 1908. Orig on Milnes Daimler chassis of Thomas Tilling
LF 9967	On loan to British Commercial Vehicle Museum at Leyland
CC 1087	Registered LP8597 by War Office in 1915. Registered XA8086 in 1921; reverted to CC1087 in 1980.
C 2367	On loan to Manchester Museum of Transport
BD 209	Formerly a Dodson demonstrator and Olympia Commercial Motor Show exhibit 1921
YG 7831	Rebuilt to recovery vehicle; to be restored back to a bus

North East Bus Preservation Trust Ltd

Contact address: The Secretary. 8 Seaburn Hill, Sunderland SR6 8BS
Phone: 0191 548 7367
E-mail: northbritish@supanet.com
Affiliation: NARTM
Brief description: The collection is displayed at an 1826 former locomotive shed on the Bowes Railway, Gateshead. This accommodates up to 10 vehicles, and so vehicles rotate between this and other locations. If you wish to view a particular vehicle, you will need to mention this when making arrangements to view.
Opening days/times: Viewing by prior arrangement only.

Above: AEC Regent V KHC 367 was new to Eastbourne Corporation in 1963 as its No 67, and is now with the Medstead Depot Omnibus Group.

Below: One of the SELNEC Preservation Society's large number of preserved Manchester-area buses is 1972 Seddon Pennine IV 1700 (YDB 453L).

Registration	Date	Chassis	Body	New to	Fleet No	Status
CN 4740	1931	SOS IM4	Short B34F	Northern General Transport Co	540	A
CN 6100	1934	Northern General Transport SE6 (LSE4)	Short B44F	Northern General Transport Co	604	RP
DPT 848	1939	Leyland Tiger TS8	Roe B32F	Sunderland District Omnibus Co	159	R
EF 7380	1942	Leyland Titan TD7	Roe H26/22C	West Hartlepool Corporation	36	R
GSR 244	1943	Commer Q4	Scottish Aviation C29F	Meffan of Kirriemiur		RP
AHL 694	1947	Leyland Tiger PS1/1	Barnaby C33F	J. Bullock & Sons of Featherstone	284	R
KTJ 502	1947	Leyland Tiger PS1	Burlingham B35F	Haslingden Corporation	2	RP
ENT 776	1948	Leyland Tiger PS1	Burlingham C33F	Premier of Watford		R
ABR 433	1949	Crossley DD42/7C	Crossley H56R	Sunderland Corporation	100	RP
CFK 340	1949	AEC Regal III 6821A	Burlingham C33F	H. & E. Burnham of Worcester		R
LYM 729	1951	AEC Regal IV 9621E	ECW C—F	Tillings Transport		RP
CBR 539	1952	Guy Arab III	Roe H33/25R	Sunderland Corporation	139	RP
PHN 831	1952	Bristol LS5G	ECW B45F	United Automobile Services	BU2	A
SHN 301	1952	AEC Regal IV 9821E	Burlingham C41C	Scotts Greys of Darlington	5	R
DCN 83	1953	AEC Beadle	Beadle C35F	Northern General Transport Co	1483	A
SPT 65	1955	Guy Arab LUF	Weymann B44F	Northern General Transport Co	1665	RP
UUA 212	1955	Leyland Titan PD2/11	Roe H33/25R	Leeds City Transport	212	R
JHL 701	1956	Bedford SBG	Plaxton C41F	Swan of Berwick		R
UFJ 292	1957	Guy Arab IV	Massey H30/26R	Exeter Corporation	52	R
WTS 708A	1957	Bristol LS5G	ECW B45F	United Automobile Services	BU250	A
AFT 930	1958	Leyland Titan PD3/4	Metro-Cammell H41/32R	Tynemouth & District Omnibus Co	230	RP
OSK 831	1958	Karrier BFD3023	Plaxton C14F	Brocksbank of Leeds		RP
TCO 537	1960	Leyland Atlantean	Metro-Cammell H44/33F	Plymouth Corporation	137	R
204 UXJ	1961	AEC Routemaster	Park Royal H36/28R	London Transport	RM1058	RP
6249 UP	1963	Leyland Leopard PSU3/3RT	Alexander DP51F	Venture Transport Co of Consett	249	RP
ACU 304B	1963	Leyland Leopard PSU3/3R	Plaxton B55F	Stanhope Motor Services		R
PCN 762	1964	AEC Routemaster 3R2RH	Park Royal H41/31F	Northern General Transport Co	2099	R
WBR 248	1964	Atkinson Alpha PM746HL	Marshall B45D	Sunderland Corporation	48	R
FBR 53D	1966	Leyland Panther PSUR1/1R	Strachan B47D	Sunderland Corporation	53	R
JJD 551D	1966	AEC Routemaster	Park Royal H40/32R	London Transport	RML2551	R
ZV 1510	1966	Leyland Atlantean PDR1/1 Mk2	Metro-Cammell O44/34F	Newcastle Corporation	118	A
ECU 201E	1967	Bristol RESL6L	ECW B45D	South Shields Corporation	1	R
SMK 686F	1967	AEC Routemaster	Park Royal H40/32R	London Transport	RML2686	R
SMK 732F	1967	AEC Routemaster	Park Royal H40/32R	London Transport	RML2732	R
VVK 149G	1969	Bedford J6	Nicolou B33D	Cyprus		R
WHN 411G	1969	Bristol VRTSL6LX	ECW H39/31F	United Automobile Services	601	A
WHA 237H	1970	Leyland Leopard PSU3A/4R	Plaxton C49F	BMMO ('Midland Red')	6237	RP
VTY 543J	1970	Leyland Leopard PSU3A/4R	Plaxton C45F	Tyne Valley of Acomb		A
GAN 744J	1971	Leyland Leopard PSU5/4RT	Plaxton C57F	Banfield Coaches		RP
GAN 745J	1971	Leyland Leopard PSU5/4RT	Plaxton C57F	Banfield Coaches		RP
PCW 203J	1971	Bristol RESL6L	Pennine B45F	Burnley, Colne & Nelson	103	R
SWV 155J	1971	Daimler Fleetline CRG6LX	Northern Counties H-/-F	Swindon Corporation		RP
GBB 524K	1972	Leyland Atlantean PDR2/1	Alexander H48/30D	Tyne & Wear PTE	688	RP
MCN 30K	1972	Leyland/NGT Tynesider	Weymann/Northern General H39/29F	Northern General Transport Co	3000	R
NHN 250K	1972	Daimler Fleetline SRG6LX-36	Roe B48D	Darlington Corporation	50	R
E901 DRG	1973	Bedford YRQ	Plaxton C45F	Smith of Durham		RP
JFT 228N	1974	Leyland Leopard AN68/1R	Park Royal O43/34F	Northern General Transport Co		RP
GUP 907N	1975	Bristol LH6L	ECW B43F	United Automobile Services	1623	R
E903 DRG	1975	Ford R1114	Plaxton C53F	Smith of Durham		RP
OCU 769R	1977	Scania BR111DH	MCW H45/29D	Tyne & Wear PTE	769	RP
OCU 807R	1977	Leyland Fleetline FE30AGR	Alexander H44/30F	Tyne & Wear PTE	807	A
RCU 588S	1977	Leyland Atlantean AN68/2R	Willowbrook H48/34F	Tyne & Wear PTE	588	RP
RCU 838S	1978	Daimler Fleetline FE30AGR	Alexander H44/30F	Tyne & Wear PTE	838	R
SCN 268S	1978	Leyland Atlantean AN68A/2R	Alexander H49/37F	Tyne & Wear PTE	268	R
JPT 901T	1978	Bristol VRTSL3/501	ECW H43/31F	Northern General Transport Co	3401	R
EJR 110W	1980	Leyland Atlantean AN68A/2R	Alexander H49/38F	Tyne & Wear PTE	110	R
EJR 111W	1980	Leyland Atlantean AN68A/2R	Alexander H49/38F	Tyne & Wear PTE	111	RP
FTN 710W	1981	Leyland National 2	Leyland National B49F	Northern General Transport Co	4710	RP

Registration	Date	Chassis	Body	New to	Fleet No	Status
PAJ 829X	1981	Bristol VRT/3/6LXB	ECW H43/31F	United Automobile Services	829	RP

Notes:

GSR 244	1943 military chassis lengthened and body fitted 1950		WHA 237H	Towing vehicle
ABR 433	Fitted with Gardner 5LW engine		MCN 30K	Rebuilt from 1958 Leyland Titan PD3/4 new to Tyneside
WTS 708A	Originally registered 650 CHN.			Tramways & Tramroads Co (49) registered NNL 49
OSK 831	Originally registered 6666 U		E901 DRG	Built 1973, stored until 1988
ACU 304B	Originally registered 6 MPT		JFT 228N	Originally H43/28D. Converted to open-top 1986
PCN 762	Originally registered RCN 699		E903 DRG	Built 1975, stored until 1988
ZV 1510	Originally H44/34F, registered KBB 118D		RCU 838S	Originally H44/27D
VVK 149G	Original Cyprus registration TEC 598.			
	Replica body constructed 2003			

Peter Stanier Collection

Phone: 01474 814476
Brief description: A collection of preserved Leyland petrol-engined vehicles with their origins in the island of Jersey
Opening days/times: Not normally open for viewing. Arrangements to visit can be made, strictly by appointment, telephoning first for details

Registration	Date	Chassis	Body	New to	Fleet No	Status
DM 6228	1929	Leyland Lioness LTB1	Burlingham C26D	Brooks Bros of Rhyl	7	
SV 6107	1929	Leyland Titan TD1	Leyland L24/24R (1931)	Jersey Motor Transport Co	24	

Notes:

SV 6107	Rebodied in 1934; originally registered J 1199

Ribble Vehicle Preservation Trust

Contact address: 34 Greystoke Park, Gosforth, Newcastle upon Tyne NE3 2DZ
Affiliation: NARTM
Brief description: The Trust promotes the preservation and restoration of vehicles from Ribble and associated companies.

Registration	Date	Chassis	Body	New to	Fleet No	Status
CK 4474	1931	Leyland Tiger TS3	Leyland C26F	Ribble Motor Services	1117	A
RN 7588	1935	Leyland Tiger TS7	Burlingham B35F	Ribble Motor Services	209	R
TJ 6760	1935	Leyland Lion LT5A	Leyland B32R	Lytham St Annes Corporation	24	RP
BTF 25	1937	Leyland Titan TD4c	Leyland FH30/24R	Lytham St Annes Corporation	45	A
RN 8622	1939	Leyland Titan TD5	Alexander L27/26R	Ribble Motor Services	2057	R
ACK 796	1944	Guy Arab II	Northern Counties / Bond L27/26R	Ribble Motor Services	2413	A
ACB 904	1947	Guy Arab II	Northern Coachbuilders	Blackburn Corporation	502	A
CCK 359	1948	Leyland Titan PD2/3	Leyland L27/26R	Ribble Motor Services	2584	A
DRN 289	1950	Leyland Titan PD2/3	Leyland L27/26RD	Ribble Motor Services	1349	A
MTC 540	1950	AEC Regent III 9613E	Park Royal H30/26R	Morecambe & Heysham L27/26R	72	RP
ERN 700	1952	Leyland Royal Tiger PSU1/13	Leyland B44F	Ribble Motor Services	377	R

Registration	Date	Chassis	Body	New to	Fleet No	Status
FCK 884	1954	Leyland Tiger Cub PSUC1/1T	Saunders Roe B44F	Ribble Motor Services	452	R
HRN 31	1955	Leyland Titan PD2/13	Metro Cammell H33/28RD	Ribble Motor Services	1391	A
HRN 39	1955	Leyland Titan PD2/13	Metro Cammell H33/28RD	Ribble Motor Services	1399	A
JFV 527	1955	Commer TS3	Harrington C41C	Abbott of Blackpool		RP
JCK 542	1956	Leyland Titan PD2/12	Burlingham H33/28RD	Ribble Motor Services	1467	RP
JRN 41	1956	Leyland Tiger Cub PSUC1/2T	Burlingham C41F	Ribble Motor Services	975	A
528 CTF	1957	Leyland Titan PD2/40	Weymann L29/28RD	J. Fishwick & Sons of Leyland	5	R
881 BTF	1958	Leyland Titan PD2/41	East Lancs H35/28R	Lancaster City Transport	881	A
KCK 869	1958	Leyland Titan PD3/4	Burlingham FH41/31F	Ribble Motor Services	1523	A
KCK 914	1958	Leyland Titan PD3/4	Burlingham FH41/31F	Ribble Motor Services	1553	A
MBN 177	1958	Leyland Titan PD3/5	East Lancs H41/33R	Bolton Corporation	122	RP
NRN 586	1960	Leyland Atlantean PDR1/1	Metro Cammell H44/33F	Ribble Motor Services	1686	R
SFV 421	1960	Leyland Atlantean PDR1/1	Weymann CH34/16Ft	W. C. Standerwick	25	A
PCK 618	1961	Leyland Leopard L2	Harrington C32F	Ribble Motor Services	1036	R
PRN 145	1961	Leyland Atlantean PDR1/1	Metro Cammell H44/33F	Scout Motor Services of Preston	5	RP
PRN 906	1961	Leyland Titan PD3/4	Metro Cammell H39/31F	Preston Corporation	14	RP
RRN 428	1962	Leyland Atlantean PDR1/1	Weymann CH39/20F	Ribble Motor Services	1279	R
TCK 465	1963	Leyland Leopard PSU3/1R	Marshall B53F	Ribble Motor Services	465	A
TCK 726	1963	Leyland Leopard PSU3/3RT	Harrington C49F	Ribble Motor Services	726	RP
TRN 731	1964	Leyland Leopard PSU3/3R	Plaxton C49F	W. C. Standerwick	731S	R
ARN 811C	1965	Leyland Leopard PSU3/3RT	Weymann DP49F	Ribble Motor Services	811	R
FPT 6G	1969	Leyland Leopard PSU3/3RT	Plaxton C51F	Weardale Motor Services of Frosterley		A
HRN 249G	1969	Bristol RELL6G	ECW B41D	Ribble Motor Services	249	A
LRN 321J	1970	Bristol RESL6L	Marshall B47F	Ribble Motor Services	321	A
NCK 106J	1971	Leyland Leopard PSU4	Plaxton C43F	Ribble Motor Services	1006	RP
NCK 338J	1971	Bristol RESL6L	ECW B47F	Ribble Motor Services	338	R
PRN 79K	1972	Bristol VRL/LH/6L	ECW CH42/18Ct	W. C. Standerwick	79	A
PTF 718L	1972	Leyland National 1151/2R/0401	Leyland National B48D	Ribble Motor Services	372	RP
PTF 727L	1972	Leyland National 1151/2R	Leyland National B48D	Ribble Motor Services	386	R
UTF 732M	1974	Leyland Leopard PSU3B/4R	Duple C49F	Ribble Motor Services	1052	A
MFR 306P	1976	Leyland Leopard PSU3C/2R	Alexander B53F	Lancaster City Transport	306	R
XCW 955R	1978	Leyland National 11351A/1R	Leyland National B49F	J. Fishwick & Sons of Leyland	24	R
TRN 481V	1979	Leyland Atlantean AN68A/1R	ECW H43/31F	Ribble Motor Services	1481	R
DBV 100W	1980	Leyland Olympian ONLXB/1R	ECW H45/33F	Ribble Motor Services	2100	
DBV 831W	1980	Leyland National 2 NL106L11/1R	Leyland National B44F	Ribble Motor Services	831	R

Notes:

RN 7588	Rebodied 1949	SFV 421	'Gay Hostess' double-deck motorway coach
RN 8622	Chassis refurbished and rebodied in 1949	NCK 106J	In Ireland 1982-2005 registered 411 LIP
ACB 904	Breakdown vehicle	PTF 727L	Used as exhibition bus
ERN 700	Originally B44F		

The Roger Burdett Collection

Contact Address: 2 Pennyfields Boulevard, Long Eaton, NG10 3QS
E-mail: rogerrbctc@aol.com
Affiliation: NARTM
Brief Description: A collection of distinctive coaches supplemented by four double deckers of interest to the collection owner. All vehicles with the exception of the Bristol RE are either unique or one of a small number of survivors.
Opening days/times: Vehicles regularly attend rallies and events and the collection can be viewed by appointment. Please write to the address given.

Registration	Date	Chassis	Body	New to	Fleet No	Status
VG 5541	1933	Bristol GJW	Weymann O28/26R	Norwich Electric Tramways		RP
JYC 855	1948	Leyland Tiger PS1	Harrington C33F	Scarlet Motors of Minehead		R
GOU 732	1949	Tilling Stevens K6LA7	Scottish Aviation C33F	Altonian Coaches of Alton		R
FNV 557	1950	Leyland Tiger PS2/3	Whitson FC33F	Church ('Royal Blue') of Pytchley		R
GKV 94	1950	Daimler CVA6	Metro Cammell H31/29R	Coventry City Transport	94	RP
LTA 813	1950	Bristol KS5G	ECW L27/28R	Western National Omnibus Co	994	R
NTU 125	1951	Foden PVRF6	Metalcraft C41C	Hollinshead of Biddulph		R
EHL 336	1952	Leyland Tiger PS2/13A	Roe C35F	West Riding Automobile Co	725	R
NXL 847	1953	AEC Regal III 6821A	Duple C39F	Eastern Belle of Bow London		R
OTT 43	1953	Bristol LS6G	ECW C39F	Western National Omnibus Co (Royal Blue)	2200	R
WKJ 787	1956	Beadle-Commer	Beadle C41C	Beadle Demonstrator		R
780 GHA	1959	BMMO C5	BMMO C41F	BMMO ('Midland Red')	4780	RP
56 GUO	1961	Bristol MW6G	ECW C39F	Western National Omnibus Co (Royal Blue)	2267	RP
5056 HA	1962	BMMO S15	BMMO B40F	BMMO ('Midland Red')	5056	R
EHA 424D	1966	BMMO D9	BMMO/Willowbrook H40/32RD	BMMO ('Midland Red')	5424	R
OTA 640G	1969	Bristol RELH6G	ECW C45F	Southern National Omnibus Co (Royal Blue)	2380	R

Notes:

VG 5541 Converted to diesel 1938 and open-top 1950

Rotherham Trolleybus Group

Contact address: 113 Tinker Lane, Walkley, Sheffield S6 5EA
Phone: 0114 266 3173
Affiliation: Trolleybus Museum at Sandtoft
Brief description: This group is open to all with an interest in Rotherham area trolleys, the vehicles and the system.
Active restoration of the vehicles takes place and the group works closely with the Trolleybus Museum at Sandtoft.
A video *Remember the Trackless* is sold to raise funds for restoration. Vehicles can be viewed by contacting the group.

Registration	Date	Chassis	Body	New to	Fleet No	Status
CET 613+	1943	Sunbeam MS2c	East Lancs B39C	Rotherham Corporation	88	RP
FET 617+	1950	Daimler CTE6	Roe H40/30R	Rotherham Corporation	37	R

+ Trolleybus

Notes:

FET 617 Rebodied 1956 (formerly single-decker). On display at the Trolleybus Museum at Sandtoft

RTW Bus Group

Contact address: 7 Oldbury Close, St Mary Cray BR5 3TH
Affiliation: Cobham Bus Museum, HCVS
Brief description: The group was formed in 1999 and comprises the owners of the preserved RTW vehicles and those interested in the type.
The vehicles appear at rallies from time to time. A DVD on the history of the RTW is available from the group.

Registration	Date	Chassis	Body	New to	Fleet No	Status
KGK 529	1949	Leyland Titan 6RT	Leyland H30/26R	London Transport	RTW29	R
KGK 575	1949	Leyland Titan 6RT	Leyland H30/26R	London Transport	RTW75	R
KLB 908	1949	Leyland Titan 6RT	Leyland H30/26RD	London Transport	RTW178	R
KLB 915	1949	Leyland Titan 6RT	Leyland H30/26R	London Transport	RTW185	R
KXW 435	1949	Leyland Titan 6RT	Leyland H30/26RD	London Transport	RTW335	RP
LLU 957	1950	Leyland Titan 6RT	Leyland H30/26R	London Transport	RTW467	R
LLU 987	1950	Leyland Titan 6RT	Leyland H30/26R	London Transport	RTW497	R

Notes:

KGK 575   Owned by Blue Triangle and operated as a PSV

KLB 908   Originally H30/26R. Acquired by Stevensons of Spath in 1966 and fitted with platform doors and saloon heaters

SELNEC Preservation Society

Contact address: 267 Rivington Crescent, Pendlebury, Swinton, Manchester M27 8TQ

Affiliation: NARTM

Brief description: A collection of buses from the SELNEC era including SELNEC Standards, the trail-blazing 'Mancunian' and other vehicles from the Greater Manchester area.

Events planned: The operational vehicles will appear at a range of local rallies and shows.

Registration	Date	Chassis	Body	New to	Fleet No	Status
EN 9965	1950	Leyland Titan PD2/4	Weymann	Bury Corporation	165	RP
DNF 708C	1965	Daimler Fleetline CRG6LX	Metro Cammell O43/29C	Manchester Corporation	4708	A
END 832D	1966	Leyland Atlantean PDR1/2	Metro Cammell H43/32F	Manchester Corporation	3832	RP
GNB 518D	1966	Bedford VAL14	Plaxton C47F	Manchester Corporation	205	A
LNA 166G	1968	Leyland Atlantean PDR2/1	Park Royal H26/7D	Manchester City Transport	1066	R
NNB 547H	1969	Leyland Atlantean PDR2/1	East Lancs H47/32F	Manchester City Transport	1142	A
NNB 589H	1970	Daimler Fleetline CRG6LXB	Park Royal H47/28D	SELNEC PTE	2130	A
ONF 865H	1970	Leyland Atlantean PDR2/1	Park Royal H47/28D	SELNEC PTE	1177	A
PNF 941J	1971	Leyland Atlantean PDR1A/1	Northern Counties H43/32F	SELNEC PTE	EX1	R
RNA 220J	1971	Daimler Fleetline CRG6LXB	Park Royal H47/29D	SELNEC PTE	2220	A
TNB 759K	1972	Daimler Fleetline CRG6LXB	Northern Counties H45/27D	SELNEC PTE	EX19	A
VNB 132L	1972	Leyland Atlantean AN68/1R	Park Royal O43/32F	SELNEC PTE	7032	R
VNB 173L	1972	Leyland Atlantean AN68/1R	Northern Counties H43/32F	SELNEC PTE	7147	A
VNB 177L	1972	Daimler Fleetline CRG6LXB	Northern Counties H45/27D	SELNEC PTE	7206	R
VNB 203L	1972	Daimler Fleetline CRG6LXB	Northern Counties H31/4D	SELNEC PTE	7232	R
WBN 955L	1972	Leyland Atlantean AN68/1R	Park Royal O43/32F	SELNEC PTE	7077	R
YDB 453L	1972	Seddon Pennine IV-236	Seddon DP25F	SELNEC PTE	1700	R
AJA 408L	1973	Bristol VRTSL/6LX	ECW H43/32F	SELNEC Cheshire Bus Co	408	R
WWH 43L	1973	Daimler Fleetline CRG6LXB	Park Royal H43/32F	SELNEC PTE	7185	R
XJA 534L	1973	Leyland Atlantean AN68/1R	Park Royal H43/32F	SELNEC PTE	7143	A
XVU 341M	1973	Seddon Pennine IV-236	Seddon B23F	SELNEC PTE	1711	A
YNA 321M	1973	Daimler Fleetline CRG6LXB	Northern Counties H43/32F	SELNEC PTE	7366	A
XVU 363M	1974	Seddon Pennine IV-236	Seddon B19F	Greater Manchester PTE	1733	A
BNE 729N	1974	Seddon Pennine IV-236	Seddon B19F	Greater Manchester PTE	1735	A
BNE 751N	1974	Leyland Atlantean AN68/1R	Northern Counties H43/32F	Greater Manchester PTE	7501	A
BNE 764N	1974	Bristol LH6L	ECW B43F	Greater Manchester PTE	1321	A
HNB 24N	1975	Leyland National 10351/1R	Leyland National B41F	Greater Manchester PTE	105	R
OBN 502R	1977	Leyland Fleetline FE30GR	Northern Counties H43/32F	Lancashire United Transport	485	A
PTD 640S	1977	Leyland Fleetline FE30GR	Northern Counties H43/32F	Lancashire United Transport	496	A
XBU 1S	1978	Leyland Fleetline FE30GR	Northern Counties H43/32F	Greater Manchester PTE	8001	R
ANE 2T	1979	Leyland Titan TNLXB1RF	Park Royal H47/26F	Greater Manchester PTE	4002	A
BNC 960T	1979	Leyland Atlantean AN68A/1R	Park Royal H43/32F	Greater Manchester PTE	7960	RP

Registration	Date	Chassis	Body	New to	Fleet No	Status
GBU 1V	1979	MCW Metrobus DR101/6	MCW H43/30F	Greater Manchester PTE	5001	R
GNF 15V	1980	Leyland Titan TNTL11/1RF	Park Royal H47/26F	Greater Manchester PTE	4015	A
GNF 16V	1980	Leyland Fleetline FE30GR	Northern Counties H43/32F	Greater Manchester PTE	8141	RP
MNC 525W	1980	Leyland Atlantean AN68A/1R	Northern Counties H43/32F	Greater Manchester PTE	8325	A
NJA 568W	1980	Leyland Olympian ONTL11/1R	Northern Counties H43/30F	Greater Manchesters PTE	1451	RP
DWH 706W	1981	Leyland Fleetline FE30GR	Northern Counties H43/32F	Lancashire United Transport	613	R
SND 455X	1981	Leyland Atlantean AN68B/1R	Northern Counties H43/32F	Greater Manchester PTE	8455	A
SND 460X	1981	Leyland Atlantean AN68B/1R	Northern Counties H43/32F	Greater Manchester PTE	8460	R
SND 501X	1982	Leyland Atlantean AN68B/1R	Northern Counties H43/32F	Greater Manchester PTE	8501	A
WRJ 448X	1982	Volvo Ailsa B55-10	Northern Counties H44/35F	Greater Manchester PTE	1448	A
ANA 1Y	1982	Leyland Olympian ONTL11/1R	Northern Counties H43/30F	Greater Manchester PTE	3001	R
ANA 601Y	1983	Leyland Atlantean AN68D/1R	Northern Counties H43/32F	Greater Manchester PTE	8601	A
ANA 645Y	1983	Leyland Atlantean AN68D/1R	Northern Counties H43/32F	Greater Manchester PTE	8645	RP
FWH 461Y	1983	Scania BR112DH	Northern Counties H43/32F	Greater Manchester PTE	1461	A
A472 HNC	1984	Dennis Falcon V DD	Northern Counties H43/37F	Greater Manchester PTE	1472	A
A700 HNB	1984	Leyland Atlantean AN68D/1R	Northern Counties H43/32F	Greater Manchester PTE	8700	RP
A701 LNC	1984	Leyland Atlantean AN68D/1R	Northern Counties H43/32F	Greater Manchester PTE	8701	A
A765 NNA	1984	Leyland Atlantean AN68D/1R	Northern Counties H43/32F	Greater Manchester PTE	8765	RP
A30 ORJ	1984	Leyland Olympian ONLXB/1R	Northern Counties H43/30F	Greater Manchester PTE	3030	RP
B101 SJA	1985	Leyland Olympian ONLXB/1R	Northern Counties H44/30F	Greater Manchester PTE	3101	A
B901 TVR	1985	Dennis Dominator DDA	Northern Counties H43/32F	Greater Manchester PTE	2001	RP
C751 YBA	1985	Dennis Domino SDA	Northern Counties B24F	Greater Manchester PTE	1751	R
C201 CBU	1986	Leyland Olympian ONLXB/1R	Northern Counties H43/30F	Greater Manchester PTE	3201	A
C225 CBU	1986	Leyland Olympian ONLXB/1R	Northern Counties H43/30F	Greater Manchester PTE	3225	A
C481 CBU	1986	Volvo Citybus B10M-50	Northern Counties H46/33F	Greater Manchester PTE	2482	A
C823 CBU	1986	Dodge S 56	Northern Counties B18F	Greater Manchester PTE	1823	RP
D302 JVR	1986	MCW Metrobus DR102/51	Northern Counties CH43/29F	Greater Manchester PTE	5302	A
D501 LNA	1986	Leyland Lynx	Leyland B48F	Greater Manchester Buses	501	A
D320 LNB	1987	MCW Metrobus DR102/51	Northern Counties CH43/29F	Greater Manchester Buses	5320	R
D509 MJA	1987	Iveco 49-10	Robin Hood B21F	Greater Manchester Buses	1509	A
F305 DRJ	1989	Leyland Olympian ONLXB/1RZ	Northern Counties H43/30F	Greater Manchester Buses	3305	A

Notes:

EN 9965	Converted to breakdown vehicle	OBN 502R	Passed to Greater Manchester PTE (6901) in 1981
DNF 708C	Originally H43/32F	XBU 1S	First GMT Leyand Fleetline Standard
LNA 166G	Originally H47/29D; converted by Greater Manchester	BNC 960T	Last Park Royal Bodied Standard
	PTE for use as 'Exhibus' exhibition vehicle - restored in	GBU 1V	Greater Manchester's first Metrobus
	this condition	NJA 568W	Exhibited at 1980 Commercial Motor Show.
NNB 547H	Mancunian		Greater Manchester's first Olympian
NNB 589H	Mancunian	GNF 15V	Greater Manchester's last Titan
ONF 865H	Mancunian	SND 455X	Seating reduced - converted to driver training vehicle
RNA 220J	Mancunian	DWH 706W	Passed to Greater Manchester PTE (6990) in 1981.
PNF 941J	Exhibited at 1970 Commercial Motor Show as prototype		Greater Manchester's last Fleetline
	SELNEC Standard	ANA 1Y	Exhibited at 1982 Commercial Motor Show
VNB 132L	Converted to open top.	A472 HNC	One of only 6 built
VNB 177L	Exhibited at 1972 Commercial Motor Show	A765 NNA	Greater Manchester's last Atlantean
VNB 203L	Originally H45/27D. Used as exhibition vehicle.	C751 YBA	Exhibited at 1984 Commercial Motor Show
WBN 955L	Converted to open top.	C481 CBU	One of 3 prototypes
PTD 640S	Rebodied 1983. Passed to GMPTE in 1981 as 6912.	D320 LNB	Greater Manchesters last Metrobus

Southampton & District Transport Heritage Trust

Contact address: 104 Oak Tree Road,, Southampton SO18 1PH
Affiliation: NARTM; WOMP
Brief description: The collection includes a selection of Southampton's fleet from the early 1970s. The small membership carries out restoration work. Several of the vehicles are privately owned by Trust members.

Registration	Date	Chassis	Body	New to	Fleet No	Status
FTR 511	1949	Guy Arab III	Park Royal O30/26R	Southampton Corporation	64	R
LOW 217	1954	Guy Arab III	Park Royal H30/26R	Southampton Corporation	71	R
JOW 928	1955	Guy Arab UF	Park Royal B39F	Southampton Corporation	255	RP
318 AOW	1962	AEC Regent V 2D3RA	Park Royal H37/29R	Southampton Corporation	318	RP
335 AOW	1963	Leyland Titan PD2A/27	Park Royal H37/29R	Southampton Corporation	335	RP
370 FCR	1963	AEC Regent V 2D3RA	East Lancs H37/29R	Southampton Corporation	350	R
BOW 507C	1965	AEC Regent V 2D3RA	East Lancs Neepsend H37/29R	Southampton Corporation	371	RP
JOW 499E	1967	AEC Swift MP2R	Strachan B47D	Southampton Corporation	1	RP
KOW 909F	1967	AEC Regent V 3D2RA	East Lancs Neepsend H40/30R	Southampton Corporation	401	RP
KOW 910F	1967	AEC Regent V 3D2RA	East Lancs Neepsend H40/30R	Southampton Corporation	402	RP
PCG 888G	1968	AEC Reliance 6U3ZR	Plaxton C55F	Coliseum Coaches of Southampton		A
PCG 889G	1968	AEC Reliance 6MU3R	Plaxton C45F	Coliseum Coaches of Southampton		A
TTR 167H	1970	Leyland Atlantean PDR1A/1	East Lancs H45/31F	Southampton Corporation	133	R
HNP 989J	1971	Leyland Atlantean PDR1A/1	East Lancs O45/31F	Southampton Corporation	139	RP
BCR 379K	1972	Seddon Pennine RU	Pennine B44F	Southampton Corporation	15	RP

Notes:

FTR 511	Converted to Open Top. Owned by Southampton City Museums
LOW 217	Owned by Southampton City Museums
OW 928	Originally B36D
PCG 888G	Originally C57F
HNP 989J	Originally registered WOW 531J; preserved in Guide Friday livery.

Southdown Historic Vehicle Group

Contact address: 173 Cuckfield Crescent, Worthing, West Sussex
E-mail: southdownqueenmary@ntlworld.com
Website: http://home.fastnet.co.uk/gerrycork/worthingbusrally/worthingbusrally.htm
Brief description: A private collection of vehicles, most of which operated for Southdown Motor Services or which have south coast connections or have taken our fancy. The collection is not on public view but vehicles are rallied and often appear in service at running days.
Event planned: 29 July 2007 — Worthing Bus Rally and Running Day.

Registration	Date	Chassis	Body	New to	Fleet No	Status
GUF 191	1945	Guy Arab II	Northern Counties O30/26R	Southdown Motor Services	451	RP
LRV 992	1956	Leyland Titan PD2/12	Metro Cammell O33/26R	Portsmouth Corporation	2	R
XUF 141	1960	Leyland Tiger Cub PSUC1/2	Weymann C41F	Southdown Motor Services	1141	R
70 AUF	1962	Commer Avenger IV	Harrington C—F	Southdown Motor Services	70	A
548 BUF	1963	Leyland Leopard L2	Harrington	Southdown Motor Services	1748	A
972 CUF	1964	Leyland Titan PD3/4	Northern Counties FH39/30F	Southdown Motor Services	972	R
416 DCD	1964	Leyland Titan PD3/4	Northern Counties FCO39/30F	Southdown Motor Services	416	R
419 DCD	1964	Leyland Titan PD3/4	Northern Counties FCO39/30F	Southdown Motor Services	419	R
AOR 158B	1964	Leyland Titan PD3/4	Northern Counties FCO39/30F	Southdown Motor Services	412	R

Registration	Date	Chassis	Body	New to	Fleet No	Status
PRX 187B	1964	Leyland Titan PD3/4	Northern Counties FCO39/30F	Southdown Motor Services	415	RP
PRX 200B	1964	Leyland Titan PD3/4	Northern Counties FCO39/30F	Southdown Motor Services	418	R
PRX 206B	1964	Leyland Titan PD3/4	Northern Counties FCO39/30F	Southdown Motor Services	401	R
BUF 122C	1965	Leyland Leopard PSU3/1RT	Marshall B45F	Southdown Motor Services	122	R
BUF 260C	1965	Leyland Titan PD3/4	Northern Counties FC39/30F	Southdown Motor Services	260	R
BUF 277C	1965	Leyland Titan PD3/4	Northern Counties FC39/30F	Southdown Motor Services	277	R
BUF 426C	1965	Leyland Titan PD3/4	Northern Counties FCO39/30F	Southdown Motor Services	426	R
BUF 427C	1965	Leyland Titan PD3/4	Northern Counties FCO39/30F	Southdown Motor Services	427	R
BJK 672D	1966	Leyland Titan PD2A/30	East Lancs H32/28R	Eastbourne Corporation	72	R
FCD 294D	1966	Leyland Titan PD3/4	Northern Counties FH39/29F	Southdown Motor Services	294	R
DHC 784E	1967	Leyland Titan PD2A/30	East Lancs O32/28R	Eastbourne Corporation	84	R
KUF 199F	1968	Leyland Leopard PSU3/1RT	Willowbrook B45F	Southdown Motor Services	199	R
LFS 296F	1968	Bristol VRTLL/6LX	ECW O41/36F	Scottish Omnibuses (Eastern Scottish)	AA296	R
PUF 165H	1969	Leyland Leopard PSU3/1RT	Northern Counties DP49F	Southdown Motor Services	465	R
TCD 374J	1970	Daimler Fleetline CRG6LX	Northern Counties H-/-F	Southdown Motor Services	374	R
TCD 383J	1970	Daimler Fleetline CRG6LX	Northern Counties H-/-F	Southdown Motor Services	383	RP
TCD 481J	1970	Bristol RESL6L	Marshall B45F	Southdown Motor Services	481	R
TCD 490J	1970	Bristol RESL6L	Marshall B45F	Southdown Motor Services	490	RP
UUF 116J	1971	Bristol VRTSL6LX	ECW O-/-F	Southdown Motor Services	516	RP
UUF 328J	1971	Leyland Leopard PSU3B/4RT	Plaxton C53F	Southdown Motor Services	1828	R
UUF 335J	1971	Leyland Leopard PSU3B/4RT	Plaxton C47F	Southdown Motor Services	1835	R
SCD 731N	1974	Leyland Atlantean AN68/1R	Park Royal - Roe H43/30F	Southdown Motor Services	731	R
RUF 37R	1977	Leyland National 11351A/2R	Leyland National B44D	Southdown Motor Services	37	R
ANJ 306T	1978	Leyland Leopard PSU3E/4RT	Plaxton C53F	Southdown Motor Services	1306	A
HNP 154S	1978	Leyland Atlantean AN68A/1R	East Lancs O43/31F	Brighton Corporation	3	R
TYJ 4S	1978	Leyland Atlantean AN68A/1R	East Lancs H43/31F	Brighton Corporation	4	R
USV 324	1979	Leyland Leopard PSU3E/4RT	Plaxton C48F	Southdown Motor Services	1320	RP
KAZ 6703	1979	Leyland Leopard PSU5C/4R	Duple C53F	Southdown Motor Services	1339	RP
OPV 821	1979	Leyland Leopard PSU3E/4RT	Plaxton C48F	Southdown Motor Services	1321	RP
JWV 275W	1981	Bristol VRTSL3/680	ECW H43/31F	Southdown Motor Services	275	A
MAP 340W	1981	Leyland Leopard PSU3F/4R	Plaxton C48F	Southdown Motor Services	1340	R

Notes:

LRV 992	Originally H33/26R
548 BUF	Converted to car transporter
AOR 158B	Originally registered 412 DCD
PRX 200B	Originally registered 418 DCD
PRX 187B	Originally registered 415 DCD
PRX 206B	Originally registered 401 DCD
LFS 296F	Originally H47/32F
UUF 116J	Originally H39/31F
HNP 154S	Originally H43/31F registered TYJ 3S
OPV 821	Originally registered EAP 921V
USV 324	Originally registered BYJ 920T
KAZ 6703	Originally registered EAP 939V

St Margaret's Transport Society

Contact Information: St Margaret's High School, Aigburth Road, Liverpool L17 6AB
Telephone: 0151 427 1825
Affiliation: NARTM
Brief Description: Formed in 1979, the Society specialises in single deck half-cabs from the 1940s and 1950s. Meetings are held regularly to carry out restoration of the vehicles. Visitors are welcome but prior appointment is essential. Please contact the address given.

Registration	Date	Chassis	Body	New to	Fleet No	Status
CMS 201	1949	Leyland Tiger PS1	Alexander C35F	Alexander	PA133	R
GWM 816	1951	Crossley SD42/7	Crossley B32F	Southport Corporation	116	RP

Telford Bus Group

Contact address: 2 Clifton Avenue, Brownhills, Walsall, West Midlands WS8 7DU
Contact number: 07968 410306
Website: www.telfordbus.org.uk
Brief description: The Telford Bus Group has a collection of privately-owned buses and coaches in various parts of England.
The Group has become known for its Bedford VALs of which 12 examples are preserved, with examples of several body types. Other vehicles include Daimler Fleetline 'Mancunian', Seddon Pennine VI, Commer Avenger and Leyland Leopard 'Midland Red S27 type'.
Not all vehicles are restored and some are long term projects.

Registration	Date	Chassis	Body	New to	Fleet No	Status
386 DD	1961	Bedford J2	Plaxton C20F	Talbott of Moreton-in-Marsh		RP
3190 UN	1962	Commer Avenger IV	Plaxton C41F	Wright of Penycae		R
9797 DP	1964	Bedford VAL 14	Duple C52F	Smiths of Reading		RP
EHL 472D	1966	Bedford VAL 14	Plaxton C52F	West Riding Automobile Co	3	R
JTH 100F	1968	Bedford VAM 14	Duple C45F	Davies of Pencader		RP
UWX 981F	1968	Bedford VAL 70	Plaxton C52F	Mosley of Barugh Green		R
RBC 345G	1969	Bedford VAL 70	Duple C52F	Cook of Dunstable		RP
WWY 115G	1969	Bedford VAL 70	Plaxton C53F	Abbey Coachways of Selby		R
FYG 663J	1970	Bedford VAL 70	Willowbrook B56F	Wigmore of Dinnington		RP
VBD 310H	1970	Bedford VAL 70	Plaxton C48F	Coales of Woolaston		R
BHO 670J	1971	Bedford VAL 70	Duple C53F	Castle Coaches of Waterlooville		R
RNA 236J	1971	Daimler Fleetline CRG6LXB-33	Park Royal H47/29D	SELNEC PTE	2236	A
CDC 166K	1972	Seddon Pennine VI	Plaxton C45F	Bob's of Middlesbrough	26	RP
CDC 168K	1972	Seddon Pennine VI	Plaxton C41F	Bob's of Middlesbrough	28	RP
FAR 724K	1972	Bedford VAL 70	Duple C53F	Langley Coaches of Slough		A
JHA 227L	1973	Leyland Leopard PSU3B/2R	Marshall DP49F	Midland Red Omnibus Co	227	RP
BOK 1V	1979	MCW Metrobus DR102/12	MCW H43/30F	West Midlands PTE	2001	RP
D536 NDA	1986	Freight Rover Sherpa 350	Carlyle B18F	West Midlands PTE	536	RP

Notes:
RNA 236J   Mancunian

TH Collection

Contact Information: Telephone 01263 834829
E-mail: nick@topolino.demon.co.uk
Affiliation: NARTM
Brief Description: A private collection representing coachwork built by Thomas Harrington of Hove. It is believed the vehicles are now all unique examples of the chassis and body combination.
Opening days/times: The collection is not on public view and all vehicles are at varying stages of restoration. Arrangements to visit can be made, strictly by appointment, telephoning first for details.

Registration	Date	Chassis	Body	New to	Fleet No	Status
KD 5296	1928	Leyland Tiger TS2	Harrington C31F	Imperial Motor Services of Liverpool		A
VRF 372	1951	Foden PVRF6	Harrington C41C	Bassett's Coaches of Tittensor		A
JAP 698	1954	Harrington Contender	Harrington C41C	Audawn Coaches of Corringham		RP
YYB 118	1957	Dennis Lancet UF	Harrington B42F	Hutchings & Cornelius Services of South Petherton		RP
PFR 747	1959	Bedford SB3	Harrington C41F	Abbotts of Blackpool		A
487 GFR	1964	AEC Reliance 2U3RA	Harrington C34F	Abbotts of Blackpool		R

Notes:
KD 5296   Rebodied in 1939   JAP 698   Former Harrington demonstrator

Three Counties Bus and Commercial Vehicle Museum

Contact address: 83 Millwright Way, Flitwick, Beds MK45 1BQ
Phone: 01525 712091
E-mail: nick.doolan@btopenworld.com
Web site: www.3cbcvm.org.uk
Affiliation: NARTM
Brief description: Established to provide a focus for the preservation, and historical record of buses in Bedfordshire, Buckinghamshire and Hertfordshire. Seeks to ensure a long-term future for the vehicles.
Events planned: Please see enthusiast press for planned Operating Days. Operational vehicles frequently attend local rallies

Registration	Date	Chassis	Body	New to	Fleet No	Status
FXT 122	1939	Leyland Cub REC	LPTB B20F	London Transport	CR16	RP
DBL 154	1946	Bristol K6A	ECW L27/28R	Thames Valley Traction Co	446	R
CFN 104	1947	Leyland Tiger PS1/1	Park Royal C32R	East Kent Road Car Co		R
JWU 307	1950	Bedford OB	Duple C29F	Lunn of Rothwell		RP
LYR 915	1952	AEC Regent III O961 RT	Weymann H30/26R	London Transport	RT3496	R
MXX 434	1952	AEC Regal IV 9821LT RF	Metro Cammell B39F	London Transport	RF457	R
MXX 332	1953	Guy Special NLLVP	ECW B26F	London Transport	GS32	R
MXX 489	1953	AEC Regal IV 9821LT RF	Metro Cammell B39F	London Transport	RF512	RP
RSJ 747	1956	Albion Victor FT39AN	Heaver C27F	Guernsey Motor Co	69	R
VYO 767	1959	Bristol MW6G	ECW C41F	Tilling		RP
OVL 473	1960	Bristol Lodekka FS5G	ECW H33/27RD	Lincolnshire Road Car Co	2378	R
EFM 631C	1965	Bristol Lodekka FS6G	ECW H33/27RD	Crosville Motor Services	DFG182	R
DEK 3D	1966	Leyland Titan PD2/37	Massey H37/27F	Wigan Corporation	140	R
KBD 712D	1966	Bristol Lodekka FS6G	ECW H33/27RD	United Counties Omnibus Co	712	R
KBD 715D	1966	Bristol Lodekka FS6G	ECW H60RD	United Counties Omnibus Co	715	RP
OWC 182D	1966	Bristol MW6G	ECW C41F	Tillings Transport	182	R
NBD 311F	1967	Bristol RELL6G	ECW B53F	United Counties Omnibus Co	311	RP
RBD 319G	1968	Bristol RELL6G	ECW B53F	United Counties Omnibus Co	319	RP
UXD 129G	1968	Bristol RELL6L	ECW B48D	Luton Corporation	129	RP
UBD 757H	1969	Bristol VRTSL6LX	ECW H39/31F	United Counties Omnibus Co	757	A
VLW 444G	1969	AEC Merlin 4P2R	MCW B25D	London Transport	MBS444	A
VMO 234H	1969	Bristol LH6L	ECW B41F	Thames Valley Traction Co	214	RP
WRP 767J	1971	Bristol VRTSL6LX	ECW H39/31F	United Counties Omnibus Co	767	RP
ANV 775J	1971	Bristol VRTSL6LX	ECW H39/31F	United Counties Omnibus Co	775	R
JPL 153K	1972	Leyland Atlantean PDR1A/1	Park Royal H43/29D	London Country Bus Services	AN53	RP
GPD 313N	1974	Bristol LHS6L	ECW B35F	London Country Bus Services	BN45	RP
RBD 111M	1974	Bedford YRT	Willowbrook B53F	United Counties Omnibus Co	111	A
UPE 203M	1974	Leyland National 10351/1R	Leyland National B41F	London Country Bus Services	SNB103	A
HPF 318N	1975	Leyland National 10351/1R/SC	Leyland National DP39F	London Country Bus Services	SNC168	R
SBD 525R	1977	Leyland National 11351A/1R	Leyland National B49F	United Counties Omnibus Co	525	RP
SOA 674S	1977	Leyland Leopard PSU3E/4R	Plaxton C49F	Midland Red Omnibus Co	674	R
UPB 312S	1977	Leyland National 10351A/1R	Leyland National B41F	London Country Bus Services	SNB312	R
GCK 279S	1978	Bedford YLQ	Plaxton C46F	Battersbys Silver Grey Coaches		RP
XPK 51T	1978	AEC Reliance 6U2R	Duple C53F	London Country Bus Services	RB51	R
SVV 587W	1980	Leyland National 2 NL116L11/1R	Leyland National 2 B49F	United Counties Omnibus Co	587	R
GUW 443W	1981	Leyland National 2 NL106AL11/2R	East Lancs National Greenway B25D	London Transport	GLS443	A
GUW 444W	1981	Leyland National 2 NL106AL11/2R	Leyland National 2 DP43F	London Transport	LS444	RP
TPD 109X	1982	Leyland Olympian ONTL11/1R	Roe H43/29F	London Country Bus Services	LR9	A
C24 NVV	1985	Ford Transit	Carlyle B16F	United Counties Omnibus Co	24	A

Notes:

RSJ 747	Original Guernsey registration was 1529
OWC 182D	Passed to Eastern National (392) in 1968 and to Tilling's Travel (9392) in 1971

Wealdstone & District Vintage Vehicle Collection

Contact address: 91 Graham Road, Wealdstone, Middx HA3 5RE
E-mail: oldbusgarage@sftt.co.uk
Web site: www.sftt.co.uk/busgarage
Affiliation: NARTM
Brief description: A small collection of mainly London buses from the 1950s, examples of which regularly attend rallies. Anyone wishing to visit or assist with the vehicles is welcome. Please write to the address given.

Registration	Date	Chassis	Body	New to	Fleet No	Status
DL 9706	1935	Dennis Lancet I	ECW B36R	Southern Vectis Omnibus Co	516	RP
KYY 622	1950	AEC Regent III O961 RT	Park Royal H30/26R	London Transport	RT1784	R
MLL 817	1952	AEC Regal IV 9821LT RF	Metro Cammell B37F	London Transport	RF280	R
MXX 410	1953	AEC Regal IV 9821LT RF	Metro Cammell B41F	London Transport	RF433	R
MXX 430	1953	AEC Regal IV 9821LT RF	Metro Cammell B39F	London Transport	RF453	R
NLE 939	1953	AEC Regent III O961 RT	Park Royal H30/26R	London Transport	RT4275	RP

Notes:
DL 9706   Rebodied 1944

The West Country Historic Omnibus & Transport Trust

Contact address: The Secretary, 33 Broad View, Broadclyst, Exeter EX5 3HA
Web site: www.busmuseum.org.uk
Affiliation: NARTM
Brief description: An Historic Bus, Coach and Lorry Rally is held annually in September at the Westpoint Showground, Clyst St Mary, near Exeter (junction 30, M5). The Trust plans to establish a museum and archive of West Country commercial road transport at this location in the near future.

Registration	Date	Chassis	Body	New to	Fleet No	Status
86 GFJ	1963	Leyland Titan PD2A/30	Massey H31/26R	Exeter City Transport	86	R
OTA 632G	1969	Bristol RELH6G	ECW C45F	Southern National Omnibus Co (Royal Blue)	1460	R
TDV 217J	1970	Leyland Panther PSUR1B/1R	Marshall B—D	Devon General	217	R
VDV 137S	1977	Bristol VRT/SL3/6LXB	ECW CO43/31F	Western National Omnibus Co (Devon General)	937	R
AFJ 726T	1979	Bristol LH6L	Plaxton C41F	Western National Omnibus Co	3306	A
AFJ 727T	1979	Bristol LH6L	Plaxton C41F	Western National Omnibus Co	3307	RP
AFJ 764T	1979	Bristol VRT/SL3/6LXB	ECW H43/31F	Western National Omnibus Co	1157	R
A927 MDV	1983	Ford Transit 160D	Carlyle B16F	Devon General Ltd	7	R
C801 FRL	1985	Mercedes L608D	Reeve Burgess B20F	Western National Ltd	104	A
C705 FFJ	1986	Ford Transit	Robin Hood B16F	Devon General Ltd	705	RP
L929 CTT	1994	Iveco 59-12	Mellor B21D	Devon General Ltd	1000	R
M627 HDV	1994	Iveco 59-12	Wadham Stringer B21D	Devon General Ltd	1029	A

Notes:
TDV 217J   Ordered by Exeter City Transport. Prev B47D. Originally B47D; converted to publicity vehicle in 1980
VDV 137S   Warship class named 'Victory'

West Midlands Bus Preservation Society

Contact address: Secretary, 22 Beaumont Way, Norton Canes, Cannock WS11 9FQ
Brief description: The main core of the collection is of vehicles from the West Midlands PTE in the period 1969 to 1986. Other artefacts are being collected for inclusion in a planned transport museum.
Opening days/times: Vehicles can be viewed by special arrangement, contact secretary.

Registration	Date	Chassis	Body	New to	Fleet No	Status
DUK 278	1946	Guy Arab II	Roe H31/25R	Wolverhampton Corporation	378	A
UHY 362	1955	Bristol KSW6B	ECW H32/28R	Bristol Tramways	8322	R
436 KOV	1964	Daimler Fleetline CRG6LX	Park Royal H43/33F	Birmingham City Transport	3436	A
NOV 880G	1969	Daimler Fleetline CRG6LX	Park Royal H43/29D	Birmingham City Transport	3880	RP
TOB 997H	1970	Daimler Fleetline CRG6LX-33	Park Royal H47/33D	West Midlands PTE	3997	A
JOV 738P	1976	Volvo Ailsa B55-10	Alexander H44/35F	West Midlands PTE	4738	R
NOC 600R	1976	Leyland Fleetline FE30AGR	Park Royal H43/33F	West Midlands PTE	6600	R
WDA 956T	1979	Leyland Fleetline FE30AGR	MCW B37F	West Midlands PTE	1956	A
D553 NOE	1986	Ford Transit	Carlyle B20F	West Midlands PTE	553	R

Notes:

DUK 278	Body built 1952
TOB 997H	Gardner 6LXB engine fitted after acquisition by C J Partridge & Son of Hadleigh
WDA 956T	Originally double-deck bus (H43/33F) 6956; rebuilt as single-decker in 1994

West of England Transport Collection

Contact address: 15 Land Park, Chulmleigh, Devon, EX18 7BH
Phone: 01769 580811
Affiliation: NARTM
Brief description: A large private collection of vehicles, mainly from West Country major operators. The collection includes buses, coaches and transport memorabilia.
Events planned: 7 October 2007 — Annual WETC Open Day, Winkleigh
Opening days/times: Viewing at other times by prior arrangement with C. T. Shears, tel: 01769 580811.

Registration	Date	Chassis	Body	New to	Fleet No	Status
UO 2331	1927	Austin 20 5PL	Tiverton B13F	Sidmouth Motor Co		RP
PSL 234	1931	Maudslay ML3BC	Thurgood C31F	Church ('Royal Blue') of Pytchley		A
JY 124	1932	Tilling Stevens B10A2 Express	Beadle B—R	Western National Omnibus Co	3379	RP
OD 5489	1933	Vauxhall Cadet VY	Mount Pleasant B7	Davis of Rockbeare		R
OD 5868	1933	Leyland Lion LT5	Weymann B31F	Devon General	68	A
OD 7500	1934	AEC Regent O661	Brush H30/26R	Devon General	DR213	R
ADV 128	1935	Bristol JO5G	Beadle B—R	Western National Omnibus Co	222	RP
ATT 922	1935	Bristol JJW6A	Beadle B35R	Western National Omnibus Co	172	RP
AUO 74	1935	Leyland Lion LT5A	(chassis only) -	Devon General	SL79	A
FV 5737	1936	Leyland Tiger TS7	Duple C31F	Ribble Motor Services	753	R
ADR 813	1938	Leyland Titan TD5c	Leyland L27/26R	Plymouth Corporation	141	R
BOW 169	1938	Bristol L5G	-	Hants & Dorset Motor Services	TS676	A
EFJ 241	1938	Leyland Titan TD5	Leyland H30/26R	Exeter Corporation	26	RP
EFJ 666	1938	Leyland Tiger TS8	Cravens B32R	Exeter Corporation	66	R
ETT 946	1938	Bristol L5G	Beadle B36R	Southern National Omnibus Co	280	A

Registration	Date	Chassis	Body	New to	Fleet No	Status
DOD 474	1940	AEC Regal O662	Weymann B35F	Devon General	SR474	RP
GTA 395	1941	Bristol LL5G	Brislington Body Works B39R	Southern National Omnibus Co	373	RP
FFY 401	1947	Leyland Titan PD2/3	Leyland O30/26R	Southport Corporation	84	RP
KHU 624	1947	Bristol K6B	ECW H30/26R	Bristol Omnibus Co	3705	RP
GLJ 957	1948	Leyland Titan PD1A	ECW L27/26R	Hants & Dorset Motor Services	PD959	A
JFJ 606	1949	Daimler CVD6	Brush H30/26R	Exeter Corporation	43	A
LTV 702	1951	AEC Regal III 9621E	East Lancs B35R	Nottingham City Transport	702	A
WRL 16	1956	Rowe Hillmaster	Reading B42F	Millbrook Steamboat & Trading Co		A
974 AFJ	1960	Guy Arab IV	Massey H31/26R	Exeter Corporation	74	R
484 EFJ	1962	Leyland Titan PD2A/30	Massey H31/26R	Exeter City Transport	84	A
815 KDV	1963	Bristol Lodekka FLF6B	ECW H38/30F	Western National Omnibus Co	2010	A
991 MDV	1963	AEC Reliance 2MU3RV	Marshall B41F	Devon General	991	A
OAE 957M	1973	Bristol RELL6L	ECW B—F	Bristol Omnibus Co	1335	A
GNM 235N	1975	Bristol LH6L	Plaxton C51F	Caroline Seagull of Great Yarmouth		R
JFJ 500N	1975	Bristol LH6L	Plaxton C45F	Greenslades Tours	320	A
MPX 945R	1977	Ford Transit	Robin Hood C–F	Angela of Bursledon		A
PTT 106R	1977	Bristol LH6L	Plaxton C37F	Western National Omnibus Co	3406	RP
CRM 927T	1979	Leyland/DAB	Leyland B64T	South Yorkshire PTE	2006	A
Q995 CPE	1979	AEC Regent III O961 RT	Park Royal O30/26R	London Transport	RT4588	A
DBV 43W	1980	Leyland Leopard		Burnley and Pendle		A
RLN 237W	1981	Leyland-DAB 6-35-690/4	Roe AB—T	British Airways	C310	A
YNW 33X	1982	Leyland Leopard	Plaxton C51F	Shilton of Leeds		R
A749 NTA	1984	Ford Transit	Ford M8L	Devon County Council		A
C748 FFJ	1985	Ford Transit 190D	Carlyle B16F	Devon General Ltd	748	A
C671 FFJ	1986	Ford Transit	Carlyle B16F	Devon General Ltd	671	RP
K361 LWS	1992	Leyland DAF 400	G & M B16	Rothwell of Plymouth		A

Notes:

UO 2331	Body new 1940
PSL 234	Body new 1948. Originally registered NV 30.
JY 124	New body and engine fitted in 1947
OD 5489	Body fitted 1946
OD 7500	Rebodied 1949
ATT 922	Rebodied in the late 1940s
ADV 128	Rebodied 1950
AUO 74	Front end of chassis only
FV 5737	Rebodied 1950
ETT 946	Rebodied 1950
BOW 169	New with Beadle body; acquired by Wilts & Dorset Motor Services (505) in 1952 and converted to breakdown vehicle in 1956
EFJ 666	Used as a snow plough 1952-6
EFJ 241	Converted to tree-cutter in 1958
ADR 813	Rebodied 1953. Originally torque convertor. Now with crash gearbox.
GTA 395	Lengthened and rebodied in 1954
FFY 401	Originally H30/26R
Q995 CPE	Original registration NLP581
CRM 927T	Articulated prototype (57 ft long)
RLN 237W	Front portion converted to playbus
A749 NTA	Fitted with tail lift for wheelchairs
K361 LWS	Originally a British Gas van

Westgate Museum

Contact address: Enquiries: Caretaker — Tony Ferris, 107 Westgate Road, Belton DN9 1PY
Brief description: The collection, near Doncaster, is housed in a former Methodist Chapel built in 1865. The site operates under the auspices of the Trolleybus Museum at Sandtoft and the vehicles operate there from time to time.
Opening days/times: Viewing strictly by appointment.

Registration	Date	Chassis	Body	New to	Fleet No	Status
RC 8472+	1944	Sunbeam W	Weymann UH30/26R	Derby Corporation	172	R
RC 8575+	1945	Sunbeam W	Park Royal UH30/26R	Derby Corporation	175	RP
SVS 281	1945	Daimler CWA6	Duple UH30/26R	Douglas Corporation	52	R
DRD 130+	1949	BUT 9611T	Park Royal H33/26RD	Reading Corporation	144	R
LDP 945	1955	AEC Regent III 6812A	Park Royal L31/26RD	Reading Corporation	98	R
WLT 529	1960	AEC Routemaster R2RH	Park Royal H36/28R	London Transport	RM529	R

+ Trolleybus

Notes:
SVS 281   Originally registered FMN 955.

Workington Heritage Transport Trust

Contact Information: 22 Calva Road, Seaton, Workington, Cumbria, CA14 1DF
Telephone: 01900 67389
E-mail: wthc@btopenworld.com
Affiliation: NARTM, Transport Trust
Brief Description: A collection based around buses and rail vehicles from the West Cumberland area. It is the aim to open to the public once a suitable building and funding have been arranged.

Registration	Date	Chassis	Body	New to	Fleet No	Status
109 DRM	1961	Bristol Lodekka FS6G	ECW H33/27RD	Cumberland Motor Services	550	R
AAO 34B	1964	Bristol MW6G	ECW B45F	Cumberland Motor Services	231	R
GRM 353L	1973	Leyland National 1151/1R/0401	Leyland National B52F	Cumberland Motor Services	353	RP
KHH 378W	1980	Leyland National 2 116L11/1R	Leyland National B52F	Cumberland Motor Services	378	R

Notes:
KHH 378W   Restored to post-NBC CMS Cumberland livery

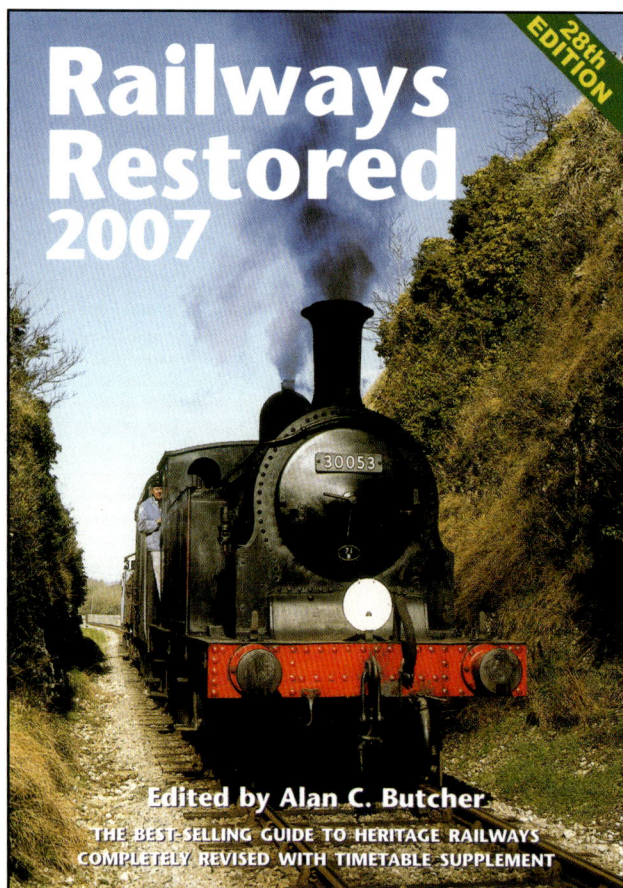

Part 3

Privately Preserved Buses

Reading Transport 113 (ARD 676) is an AEC
661T trolleybus with Park Royal bodywork.
Also in view is AEC Regent 47 (RD 7127)
from the same company.

PRIVATELY PRESERVED BUSES

This section is included with the help and co-operation of the British Bus Preservation Group (BBPG). There are known to be many excellent privately preserved buses, coaches and some trolleybuses in this country and the list which follows is prepared from data provided by the Group. All the vehicles are owned by BBPG members and every effort has been made to ensure that the information given is correct at the time of going to press.

Condition of the vehicles varies, some having been fully restored (even to public operational standard in some cases); others are undergoing restoration, often a lengthy job with limited resources; some awaiting their turn for the day when the restoration task can be started. Those vehicles which are restored generally make visits to bus rallies up and down the country and details of such events can be found in the bus enthusiast magazines, regularly published.

If you are the owner of a preserved bus, coach or trolleybus which is not listed, you may wish to become a member of the BBPG. Services to their members include a regular Newsletter 'British Bus News', the chance to contact others with similar interests and the ability to share information on vehicle restoration problems, projects and, of course, sources of spare parts. Membership costs is £13 per annum and the BBPG may be contacted at the address below.

British Bus Preservation Group

Contact address: BBPG, 25 Oldfield Road, Bexleyheath, Kent DA7 4DX.
E-mail: info@bbpg.co.uk
Web site: www.bbpg.co.uk
Affiliation: NARTM

Registration	Date	Chassis	Body	New to	Fleet No	Status
PY 6170	1926	Morris Commercial Z 15.9hp	Ch16	Robinsons of Scarborough		R
DB 5221	1929	Tilling Stevens B10A	no body	North Western Road Car Co	321	A
FM 6397	1931	Leyland Titan TD1	Leyland L51R	Crosville Motor Services	45	RP
FM 6435	1931	Leyland Lion LT2	Leyland B32F	Crosville Motor Services	L7	RP
MV 8996	1931	Bedford WLB	Duple B20F	Howards of West Byfleet		R
BU 7108	1932	Leyland Titan TD2	Massey H-/-R	Oldham Corporation	69	RP
FM 7443	1932	Leyland Cub KP2	Brush B20F	Crosville Motor Services	716	RP
AOG 638	1934	Daimler COG5		Birmingham City Transport	51	RP
AUF 670	1934	Leyland Titan TD3	East Lancs H26/26R	Southdown Motor Services	970	R
FM 9984	1936	Leyland Tiger TS7	Harrington C32F	Crosville Motor Services	K101	RP
JA 5528	1936	Bristol JO5G	Brush B31R	North Western Road Car Co	728	RP
BFM 144	1937	Leyland Tiger TS7	ECW B32F	Crosville Motor Services	KA27	R
EUF 181	1938	Leyland Titan TD5		Southdown Motor Services	0181	RP
FHT 112	1938	Bristol K5G	ECW O30/26R	Bristol Tramways	C3209	RP
JA 7770	1938	Bristol L5G	Burlingham B35R	North Western Road Car Co	346	RP
JK 8418	1939	Leyland Lion LT9	Leyland B32F	Eastbourne Corporation	12	R
EFM 581	1940	Leyland Tiger TS8	ECW B32F	Crosville Motor Services	KA158	RP
EVC 244	1940	Daimler COG5/40	Park Royal B38F	Coventry City Transport	244	R
FNY 933	1944	Bristol K6A	Park Royal H30/26R	Pontypridd UDC	40	RP
HHA 26	1944	Guy Arab II	Weymann H30/26R	BMMO ('Midland Red')	2574	RP
HKE 867	1945	Bristol K6A	Weymann H30/26R	Maidstone & District Motor Services	DH159	R
HKL 826	1946	AEC Regal I O662	Beadle OB35F	Maidstone & District Motor Services	OR2	R
ACH 627	1947	Daimler CVD6	Brush H30/26R	Derby Corporation	27	RP
ANH 154	1947	Daimler CVG6	Northern Coachbuilders H30/26R	Northampton Corporation	154	R
CUH 856	1947	Leyland Tiger PS1	ECW B35R	Western Welsh Omnibus Co	856	RP
GOE 486	1947	Daimler CVA6	MCW H30/24R	Birmingham City Transport	1486	RP
HLW 214	1947	AEC Regent III O961 RT	Park Royal H30/26RD	London Transport	RT277	R
HTC 661	1947	Bedford OB	Scottish Motor Traction C29F	Dean & Pounder of Morecombe		R
JK 9915	1947	Leyland PD1	East Lancs O30/26R	Eastbourne Corporation	17	A
ENT 778	1948	Leyland Tiger PS1	Burlingham C33F	Gittins of Crickheath		R
JXN 46	1948	AEC Regent III O961 RT	Weymann H30/26R	London Transport	RT1018	R

Registration	Date	Chassis	Body	New to	Fleet No	Status
KHA 311	1948	BMMO C1	Duple C30C	BMMO ('Midland Red')	3311	R
KNN 254	1948	Leyland Titan PD1A	Duple L29/26F	Barton Transport of Chilwell	580	RP
EVD 406	1949	Crossley DD42/7	Roe H31/25R	Baxter's Bus Service of Airdrie	34	R
LHY 937	1949	Bristol K6B	ECW H31/28R	Bristol Tramways	3774	RP
LUC 250	1949	Leyland Titan 7RT	(chassis only)	London Transport	RTL1073	RP
HWY 36	1950	Leyland Titan PD2/1	Leyland L27/26R	Todmorden Joint Omnibus Committee	18	RP
JOJ 231	1950	Leyland Tiger PS2	Weymann B34F	Birmingham City Transport	2231	RP
JOJ 827	1950	Daimler CVG6	Crossley H30/25R	Birmingham City Transport	2827	RP
JXX 487	1950	Bedford OB	Duple B30F	Ministry of Supply		A
KEL 405	1950	Bristol LL6B	ECW FB37F	Hants & Dorset Motor Services	677	R
KNG 711	1950	Bristol L5G	ECW B35R	Eastern Counties Omnibus Co	LL711	RP
KYY 529	1950	AEC Regent III O961 RT	Park Royal H30/26RD	London Transport	RT1702	R
KYY 615	1950	AEC Regent III O961 RT	Park Royal H30/26R	London Transport	RT1777	RP
KYY 647	1950	Leyland Titan 7RT	H30/26R	London Transport	RTL1004	R
DMS 130	1951	AEC Regal III 6821A	Alexander C35F	W. Alexander & Sons	A104	RP
FFN 446	1951	Leyland/Beadle Titan TD5	Beadle C35F	East Kent Road Car Co		RP
HDL 280	1951	Bristol LL5G	ECW B39R	Southern Vectis Omnibus Co	39	RP
JND 629	1951	Leyland Titan PD2/3	Metro Cammell H32/26R	Manchester Corporation	3228	R
JOJ 207	1951	Daimler CVD6		Birmingham City Transport	2707	RP
LUC 381	1951	AEC Regal IV 9821E	ECW C39F	London Transport	RFW6	RP
LYF 104	1951	Leyland Titan 7RT	Park Royal H30/26R	London Transport	RTL1163	R
LYF 316	1951	AEC Regent III O961 RT	Park Royal H30/26R	London Transport	RT2591	R
LYR 672	1951	AEC Regent III O961 RT	Park Royal H30/26R	London Transport	RT2688	RP
MFM 39	1951	Bedford OB	Duple C29F	Crosville Motor Services	SL71	R
RSK 615	1951	Leyland Royal Tiger PSU1/15	Duple DP41F	Jackson of Castle Bromwich		A
URE 281	1951	AEC Regal III 9612A	Harrington FC33F	Lymers of Tean		R
LTX 311	1952	Leyland Tiger PS2/5	Massey B35F	Caerphilly Corporation	1	R
MLL 555	1952	AEC Regal IV 9821LT RF	Metro Cammell B37F	London Transport	RF168	RP
MLL 722	1952	AEC Regal IV 9822E	Park Royal RDP—C	British European Airways	1080	A
NLE 534	1952	AEC Regal IV 9821LT RF	Metro Cammell B39F	London Transport	RF 534	R
JDL 40	1953	Bristol KSW5G	ECW L-/-RD	Southern Vectis Omnibus Co	766	A
LWR 424	1953	Bristol KSW6G	ECW -	West Yorkshire Road Car Co	4044	R
MXX 283	1953	AEC Regal IV 9821LT RF	Metro Cammell B41F	London Transport	RF395	RP
MXX 292	1953	AEC Regal IV 9821LT RF	Metro Cammell	London Transport	RF404	RP
MXX 421	1953	AEC Regal IV 9821LT RF	Metro Cammell B39F	London Transport	RF444	R
NLE 673	1953	AEC Regal IV 9821LT RF	Metro Cammell B39F	London Transport	RF673	R
RAL 795	1954	Daimler CVG6	Massey H33/28RD	Gash of Newark	DD10	RP
UAS 954	1954	GMC PD4501 Scenicruiser	GMC RC43F	Greyhound	T-902	RP
395 DEL	1955	Albion Victor	Heaver B35F	Guernsey Motor Co	71	RP
JVH 381	1955	AEC Regent III 9613E	East Lancs H35/28R	Huddersfield Corporation	181	A
MDL 954	1956	Bristol Lodekka LD6G	ECW O33/27R	Southern Vectis Omnibus Co	544	R
WUA 832	1956	AEC Regent V MD2RA	Roe H33/27R	Leeds City Transport	832	A
783 EFM	1957	Bristol SC4LK	ECW B35F	Crosville Motor Services	SC13	R
XCV 326	1957	Bedford SBG	Duple B42F	Harper & Kellow of St Agnes		A
GEN 201	1958	Leyland Titan PD3/6	Weymann H41/32RD	Bury Corporation	201	R
PFW 935	1958	Bristol SC4LK	ECW B35F	Lincolnshire Road Car Co	2453	RP
TAX 235	1958	Bristol Lodekka LD6G	ECW H33/27RD	Red & White Services	L358	RP
UNB 524	1958	Leyland Titan PD2/40	Metro Cammell H37/28R	Manchester Corporation	3524	R
VFJ 995	1958	Leyland Titan PD2/40	Weymann H31/26R	Exeter Corporation	60	R
120 JRB	1959	Daimler Freeline D650HS	Burlingham C37F	Tailby & George ('Blue Bus Services') of Willington		A
129 DPT	1959	AEC Reliance 2MU3RA	Plaxton C41F	OK Motor Services		RP
3014 AH	1959	Bristol MW5G	ECW B45F	Eastern Counties Omnibus Co	LL452	RP
654 BUP	1959	Leyland Tiger Cub PSUC1/2	Plaxton C37F	Wilkinson Bros of Sedgefield	54	RP
FRE 699A	1959	Bristol SC4LK	ECW B35F	Eastern Counties Omnibus Co	LC556	RP
314 PFM	1960	Bristol Lodekka FS6G	ECW H60R	Crosville Motor Services	DFG33	R
999 PPL	1960	Bedford J4LZ2	Plaxton C29F	Comfy Coaches of Farnham		RP
PBN 668	1960	Daimler CVG6-30	East Lancs H41/32F	Bolton Corporation	150	RP
VLT 250	1960	AEC Routemaster	Park Royal H36/28R	London Transport	RM244	RP

Registration	Date	Chassis	Body	New to	Fleet No	Status
314 DBM	1961	Ford Yeoman	Duple C41F	Travel House of Dunstable		R
387 MRR	1961	Leyland Leopard		East Midland Motor Services		A
8124 WX	1961	Bristol MW6G	ECW C39F	West Yorkshire Road Car Co	CUG27	R
WKG 284	1961	AEC Reliance 2MU3RA	Willowbrook DP41F	Western Welsh Omnibus Co	1284	R
XKO 72A	1961	Leyland Atlantean PDR1/1 Mk II	Metro Cammell O44/33F	Maidstone & District Motor Services	DH572	RP
4045 JIW	1962	AEC Reliance 760	Plaxton C57F	Williams of Bradford		RP
811 BWR	1962	Bristol SUL4A	ECW B36F	West Yorkshire Road Car Co	SMA5	R
NAT 766A	1962	Daimler CVG6-30	Roe H39/31F	Grimsby-Cleethorpes Transport	57	R
RCK 920	1962	Leyland Titan PD3/5	Metro Cammell FH41/31F	Ribble Motor Services	1775	RP
3747 RH	1963	AEC Bridgemaster 2B3RA	Park Royal H43/29F	East Yorkshire Motor Services	747	RP
AMX 8A	1963	AEC Reliance 2U3RA	Harrington C51F	Valliant of Ealing		RP
HH-97-96	1963	AEC Regal V	UTIC	Carris of Lisbon		RP
ALM 37B	1964	AEC Routemaster	Park Royal H36/28R	London Transport	RM 2037	RP
BCH 156B	1964	Daimler CVG6	Roe H37/28R	Derby Corporation	156	A
BDL 583B	1964	Bristol Lodekka FLF6G	ECW H38/32F	Southern Vectis Omnibus Co	70	A
BKG 713B	1964	AEC Renown 3B3RA	Northern Counties H38/29F	Western Welsh Omnibus Co	713	RP
TFA 987	1964	Daimler CCG5	Massey H33/28R	Burton upon Trent Corporation	87	R
WOW 993T	1964	Leyland Titan PD3/4	Northern Counties FCO39/30F	Southdown Motor Services	423	RP
BED 732C	1965	Leyland Titan PD2/40	East Lancs H34/30F	Warrington Corporation	51	RP
BNH 246C	1965	Daimler CVG6	Roe H33/26R	Northampton Corporation	246	R
BOW 503C	1965	AEC Regent V 2D3RA	East Lancs Neepsend H37/29R	Southampton Corporation	366	RP
BUF 272C	1965	Leyland Titan PD3/4	Northern Counties FH39/30F	Southdown Motor Services	272	RP
CUV 116C	1965	AEC Routemaster	Park Royal H36/28R	London Transport	RM 2116	R
EKP 234C	1965	Leyland Atlantean PDR1/1	Massey H—/—F	Maidstone Borough Council	34	RP
FDB 328C	1965	Leyland Titan PD2/40	East Lancs H36/28R	Stockport Corporation	28	RP
FDB 334C	1965	Leyland Titan PD2/40	East Lancs H36/28R	Stockport Corporation	34	R
FPT 590C	1965	AEC Routemaster 3R2RH	Park Royal H41/31F	Northern General Transport	2120	R
GEE 418D	1966	Daimler Fleetline SRG6LW	Willowbrook B42D	Grimsby-Cleethorpes Transport	35	R
HAD 915D	1966	Bedford VAM 5	Plaxton C45F	Princess Mary Coaches		RP
HHW 452D	1966	Bristol MW5G	ECW B45F	Bristol Omnibus Co	2636	RP
JJD 394D	1966	AEC Routemaster	Park Royal H40/32R	London Transport	RML2394	RP
JJD 499D	1966	AEC Routemaster	Park Royal H40/32R	London Transport	RML2499	RP
JJD 539D	1966	AEC Routemaster	Park Royal H40/32R	London Transport	RML2539	RP
HDV 638E	1967	Bristol MW6G	ECW C39F	Western National Omnibus Co (Royal Blue)	1433	RP
LAX 101E	1967	Bristol RESL6L	ECW B46F	Red & White Services	RS167	R
NDM 950E	1967	Bedford VAM14	Duple Midland DP45F	Phillips of Holywell		A
SMK 676F	1967	AEC Routemaster	Park Royal H40/32R	London Transport	RML2676	RP
SMK 716F	1967	AEC Routemaster	Park Royal H40/32R	London Transport	RML2716	R
SMK 747F	1967	AEC Routemaster	Park Royal H40/32R	London Transport	RML2747	A
JVV 267G	1968	Daimler CVG6	Roe H33/26R	Northampton Corporation	267	RP
YNU 351G	1968	Bristol Lodekka FLF6G	ECW H38/32F	Midland General Omnibus Co	313	R
MJA 895G	1969	Leyland Titan PD3/14	East Lancs H38/32F	Stockport Corporation	95	RP
SVF 896G	1969	Bristol RELH6G	ECW C47F	Eastern Counties Omnibus Co	RE896	RP
UTG 313G	1969	AEC Regent V 2MD3RA	Willowbrook H34/26F	Pontypridd UDC	8	RP
WYP 203G	1969	AEC Reliance 6MU3R	Plaxton C41F	Surrey Motors		R
UHA 963H	1969	BMMO S23	BMMO/Plaxton B51F	BMMO ('Midland Red')	5963	R
XCH 425G	1969	Daimler Fleetline CRG6LX	Roe H44/34F	Derby Corporation	225	A
CRR 537J	1970	Bristol RELL6L	Marshall	East Midland Motor Services	0537	A
PKW 434J	1970	Daimler Fleetline		Bradford City Transport		A
IJI 5367	1971	Bristol RELH6L	Plaxton C49F	Greenslades Tours	300	RP
STL 725J	1971	Bedford YRQ	Willowbrook DP43F	Simmonds of Great Gonnerby		RP
TRU 947J	1971	Bristol RELL6G	ECW DP50F	Wilts & Dorset Motor Services	846	R
VOD 123K	1971	Bristol LHS	Marshall B33F	Western National Omnibus Co	1253	RP
XRD 23K	1971	Bristol VRT/LL6G	Northern Counties H47/30D	Reading Corporation	23	R
GBB 516K	1972	Leyland Atlantean PDR2/1	Alexander H48/30F	Tyneside PTE	680	RP
JMC 123K	1972	AEC Reliance 6MU4R	Plaxton C34F	Glenton Tours of London	123	RP

Registration	Date	Chassis	Body	New to	Fleet No	Status
NPD 108L	1972	Leyland National 1151/2R	Leyland National B18D	London Country Bus Services	LN8	R
RWC 637K	1972	Bedford YRQ	Plaxton C37F	Harris of Grays		RP
TDL 566K	1972	Bristol RELL6G	ECW B53F	Southern Vectis Omnibus Co	866	A
YFM 269L	1972	Bristol RELL6G	ECW DP50F	Crosville Motor Services	ERG269	RP
BPT 672L	1973	Leyland Leopard PSU3B4R	Plaxton C53F	Trimdon Motor Services		RP
CRU 301L	1972	Bristol VRT6G	ECW	Hants & Dorset Motor Services	3301	RP
HKE 680L	1973	Bristol VRTSL6LX	ECW H43/29F	Maidstone & District Motor Services	680	A
NCD 559M	1973	Bristol VRTSL6LX	ECW	Southdown Motor Services	559	RP
NPD 128L	1973	Leyland National 1151/1R/0402	Leyland National B28F	London Country Bus Services	LNC 28	R
OCH 261L	1973	Daimler Fleetline CRG6LX	Roe H44/34F	Derby Corporation	261	RP
RVO 668L	1973	Leyland Leopard PSU3B4R	Plaxton C53F	Barton Transport of Chilwell	1246	RP
OWC 720M	1973	Bristol RELL6L	ECW B53F	Colchester Corporation	20	A
PKG 587M	1973	Bristol VRT/SL2/6G	ECW	Cardiff Corporation	587	RP
TGY 102M	1973	Leyland National	Leyland National	London Transport	LS2	A
THM 515M	1973	Daimler Fleetline	MCW	London Transport	DMS1515	A
PKH 600M	1974	Bedford VAS	Plaxton C29F	Hull City Football Club		R
RPU 869M	1974	Bristol RELH6G	ECW DP49F	Eastern Counties Omnibus Co	RE849	RP
WPG 217M	1974	Leyland National 10351/1R/SC	Leyland National DP39F	London Country Bus Services	SNC117	A
GLJ 467N	1974	Bristol VRTSL2/6LXB	ECW H43/31F	Hants & Dorset Motor Services	3315	R
GUG 547N	1974	Leyland Atlantean		West Yorkshire PTE		R
HPK 503N	1974	Leyland National 11351/1R	Leyland National B49F	Alder Valley	201	RP
UMO 180N	1974	Leyland National 11351/1R	Leyland National B49F	Alder Valley	180	R
GPD 318N	1975	Bristol LHS6L	ECW B35F	London Country Bus Services	BN 50	RP
JFJ 400N	1975	Bristol LH6L	Plaxton	Greenslades Tours		A
KDW 347P	1975	Leyland National 10351/1R/SC	Leyland National DP48F	Western Welsh Omnibus Co	ND3975	RP
KDW 362P	1975	Leyland National 11351/1R/SC	Leyland National DP48F	Jones Omnibus Services	ND5475	RP
KPA 369P	1975	Leyland National	Leyland National	Alder Valley	218	RP
KJD 507P	1976	Leyland National 11351A/2R	Leyland National DP36D	London Transport	LS7	A
KOU 795P	1976	Bristol VRTSL3/6LXB	ECW H43/31F	Bristol Omnibus Co	5508	A
LWB 377P	1976	Ailsa B55-10	Van Hool McArdle H44/31D	South Yorkshire PTE	377	RP
NDP 31R	1976	Bristol VRTLL3/6LXB	Northern Counties H47/29D	Reading Transport	31	RP
NDP 38R	1976	Bristol VRTLL3/6LXB	Northern Counties H47/29D	Reading Transport	38	R
NEL 119P	1976	Bristol VRTSL3/501	ECW CH41/29F	Hants & Dorset Motor Services	3345	RP
NOE 576R	1976	Leyland National 11351A/1R	Leyland National	Red & White Services	654	A
NWO 462R	1976	Leyland National 11351A/1R	Leyland National DP48F	Western Welsh Omnibus Co	ND1776	A
ODV 287P	1976	Volvo B58	Duple	Trathens of Yelverton		A
UGR 698R	1976	Bristol VRT/SL3/6LXB	ECW H43/31F	United Automobile Services	698	RP
LOI 1859	1977	Bedford YLQ	Alexander B45F	Ulsterbus	1859	RP
AYJ 100T	1978	Leyland National	Leyland National	Southdown Motor Services	100	RP
DAR 120T	1978	Leyland National 11351A/1R	Leyland National B49F	Eastern National Omnibus Co	1898	RP
THX 220S	1978	Leyland National 10351A/1R	Leyland National B36D	London Transport	LS220	RP
VDV 107S	1978	Bristol LH6L	ECW B43F	Western National (Devon General)	127	RP
WKO 132S	1978	Bristol VRTSL3/6LXB	ECW H43/31F	Maidstone & District Motor Services	5132	RP
WKO 138S	1978	Bristol VRTSL3/6LXB	ECW H43/31F	Maidstone & District Motor Services	5138	RP
WUH 173T	1978	Leyland National 11351A/1R	Leyland National B52F	National Welsh Omnibus Services	N2978	A
YRC 420	1978	AEC Reliance 6U3ZR	Plaxton C48FL	Silver Line Coaches		
AYR 300T	1979	Leyland National 10351A/2R	Leyland National B36D	London Transport	LS300	RP
BUH 239V	1979	Leyland National 2 NL106L11/1R	Leyland National B44F	National Welsh Omnibus Services	NS8011	A
EPD 511V	1979	Leyland National	Leyland National B41F	London Country Bus Services	SNB511	A
EPD 543V	1979	Leyland National 10351B/1R	Leyland National B41F	London Country Bus Services	SNB543	A
EWW 207T	1979	Leyland Leopard PSU3E/4R	Plaxton C49F	Wallace Arnold Tours of Leeds		RP
FDV 827V	1979	Leyland Leopard PSU3E/4R	Willowbrook C49F	Devon General		RP
GSU 866T	1979	Leyland Leopard PSU3C/3R	Alexander (Belfast) B53F	Central SMT Co	T384	RP
HIL 7081	1979	Bedford CFL	Plaxton C17F	Golden Miller of Feltham		R

Registration	Date	Chassis	Body	New to	Fleet No	Status
LSU 381V	1979	Leyland Atlantean AN68A/1R	Alexander H45/33F	Strathclyde PTE	LA1324	RP
AFB 593V	1980	Bristol LH6L	ECW B43F	Bristol Omnibus Co	462	A
AUP 369W	1980	Leyland Atlantean	Roe H73F	Northern General Transport Co	3469	RP
HFG 923V	1980	Leyland National 2 NL116L11/1R	Leyland National B52F	Southdown Motor Services	123	R
SNS 823W	1980	Leyland National 2 NL116L11/1R	Leyland National B52F	Central SMT Co	N37	A
VIB 5069	1980	Leyland Leopard PSU3E/4R	Duple C49F	Grey Green		RP
JCK 852W	1981	Leyland National 2	National Greenway B41F	Ribble Motor Services	252	RP
OCW 8X	1981	Leyland Atlantean	East Lancs	Blackburn Corporation	8	R
PUA 310W	1981	Leyland Atlantean		West Yorkshire PTE		A
RLN 230W	1981	Bristol LHS	Plaxton	British Airways		RP
RNE 692W	1981	Bedford CF	Plaxton C17F	Shearings of Altrincham		R
XFG 25Y	1983	Leyland National 2 NL116L11/1R	Leyland National B49F	Brighton Borough Transport	25	A
AXI 2534	1982	Bristol RELL6G		Citybus	2534	A
PSX 189Y	1982	Leyland Leopard PSU3G/4R	Alexander B53F	Alexander (Fife)	FPE189	RP
A537 TYW	1983	Dodge G08	Wadham Stringer	British Rail		RP
VCO 802	1983	Leyland Tiger TRCTLL/3R	Plaxton	East Kent Road Car Co	8840	R
C832 KNK	1986	Bedford CF	Martyn Walker	Regency Cars		RP
E523 TOV	1988	Iveco 49-10	Carlyle	Midland Red Omnibus Co		RP
G645 WDV	1990	Volkswagen LT31	-10	Crediton Disability Group		A
VCO 772	1991	Mercedes 814D	Dormobile C33F	Pathfinder	2	R
J7 FTG	1992	Mercedes 811D	AMI B33F	Compass Travel of Worthing		R
K727 UTT	1993	Iveco 59-12	Mellor B29F	APL Travel Wilts		R
L932 CTT	1994	Iveco 59-12	Mellor B21D	Devon General Ltd		R

Notes:

AOG 638	Converted to lorry
EUF 181	Coverted to Recovery Vehicle
HKE 867	Rebodied 1953
JK 9915	Open top
LHY 937	Renumbered 1541 in 1964
EVD 406	New with Scottish Commercial body; acquired by J Wood & Son of Mirfield in 1953 and rebodied 1955
KYY 615	Previously a training bus
RSK 615	Originally registered LOE 300
FFN 446	Chassis parts from 1938 Leyland TD5
LWR 424	Originally bus 858 (later DGW4); converted to a towing vehicle and renumbered 4044 in 1972
UAS 954	Originally registered in USA
395 DEL	Guernsey registration was 2027
FRE 699A	Originally registered 3003AH
NAT 766A	Originally registered TJV 100
WOW 993T	Originally registered 423 DCD
XCH 425G	Subsequently worked in Coventry
MJA 895G	For continued preservation in Portsmouth
IJI 5367	Originally registered UFJ 229J
HIL 7081	Originally registered DJF 631T
VIB 5069	Originally registered FYX 817W
VCO 802	Originally registered FKK 840Y
THM 515M	Originally H44/24D; rebuilt as 'Supercar' publicity vehicle

Part 4

New in 1945 to Huddersfield Joint Omnibus Committee, Duple-bodied Daimler CWA6 No 217 (CCX 777) is now part of the Quantock Motor Services fleet.

Blue Triangle
Rainham

Contact address: Unit 3C, Denver Industrial Estate, Ferry Lane, Rainham, Essex, RM13 7MD.
Phone: 01708 631001
Website: www.bluetrianglebuses.com
Operations planned for 2007: Scheduled heritage services not finalised at time of publication. Please see website for details. Vehicles occasionally appear on rail replacement services.

Registration	Date	Chassis	Body	New to	Fleet No	Status
JXN 371	1949	Leyland Titan 7RT	Park Royal H30/26R	London Transport	RTL48	A
KGK 959	1949	AEC Regent III O961 RT	Weymann H30/26R	London Transport	RT2150	R
KXW 171	1950	AEC Regent III O961 RT	Saunders Roe H30/26R	London Transport	RT3062	R
KXW 22	1950	Leyland Titan 7RT	Metro Cammell H30/26R	London Transport	RTL672	A
KXW 488	1950	AEC Regent III O961 RT	Weymann H30/26R	London Transport	RT1389	A
LLU 670	1950	AEC Regent III O961 RT	Park Royal H30/26R	London Transport	RT3871	R
LLU 732	1950	AEC Regent III O961 RT	Park Royal H30/26R	London Transport	RT3933	RP
LYR 854	1950	AEC Regent III O961 RT	Weymann O30/26R	London Transport	RT3435	R
MLL 682	1950	AEC Regent III O961 RT	Saunders Roe H30/26R	London Transport	RT1320	A
LYR 969	1952	AEC Regent III O961 RT	Weymann H30/26R	London Transport	RT2799	R
MXX 289	1952	AEC Regal IV 9821LT RF	Metro Cammell B39F	London Transport	RF401	RP
VLT 85	1959	AEC Routemaster	Park Royal H36/28R	London Transport	RM85	R
VLT 268	1960	AEC Routemaster	Park Royal H36/28R	London Transport	RM268	A
VLT 298	1960	AEC Routemaster R2RH	Park Royal H36/28R	London Transport	RM298	R
215 UXJ	1962	AEC Routemaster R2RH/1	Park Royal H40/32R	London Transport	RML899	R
WLT 900	1962	AEC Routemaster R2RH/1	Park Royal H40/32R	London Transport	RML900	R
WLT 902	1962	AEC Routemaster R2RH/1	Park Royal H40/32R	London Transport	RML902	R
CUV 260C	1965	AEC Routemaster R2RH/1	Park Royal H36/29RD	London Transport	RCL2260	R
AML 1H	1970	AEC Swift 4MP2R	Marshall B42F	London Transport	SM1	RP
JPF 108K	1970	AEC Swift 3MP2R	Alexander DP45F	London Country Bus Services	SMA8	A
A103 SUU	1984	Volvo Ailsa B55-10 Mk III	Alexander H38/30F	London Transport	V3	RP

Notes:

LYR 854	Converted to open top following de-roofing in 1976
215 UXJ	Originally registered WLT 899
A103 SUU	Originally H36/28D

Buckland Omnibus Co
Woodbridge

Contact address: Ivy Cottage, 28 Marloesfield Road, Hachestan, Woodbridge, Suffolk IP13 0DP
Phone: 01728 747093
E-mail: bucklandcoaches@yahoo.co.uk
Web site: www.bucklandbuses.co.uk
Operations planned for 2007: Vehicles available for private hire. Occasional special Felixstowe sea front service — phone for details.

Registration	Date	Chassis	Body	New to	Fleet No	Status
TE 7870	1929	Dennis ES	Brush B29D	Accrington Corporation	57	R
GRP 260D	1966	Bristol MW6G	ECW C39F	United Counties Omnibus Co	260	R
KUL 331D	1966	Bedford VAS2	Willowbrook B29F	Greater London Council	331	A

Notes:

TE 7870	Body rebuilt 1974 by Wyatt

Carmel Coaches
Okehampton

Contact address: Mr A. G. Hazell, Northlew, Okehampton, Devon.
Phone: 01409 221237
Operations planned for 2007: LOD 495 is a licensed PSV and available for private hire

Registration	Date	Chassis	Body	New to	Fleet No	Status
LOD 495	1950	Albion Victor FT39N	Duple C31F	Way of Crediton		R
MTT 640	1951	Leyland Titan PD2/1	Leyland L27/26R	Devon General	DL640	R

Cosy Coaches
Killamarsh

Contact address: Cosy Coach Tours, 5 Meynell Way, Killamarsh, Derbyshire, S21 1HG.
Phone: 0114 248 9139
Operations planned for 2007: Please telephone for details.

Registration	Date	Chassis	Body	New to	Fleet No	Status
ATS 408	1948	Bedford OB	Duple C29F	James Mefflan of Kirriemuir		R
MRB 765	1949	Bedford OB	Duple C29F	H. D. Andrew of Tideswell		RP
CCB 300	1950	Albion Victor FT39N	Duple C31F	Cronshaw of Blackburn		A
ERG 164	1950	Bedford OB	Duple C29F	Paterson of Aberdeen		RP
TDT 344	1955	AEC Regent V MD3RV	Roe H34/28R	Doncaster Corporation	144	RP
YBD 201	1961	Bristol MW6G	ECW C34F	United Counties Omnibus Co	201	A

Cumbria Classic Coaches
Kirkby Stephen

Contact address: Bowber Head, Ravenstonedale, Kirkby Stephen, Cumbria, CA17 4NL.
Phone: 015396 23254
Website: www.cumbriaclassiccoaches.co.uk
E-mail: coaches@cumbriaclassiccoaches.co.uk
Operations planned for 2007: Route 569: Ravenstonedale–Kirkby Stephen–Hawes, Tues (Hawes market day) Easter to October.
Kendal Clipper (circular tour of Kendal), half-hourly, seven days a week during school summer holidays. Route 570: Hawes to Ribblehead
viaduct Tuesdays Easter to October (to be confirmed)

Registration	Date	Chassis	Body	New to	Fleet No	Status
JTB 749	1948	AEC Regal III O962	Burlingham C33F	Florence Motors of Morcambe		R
CRN 80	1949	Leyland Tiger PS1	East Lancs B34R	Preston Corporation	75	R
TSK 736	1949	Commer Commando	Scottish Aviation C29F	David Lawson	C8	RP
CWG 286	1950	Leyland Tiger PS1/1	Alexander C35F	W. Alexander & Sons (Northern)	PA184	R
MTJ 84	1951	Guy Arab III	Roe C31F	Lancashire United Transport	440	R
627 HFM	1959	Bristol Lodekka LD6B	ECW CO33/27RD	Crosville Motor Services	DLB978	R

Notes:
TSK 736   Originally registered CMS 9. To be returned to original colours.

Mac Tours and Majestic Tour
Edinburgh

Contact address: Edinburgh Vintage Bus Company, 11A James Court, Lawnmarket, Edinburgh EH1 2PB.
Phone: 0131 477 4771
Operations planned for 2007: Hop-on, hop-off open-top tours of Edinburgh operate seven days a week, most of the year.

Registration	Date	Chassis	Body	New to	Fleet No	Status
YSL 334	1951	Leyland Tiger PS1	Guernseybus OB34F	Jersey Motor Transport Co	44	
LST 873	1958	Leyland Titan PD2/40	Park Royal O27/26RO	Barrow in Furness Corporation	165	
JSJ 746	1959	AEC Routemaster	Park Royal O75R	London Transport	RM90	
JSJ 747	1959	AEC Routemaster	Park Royal O75R	London Transport	RM84	
JSJ 748	1959	AEC Routemaster	Park Royal O75R	London Transport	RM80	
JSJ 749	1959	AEC Routemaster	Park Royal O76R	London Transport	RM94	
VLT 143	1960	AEC Routemaster	Park Royal O75R	London Transport	RM143	
VLT 163	1960	AEC Routemaster	Park Royal O75R	London Transport	RM163	
VLT 235	1960	AEC Routemaster	Park Royal O75R	London Transport	RM235	
VLT 237	1960	AEC Routemaster	Park Royal O75R	London Transport	RM237	
VLT 242	1960	AEC Routemaster	Park Royal O71R	London Transport	RM242	
VLT 281	1960	AEC Routemaster	Park Royal O71R	London Transport	RM281	
WLT 371	1960	AEC Routemaster R2RH	Park Royal O63R	London Transport	RM371	
858 DYE	1961	AEC Routemaster R2RH	Park Royal O63R	London Transport	RM727	
803 DYE	1961	AEC Routemaster R2RH	Park Royal O63R	London Transport	RM1010	
485 CLT	1962	AEC Routemaster	Park Royal O57R	London Transport	RMC1485	
CUV 203C	1965	AEC Routemaster R2RH	Park Royal H36/28R	London Transport	RM2203	
CUV 210C	1965	AEC Routemaster R2RH	Park Royal O63R	London Transport	RM2210	
CUV 241C	1965	AEC Routemaster R2RH/3	Park Royal H64RD	London Transport	RCL2241	
CUV 248C	1965	AEC Routemaster R2RH/3	Park Royal H64RD	London Transport	RCL2248	
NMY 634E	1967	AEC Routemaster R2RH/2	Park Royal H32/24F	British European Airways	8241	
NMY 646E	1967	AEC Routemaster R2RH/2	Park Royal H56F	British European Airways	8253	
OSJ 636R	1977	Leyland Leopard PSU3C/3R	Alexander OB49F	Western SMT Co	L2636	

Notes:

YSL 334	Originally registered J 5567 and fitted with Reading B34F body
LST 873	Originally registered CEO 952
JSJ 746	Originally registered VLT 90. Extended and converted to open top.
JSJ 747	Originally registered VLT 84. Extended and converted to open top.
JSJ 748	Originally registered VLT 80. Extended and converted to open top.
JSJ 749	Originally registered VLT 94. Extended and converted to open top.
WLT 371	Converted to open top.
VLT 143	Extended and converted to open top.
VLT 163	Extended and converted to open top.
VLT 237	Extended and converted to open top.
VLT 235	Extended and converted to open top.
VLT 242	Extended and converted to open top.
VLT 281	Extended and converted to open top.
858 DYE	Originally registered WLT 727. Converted to open top.
803 DYE	Originally registered 10 CLT. Converted to open top.
CUV 210C	Converted to open top.
NMY 646E	Passed to London Transport (RMA9) in 1979
NMY 634E	Passed to London Transport (RMA50) in 1979; acquired by Stagecoach at Perth in 1987
OSJ 636R	Converted to open top

Memory Lane Vintage Omnibus Services
Maidenhead

Contact address: 78 Lillibrooke Crescent, Maidenhead, Berkshire, SL6 3XQ.
Phone: 01628 825050
Fax: 01628 825851
E-mail: info@memorylane.co.uk
Web site: www.memorylane.co.uk

Registration	Date	Chassis	Body	New to	Fleet No	Status
KGU 290	1949	AEC Regent III O961 RT	Weymann H30/26R	London Transport	RT1530	RP
KYY 628	1950	AEC Regent III O961 RT	Park Royal H30/26R	London Transport	RT1790	R
LYF 377	1951	AEC Regal IV 9821LT RF	Metro Cammell B37F	London Transport	RF26	R
NLE 643	1953	AEC Regal IV 9821LT RF	Metro Cammell B39F	London Transport	RF643	RP
VLT 216	1960	AEC Routemaster R2RH	Park Royal H36/28R	London Transport	RM216	R

Midland Classic Ltd
Swadlincote

Contact Address: Kiln Way, Swadlincote, Derbyshire, DE11 8ED
Telephone: 01283 213869, 08700 671505
Web site: www.midlandclassic.com
E-mail: info@midlandclassic.com
Brief Description: Midland Classic have a range of restored vehicles available for hire and also operate bus services in the Swadlincote / Burton upon Trent area.
Operations planned for 2007: Route 21 Swadlincote to Burton upon Trent. Vehicles also visit transport rallies.

Registration	Date	Chassis	Body	New to	Fleet No	Status
798 UXA	1962	AEC Routemaster	Park Royal H36/28R	London Transport	RM1168	R
799 UXA	1962	AEC Routemaster	Park Royal H36/28R	London Transport	RM1305	R
TOJ 592S	1977	MCW Metrobus	MCW H43/28F	MCW demonstrator		R
WDA 4T	1978	Leyland Titan TNLXB1RF	Park Royal H43/29F	West Midlands PTE	7004	R
C168 YBA	1985	Leyland Olympian ONLXB/1R	Northern Counties H43/30F	Greater Manchester PTE	3184	RP

Notes:

798 UXA	Originally registered 168 CLT
799 UXA	Originally registered 305 CLT
TOJ 592S	Prototype Metrobus, originally 5LXT engine and H43/28D. Rebuilt in 1990 by Stevensons of Uttoxeter

Quantock Motor Services
Wiveliscombe

Contact address: Bishop's Lydeard, Somerset.
Phone: 01823 251140
Affiliations: NARTM
Operations planned for 2007: Please telephone for details

Registration	Date	Chassis	Body	New to	Fleet No	Status
JG 9938	1937	Leyland Tiger TS8	Park Royal C32R	East Kent Road Car Co		R
AJA 132	1938	Bristol L5G	Burlingham B35R	North Western Road Car Co	372	R
GNU 750	1939	Daimler COG5/40	Willowbrook DP35F	Tailby & George ('Blue Bus Services') Willington	DR5	RP
CCX 777	1945	Daimler CWA6	Duple L27/26R	Huddersfield Joint Omnibus Committee	217	RP
EMW 893	1947	Daimler CVD6	Park Royal B35C	Swindon Corporation	57	A
HUO 510	1947	AEC Regal I O662	Weymann B35F	Devon General	SR510	A
JUO 992	1947	Leyland Titan PD1	ECW L27/26R	Southern National Omnibus Co	2932	A
ACH 441	1948	AEC Regal III O682	Windover C32F	Trent Motor Traction Co	611	R
JFM 575	1948	AEC Regal III 6821A	Strachan B35R	Crosville Motor Services		R
JNN 384	1948	Leyland Titan PD1	Duple L29/26F	Barton Transport of Chilwell	467	RP
JTE 546	1948	AEC Regent III 6811A	Park Royal H33/26R	Morecambe & Heysham Corporation	20	R
KTF 594	1949	AEC Regent III 9621E	Park Royal O33/26R	Morecambe & Heysham Corporation	65	R
LJH 665	1949	Dennis Lancet III	Duple C35F	Lee of Barnet		RP
JFJ 875	1950	Daimler CVD6	Weymann B35F	Exeter City Transport	75	R
KEL 131	1950	Leyland Titan PD2/3	Weymann FH33/25D	Bournemouth Corporation	131	RP
KFM 893	1950	Bristol L5G	ECW DP31R	Crosville Motor Services	KG131	R
LFM 302	1950	Leyland Tiger PS1	Weymann B35F	Crosville Motor Services	KA226	R
LFM 717	1950	Bristol L5G	ECW B35R	Crosville Motor Services	KG136	A
LFM 734	1950	Bristol LL5G	ECW B39R	Crosville Motor Services	KG153	A
LUO 692	1950	Leyland Tiger PS2/3	Burlingham C33F	Pridham of Lamerton		A
DCK 219	1951	Leyland Titan PD2/3	East Lancs FCL27/22RD	Ribble Motor Services	1248	R
PHN 699	1952	Guy Arab III	Roe B41C	Darlington Corporation	26	RP
BAS 563	1956	Bristol Lodekka LD6G	ECW O33/27R	Southern Vectis Omnibus Co	501	R
701 AEH	1957	Leyland Titan PD3/4	MCW O36/32F	Potteries Motor Traction Co	H701	RP
VDV 752	1957	Bristol Lodekka LDL6G	ECW O37/33RD	Western National Omnibus Co	1935	R
VDV 753	1957	Bristol Lodekka LDL6G	ECW O37/33RD	Western National Omnibus Co	1936	R
NDB 356	1958	Leyland Tiger Cub PSUC1/1	Crossley B44F	Stockport Corporation	403	R
890 ADV	1959	AEC Reliance 2MU3RV	Willowbrook C41F	Devon General Grey Cars	TCR890	R
792 UXA	1960	AEC Routemaster	Park Royal O36/28R	London Transport	RM787	R
805 EVT	1960	AEC Reliance 2MU3RV	Weymann DP41F	Potteries Motor Traction Co	SL805	R
572 CNW	1962	Daimler CVG6LX-30	Roe H39/31F	Leeds City Transport	572	R
AAO 771A	1963	Leyland Titan PD3/5	Metro Cammell FH41/31F	Ribble Motor Services	1841	R
DPV 65D	1966	AEC Regent V 2D2RA	Neepsend H37/28R	Ipswich Corporation	65	R
JJD 511D	1966	AEC Routemaster	Park Royal H40/32R	London Transport	RML2511	R
XTF 98D	1966	Leyland Titan PD3/4	East Lancs H41/32F	Haslingden Corporation	45	R
HJA 965E	1967	Leyland Titan PD2/40	East Lancs / Neepsend H36/28R	Stockport Corporation	65	R
GNH 258F	1968	Daimler CVG6	Roe H33/26R	Northampton Corporation	258	R
TDK 686J	1971	AEC Reliance 6U3ZR	Plaxton C53F	Yelloway Motor Services of Rochdale		A
HVU 247N	1975	AEC Reliance 6U3ZR	Plaxton C53F	Yelloway Motor Services of Rochdale		RP
NNC 854P	1976	AEC Reliance 6U3ZR	Plaxton C53F	Yelloway Motor Services of Rochdale		A
WDK 562T	1979	AEC Reliance 6U3ZR	Plaxton C49F	Yelloway Motor Services of Rochdale		R

Notes:

AJA 132	Rebodied 1950
KEL 131	Built with twin staircases and dual doors
DCK 219	White Lady double deck coach
BAS 563	Originally registered MDL 952
701 AEH	Converted to open top by Sundekker
792 UXA	Originally registered WLT 787
572 CNW	Converted to exhibition vehicle
AAO 771A	Driver training vehicle 1981-1998. Originally registered TCK 841.
HVU 247N	Did carry registration 146 FLD

Indices

Former Eastern National Leyland National 1702 (UOA 322L, new as WNO 551L) peeps out of the south wing of the Midland Road Transport group museum. *Andrew Bagshaw*

Index of Vehicles by Registration

Reg	Page	Reg	Page	Reg	Page	Reg	Page	Reg	Page
1 RDV	74	304 GHN	63	47638	81	657 BWB	58	858 DYE	116
101 CLT	59	304 KFC	46	484 EFJ	104	66	58	86 GFJ	102
105 UTU	52	305 KFC	46	485 CLT	116	672 COD	72	862 RAE	67
109 DRM	105	314 DBM	110	487 GFR	100	675 AAM	69	866 HAL	45
116 JTD	37	314 PFM	109	488 KOT	62	675 COD	69	869 NHT	66
116 TMD	89	318 AOW	98	501 KD	89	675 OCV	77	871 KHA	55
12 MFC	70	3190 UN	100	504 EBL	41	6769	80	872 ATA	74
120 JRB	109	326 CAA6	79	5056 HA	95	6801 FN	77	875 VFM	89
122 JTD	37	332 RJO	70	507 OHU	67	694 ZO	53	881 BTF	94
129 DPT	109	333 CRW	26	5073 HA	55	70 AUF	98	8860 VR	38
1294 RE	20	334 CRW	20	519 BTA	72	701 AEH	118	890 ADV	118
1322 WA	51	335 AOW	98	5212 HA	55	71 AHI	24	9 RDV	74
138 CLT	23	348 CLT	78	528 CTF	94	72 MMJ	86	90 HBC	87
14 LFC	46	3655 NE	37	5280 NW	78	7209 PW	52	904 OFM	67
14 PKR	82	370 FCR	98	534 RTB	85	737 DYE	36	913 DTT	74
1425 P	57	371 BKA	89	548 BUF	98	7424 SP	49	918 NRT	23
177 IK	24	372 BKA	89	557 BNG	28	7514 UA	33	924 AHY	66
191 AWL	69	373 WPU	23	56 GUO	95	756 KFC	46	928 GTA	74
1925 WA	82	3747 RH	110	561 TD	85	760 CTD	85	931 GTA	74
198 CUS	80	381 BKM	23	562 RTF	44	773 FHA	20	932 GTA	74
201 YTE	44	386 DD	100	569 KKK	27	78 D140	24	935 GTA	74
204 UXJ	92	387 MRR	110	57 GUO	67	78 D824	24	943 KHA	55
214 CLT	82	3916 UB	82	572 CNW	118	780 GHA	95	952 JUB	35
215 UXJ	114	3945 UE	24	574 TD	44	783 EFM	109	956 AJO	46
217 AJF	87	395 DEL	109	5789 AH	77	7830 LG 69	58	960 HTT	74
217 MHK	23	404 RIU	53	583 CLT	85	7874 WJ	51	9629 WU	58
2206 OI	21	4045 JIW	110	595 LCG	79	792 UXA	118	964 H87	57
221 JVK	72	410 DCD	71	596 LCG	79	798 UXA	117	969 EHW	66
236 LNO	23	414 CLT	38	6167 RU	65	799 DYE	78	972 CUF	98
248 NEA	55	416 DCD	98	6203 KW	33	799 UXA	117	972 EHW	66
256 SFM	89	419 DCD	98	6204 KW	33	80 NVO	45	974 AFJ	104
264 ERY	20	422 CAX	52	6220 KW	33	802 MHW	55	975 CWL	69
264 KTA	69	422 DCD	71	6249 UP	92	803 DYE	116	9797 DP	100
268 KTA	69	4227 FM	44	627 HFM	115	805 EVT	118	980 DAE	67
271 KTA	69	433 MDT	58	63 CLT	68	811 BWR	110	991 MDV	104
28 TKR	23	434 BTE	42	6330 WJ	51	8124 WX	110	99-64-HB	56
286 KTA	72	436 KOV	103	6342 HA	22	815 KDV	104	999 PPL	109
297 LJ	65	449 CLT	51	6370 HA	20	815 XFM	69		
301 LJ	22	461 CLT	25	643 MIP	24	8154 EL	65		
3014 AH	109	462 EOT	62	6479 HA	20	8319 JD 13	58		
3016 HA	55	4632 VM	38	654 BUP	109	85 D 2412	24		
3035 HA	20	468 FTT	72	6545 HA	55	850 ABK	46		

Reg	Page	Reg	Page	Reg	Page	Reg	Page	Reg	Page
A103 SUU	114	A913 ERM	59	ADR 813	103	AG 6470	64	ALM 37B	110
A110 WVP	21	A927 MDV	102	ADV 128	103	AH 7950	28	ALS 102Y	81
A112 HLV	89	A954 SAE	66	ADX 1	30	AHA 451J	56	AML 1H	114
A135 HLV	89	AAA 503C	62	ADX 196	30	AHA 582	54	AML 582H	88
A250 SVW	78	AAA 506C	62	ADX 63B	30	AHC 442	70	AMX 8A	110
A30 ORJ	97	AAA 508C	62	AED 31B	64	AHE 163	35	ANA 1Y	97
A323 GLV	44	AAA 756	47	AEL 170B	65	AHF 850	59	ANA 601Y	97
A472 HNC	97	AAO 34B	105	AEX 85B	28	AHG 334V	86	ANA 645Y	97
A537 TYW	112	AAO 771A	118	AFB 592V	66	AHL 694	92	ANB 851	37
A680 KDV	74	ABD 252B	69	AFB 593V	112	AHN 451B	63	ANE 2T	96
A686 KDV	72	ABH 358	64	AFJ 708T	72	AHU 803	67	ANH 154	108
A700 DDL	32	ABR 433	92	AFJ 726T	102	AIT 934	53	ANJ 306T	99
A700 HNB	97	ACB 904	93	AFJ 727T	102	AJA 132	118	ANQ 778	42
A701 LNC	97	ACH 441	118	AFJ 729T	72	AJA 139B	44	ANV 775J	101
A706 LNC	38	ACH 627	108	AFJ 764T	102	AJA 152	37	ANW 682	33
A735 PSU	81	ACK 796	93	AFN 488B	77	AJA 408L	96	AOG 638	108
A749 NTA	104	AC-L 379	57	AFN 780B	77	AJX 369	82	AOG 679	20
A765 NNA	97	ACU 304B	92	AFS 91B	49	ALJ 340B	65	AOR 158B	98
A869 SUL	46	AD 7156	84	AFT 930	92	ALJ 973	57	APR 167A	45
A910 SYE	44	ADL 459B	32	AFY 971	42	ALJ 986	28	APW 829B	30

Plate	No.	Plate	No.	Plate	No.	Plate	No.	Plate	No.
ARC 515	20	BHL 682	76	C526 DYT	88	CPU 979G	23	D553 NOE	103
ARC 666T	45	BHO 543C	79	C526 FFJ	74	CRC 911	52	D63 NOF	38
ARD 676	57	BHO 670J	100	C53 HDT	51	CRG 811	80	D676 NNE	38
ARG 17B	49	BHT 677A	89	C671 FFJ	104	CRM 927T	104	D685 SEM	89
ARN 811C	94	BHU 92C	66	C705 FFJ	102	CRN 80	115	DAR 120T	111
ARY 225K	87	BJA 425	37	C724 JJO	46	CRR 537J	110	DAU 370C	45
ASC 665B	49	BJK 672D	99	C729 JJO	70	CRS 834	80	DB 5070	37
ASF 365	47	BJX 848C	80	C748 FFJ	104	CRU 103C	65	DB 5221	108
ATA 563L	74	BK 2986	70	C751 YBA	97	CRU 180C	65	DBA 214C	38
ATD 281J	85	BKC 236K	89	C777 SFS	50	CRU 184C	78	DBC 190C	87
ATD 683	42	BKC 276K	89	C801 FRL	102	CRU 187C	65	DBE 187	35
ATF 477	47	BKG 713B	110	C823 CBU	97	CRU 197C	65	DBL 154	101
ATS 408	115	BLH 123B	24	C832 KNK	112	CRU 301L	110	DBN 978	52
ATT 922	103	BMS 222	48	C862 DYD	72	CS 3364	47	DBU 246	37
AUD 310J	70	BMS 405	48	C869 DYD	72	CSG 29C	49	DBV 43W	104
AUF 670	108	BNC 960T	96	CAH 923	30	CSG 43C	49	DBV 100W	94
AUO 74	103	BND 874C	38	CBC 921	18	CSG 773S	50	DBV 831W	94
AUP 369W	73	BNE 729N	96	CBR 539	92	CSG 792S	50	DBW 613	46
AUX 296	47	BNE 751N	96	CC 1087	90	CSL 498	78	DBY 001	80
AVX 975G	23	BNE 764N	96	CC 7745	54	CTF 627B	85	DCK 219	118
AWA 124B	49	BNH 246C	110	CC 8671	73	CTP 200	70	DCN 83	92
AWG 393	48	BNU 679G	39	CC 9305	27	CTT 23C	74	DCS 616	48
AWG 623	48	BOD 25C	72	CC 9424	73	CTT 513C	74	DDB 174C	38
AWG 639	48	BOK 1V	100	CCB 300	115	CTT 518C	82	DDL 50	32
AXI 2259	83	BON 474C	55	CCG 296K	62	CU 3593	57	DDM 652	65
AXI 2534	112	BOT 303	62	CCG 704C	79	CU 4740	48	DED 797	42
AXJ 857	37	BOW 162	65	CCK 359	93	CUB 331C	33	DEK 3D	101
AXM 649	87	BOW 169	103	CCK 663	85	CUH 856	108	DFE 383	35
AXM 693	25	BOW 503C	110	CCX 801	76	CUH 859	48	DFE 963D	67
AYJ 379	48	BOW 507C	98	CCX 777	118	CUL 260	28	DFM 347H	44
AYJ 100T	111	BP 9822	19	CD 4867	19	CUV 116C	110	DFV 146	85
AYR 300T	111	BPT 672L	111	CD 5125	19	CUV 121C	80	DGS 536	48
AYV 651	87	BPV 9	30	CD 7045	47	CUV 203C	116	DGS 625	48
AZD 203	24	BR 7132	19	CDB 224	37	CUV 208C	76	DHC 784E	99
B100 PKS	81	BRS 37	48	CDC 166K	100	CUV 210C	116	DHR 192	41
B101 SJA	97	BTA 59	71	CDC 168K	100	CUV 218C	45	DHW 293K	68
B106 XJO	46	BTF 25	93	CDJ 878	42	CUV 219C	55	DIV 83	53
B115 ORU	78	BTN 113	72	CDK 409C	86	CUV 220C	78	DJF 349	45
B177 FFS	81	BTR 361B	70	CDL 479C	32	CUV 229C	88	DJG 619C	77
B349 LSO	50	BTW 488	23	CDR 679	48	CUV 233C	23	DJP 754	37
B401 NJF	18	BU 7108	108	CDT 636	57	CUV 241C	116	DKC 301L	44
B65 PJA	38	BUF 122C	99	CDX 516	25	CUV 248C	116	DKC 330L	89
B901 TVR	97	BUF 260C	99	CEO 720W	63	CUV 260C	114	DKY 704	68
B926 KWM	60	BUF 272C	110	CEO 723W	63	CUV 290C	85	DKY 706	57
BAS 563	118	BUF 277C	99	CEO 956	63	CVF 874	30	DKY 712	65
BBA 560	37	BUF 426C	99	CEO 957	63	CVH 741	57	DKY 735	21
BBK 236B	70	BUF 427C	99	CET 613	95	CVL 850D	35	DL 5084	32
BBW 21V	46	BUH 239V	111	CFK 340	92	CVP 207	54	DL 9015	73
BCD 820L	41	BUS 181	80	CFN 104	101	CWG 206	37	DL 9706	102
BCH 156B	110	BVP 784V	21	CFN 136	73	CWG 283	48	DLJ 111L	66
BCJ 710B	78	BWG 39	48	CFN 154	73	CWG 286	115	DLU 92	25
BCK 367C	44	BWG 833L	49	CFV 851	23	CWG 696V	44	DM 2583	90
BCK 939	57	BWO 585B	52	CGJ 188	25	CWG 756V	51	DM 6228	93
BCP 671	82	BWS 105L	49	CHF 565	59	CWH 717	37	DMS 130	109
BCR 379K	98	BXA 464B	49	CHG 541	48	CWN 629C	68	DMS 325C	49
BD 209	90	BXD 576	87	CHL 772	80	CWU 146T	60	DMS 348C	80
BDJ 87	57	BXI 2583	83	CJG 959	76	CWX 671	33	DMS 359C	49
BDL 583B	110	BXI 339	83	CK 3825	37	CXX 171	25	DMS 820	48
BDY 809	28	C 2367	90	CK 4474	93	CYI 621	53	DMS 823	48
BED 731C	44	C113 CAT	73	CKC 308L	89	CYJ 252	48	DNF 204	52
BED 732C	110	C168 YBA	117	CKG 193	57	D103 DAJ	28	DNF 708C	96
BEN 177	37	C201 CBU	97	CLE 122	88	D122 PTT	46	DNW 840T	34
BFE 419	35	C208 FVU	38	CMS 201	99	D176 NON	64	DOD 474	104
BFM 144	108	C225 CBU	97	CN 2870	54	D275 OOJ	34	DPT 848	92
BFS 1L	49	C24 NVV	101	CN 4740	92	D302 JVR	97	DPV 65D	118
BFS 463L	49	C255 FRJ	38	CN 6100	92	D320 LNB	97	DPV 68D	30
BG 8557	59	C386 XFD	64	CNH 699	67	D472 OWE	58	DR 4902	40
BG 9225	59	C416 AHT	67	CNH 860	69	D501 LNA	97	DRC 224	28
BHA 399C	55	C45 HDT	58	CNH 862	69	D509 MJA	97	DRD 130	105
BHA 656C	55	C481 CBU	97	CPM 61	40	D536 NDA	100	DRD 130	57

Reg	No.	Reg	No.	Reg	No.	Reg	No.	Reg	No.
DRN 289	93	EKU 746	57	FCK 884	94	FUF 181	73	GLS 265S	50
DSD 936V	50	EKV 966	26	FDB 328C	110	FV 5737	103	GM 6384	48
DSE 980T	59	EKY 558	57	FDB 334C	110	FVA 854	80	GN 8242	25
DSG 169	48	ELP 223	78	FDL 927D	32	FW 5698	35	GNB 518D	96
DTJ 139B	85	ELP 228	25	FDL 676L	32	FW 8990	57	GNC 276N	38
DTP 823	70	EMS 362V	80	FDM 724	55	FWG 846	48	GNF 15V	97
DU 4838	46	EMW 284	68	FDO 573	35	FWH 461Y	97	GNF 16V	97
DUK 278	103	EMW 893	118	FDV 790V	72	FWL 371E	46	GNG 125C	30
DUK 833	21	EN 9965	96	FDV 803V	72	FWX 914	33	GNH 258F	118
DWB 54H	51	END 832D	96	FDV 827V	111	FXH 521	28	GNM 232N	23
DWG 526	48	ENT 776	92	FDV 829V	74	FXT 122	101	GNM 235N	104
DWH 706W	97	ENT 778	108	FEA 156	21	FXT 183	78	GNU 750	118
DX 3988	30	ENW 980D	33	FEL 105L	66	FYG 663J	100	GO 5170	25
DX 5610	30	EO 9051	63	FEL 751D	45	FYS 8	80	GO 5198	87
DX 5629	30	EO 9177	63	FES 831W	50	FYS 839	57	GOE 486	108
DX 6591	30	EOD 524D	45	FET 617	95	FYS 988	40	GOU 732	95
DX 7657	85	EOI 4857	58	FET 618	57	FYS 998	40	GOU 845	62
DX 7812	30	EPD 511V	111	FFM 135C	44	FYS 999	80	GPD 313N	101
DX 8871	40	EPD 543V	111	FFN 399	76	FZ 7897	58	GPD 318N	111
DY 5029	82	EPW 516K	77	FFN 446	109	G292 EOG	21	GRD 576D	73
E186 BNS	81	ERD 145	57	FFU 860	35	G645 WDV	112	GRM 353L	105
E523 TOV	112	ERD 152	57	FFV 447D	49	GAA 580	62	GRP 260D	114
E570 MAC	63	ERG 164	115	FFY 401	104	GAA 616	62	GRS 334E	80
E901 DRG	92	ERN 700	93	FFY 402	54	GAJ 12	57	GRS 343E	49
E903 DRG	92	ERV 938	28	FFY 404	42	GAM 216	67	GRY 48D	87
EA 4181	20	ESF 647W	50	FGS 59D	48	GAN 744J	92	GRY 60D	55
EBB 846W	73	ESF 801C	49	FHF 451	59	GAN 745J	92	GSC 667X	50
EBO 919	68	ESG 652	48	FHF 456	42	GBB 516K	110	GSI 353	53
EC 8852	64	ESV 811	39	FHN 833	35	GBB 524K	92	GSO 80V	80
ECD 524	19	ETA 280	65	FHN 923	62	GBJ 192	28	GSR 244	92
ECU 201E	92	ETJ 108	48	FHT 112	108	GBU 1V	97	GSU 866T	111
ECX 425	82	ETS 964	48	FHU 59D	66	GCD 48	71	GTA 395	104
EDB 549	37	ETT 946	103	FJ 8967	71	GCK 279S	101	GTB 903	85
EDB 562	37	EUD 256K	46	FJF 40D	87	GCM 152E	59	GTJ 694	82
EDB 575	37	EUF 181	108	FJJ 774	36	GDJ 435	42	GTP 175F	70
EDJ 248J	44	EUF 184	19	FJW 616	55	GDL 33	65	GTV 666	57
EDL 657L	32	EUP 405B	72	FKF 801D	89	GDL 764L	32	GUE 247	54
EDS 288A	49	EVA 324	48	FKF 835E	89	GDT 421	57	GUF 191	98
EDS 320A	48	EVC 244	108	FKF 933G	89	GE 2446	47	GUF 727	35
EDS 50A	48	EVD 406	109	FKU 758	57	GEA 174	21	GUG 547N	111
EDT 703	57	EVL 549E	35	FLD 447Y	81	GEE 418D	110	GUJ 608	20
EDV 555D	69	EWM 358	42	FM 6397	108	GEK 14V	44	GUP 907N	92
EF 7380	92	EWS 130D	49	FM 6435	108	GEN 201	109	GUS 926	80
EFJ 241	103	EWS 168D	49	FM 7443	108	GFN 273	76	GUW 443W	101
EFJ 666	103	EWS 812D	49	FM 9984	108	GFU 692	57	GUW 444W	101
EFJ 92	37	EWW 207T	111	FNV 557	95	GFY 406	42	GUX 188	53
EFM 181H	44	EXV 201	28	FNY 933	108	GGR 103N	72	GVD 47	48
EFM 581	108	EXV 253	88	FOI 1629	83	GHA 327D	22	GW 713	40
EFM 631C	101	EZH 155	24	FON 630	20	GHA 333	54	GWJ 724	51
EFN 178L	77	EZH 17	53	FOP 429	23	GHA 337	54	GWM 816	99
EFN 568	73	EZH 170	24	FPT 590C	110	GHA 415D	55	GWY 690N	34
EFN 584	73	EZH 231	53	FPT 6G	94	GHD 215	83	GYC 160K	67
EFN 592	76	EZH 64	53	FR 1347	40	GHN 189	62	GYS 896D	80
EGA 79	40	EZL 1	53	FRB 211H	56	GHN 574	57	GZ 7638	53
EGN 369J	25	F115 PHM	88	FRC 956	55	GHT 127	67	H74 ANG	77
EGO 426	25	F261 YTJ	89	FRE 699A	109	GHT 154	67	HA 3501	54
EGP 1J	36	F300 SSX	81	FRJ 254D	38	GJ 2098	25	HA 4963	20
EGP 33J	78	F305 DRJ	97	FRJ 511	52	GJB 254	46	HA 8047	21
EHA 424D	95	F575 RCW	86	FRP 692	69	GJF 301N	87	HAD 915D	110
EHA 767D	55	F649 FGE	59	FRP 828	69	GJG 751D	27	HAH 537L	69
EHA 775	20	F685 YOG	21	FRU 224	65	GJX 331	33	HAX 399N	67
EHL 336	95	FAE 60	67	FRU 305	53	GK 3192	87	HBD 919T	69
EHL 344	76	FAR 724K	100	FSC 182	48	GK 5323	87	HBF 679D	55
EHL 472D	100	FAS 982	48	FSL 615W	81	GK 5486	87	HCD 347E	71
EHV 65	70	FBG 910	59	FTA 634	71	GKA 74N	89	HD 7905	51
EJR 110W	92	FBN 232C	64	FTB 11	37	GKD 434	89	HDG 448	55
EJR 111W	92	FBR 53D	92	FTN 710W	92	GKP 511	57	HDL 280	109
EKA 220Y	89	FBU 827	37	FTO 614	57	GKV 94	95	HDV 624E	72
EKP 234C	110	FCD 294D	99	FTR 511	98	GLJ 467N	111	HDV 638E	110
EKU 743	57	FCI 323	24	FTT 704	67	GLJ 957	104	HDV 639E	49

HE 12	90	HYM 812	57	JND 728	52	JWV 275W	99	KJA 299G	44
HEK 705	37	HZA 230	53	JND 791	37	JWV 976W	71	KJA 871F	38
HET 513	41	HZA 279	53	JNK 681C	86	JWW 375	57	KJD 401P	88
HF 9126	48	HZD 593	53	JNN 384	118	JWW 376	57	KJD 507P	111
HFG 923V	112	IB 552	19	JO 5032	46	JWW 377	57	KL 7796	85
HFM 561D	69	IJI 5367	110	JO 5403	46	JX 7046	82	KLB 721	68
HFR 501E	80	ILI 98	24	JOJ 207	109	JX 9106	82	KLB 908	96
HFR 512E	85	IY 1940	53	JOJ 222	20	JXC 194	78	KLB 915	96
HFR 516E	85	IY 7383	24	JOJ 231	109	JXC 288	25	KLJ 346	65
HGA 983D	80	IY 7384	53	JOJ 245	55	JXC 323	68	KMN 501	89
HGC 130	25	IY 8044	24	JOJ 526	20	JXC 432	78	KMN 519	89
HGG 359	80	J 2503	42	JOJ 533	55	JXN 371	114	KNG 374	30
HGM 335E	49	J 9567	64	JOJ 548	20	JXN 46	108	KNG 711	109
HGM 346E	49	J7 FTG	112	JOJ 827	109	JXX 487	109	KNG 718	77
HH-97-96	110	JA 5506	73	JOJ 847	20	JY 124	103	KNN 254	109
HHA 26	108	JA 5528	108	JOJ 976	55	JYC 855	95	KNV 337	69
HHA 637	54	JA 7585	37	JOV 613P	56	K232 DAC	26	KO 117	85
HHN 202	72	JA 7770	108	JOV 714P	21	K361 LWS	104	KO 54	85
HHP 755	82	JAA 7086	79	JOV 738P	103	K727 UTT	112	KO 7311	85
HHW 452D	110	JAP 698	100	JOW 499E	98	KAG 856	80	KOM 150	26
HIL 7081	111	JBD 975	69	JOW 928	98	KAH 407	30	KON 311P	56
HJA 965E	118	JBN 153	37	JP 4712	37	KAH 408	28	KOU 791P	67
HJG 17	73	JC 5313	82	JP 7538	65	KAL 579	55	KOU 795P	111
HKE 680L	111	JCK 530	85	JPA 190K	25	KAZ 6703	99	KOW 909F	98
HKE 867	108	JCK 542	94	JPA 82V	80	KBD 712D	101	KOW 910F	98
HKF 820	59	JCK 852W	112	JPF 108K	114	KBD 715D	101	KOX 663F	20
HKL 826	108	JCP 60F	40	JPL 153K	101	KBO 961	68	KOX 780F	55
HKR 11	57	JDC 599	73	JPT 901T	92	KCG 627L	62	KPA 369P	111
HL 7538	65	JDL 40	109	JPT 906T	72	KCK 869	94	KPT 909	41
HLJ 44	78	JEL 257	67	JRN 29	22	KCK 914	94	KR 8385	85
HLW 159	42	JF 2378	20	JRN 41	94	KD 3185	82	KRN 422	42
HLW 214	108	JFJ 400N	111	JRR 404	55	KD 5296	100	KRR 255	39
HLX 410	25	JFJ 500N	104	JRT 82K	30	KDB 408F	38	KRU 55F	66
HNB 24N	96	JFJ 506N	69	JRX 823	88	KDB 696	77	KSV 102	84
HNP 154S	99	JFJ 606	104	JSC 900E	49	KDJ 999	44	KSX 102X	50
HNP 989J	98	JFJ 875	118	JSF 928T	50	KDL 885F	32	KTB 672	65
HNW 131D	33	JFM 238D	29	JSJ 746	116	KDT 206D	58	KTD 768	42
HOR 590E	79	JFM 575	118	JSJ 747	116	KDW 347P	111	KTF 594	118
HOR 592E	79	JFM 650J	44	JSJ 748	116	KDW 362P	111	KTJ 502	92
HOU 904	62	JFT 228N	92	JSJ 749	116	KE 4771	73	KTT 42P	74
HOV 685	54	JFV 527	94	JSX 595T	50	KED 546F	84	KTT 689	20
HPF 318N	101	JG 669	85	JT 8077	32	KEL 110	65	KTV 493	57
HPK 503N	111	JG 691	85	JTB 749	115	KEL 131	118	KTV 506	57
HPW 108	67	JG 8720	73	JTD 300B	44	KEL 133	65	KUF 199F	99
HPW 133	35	JG 9938	118	JTE 546	118	KEL 405	109	KUL 331D	114
HRG 209	48	JGA 189N	80	JTF 920B	58	KET 220	51	KUS 607E	64
HRN 249G	94	JHA 227L	100	JTH 100F	100	KFM 775	55	KVF 658E	77
HRN 31	94	JHA 868E	55	JTU 588T	50	KFM 893	118	KVH 219	57
HRN 39	94	JHL 701	92	JUB 29	82	KFN 239	76	KVH 473E	33
HRN 99N	86	JHL 708	76	JUD 597W	46	KGK 529	96	KVO 429P	45
HSC 173X	50	JHT 802	66	JUE 349	55	KGK 575	96	KW 1961	28
HSD 73V	80	JJD 394D	110	JUM 505V	34	KGK 758	78	KW 2260	33
HSD 86V	81	JJD 405D	78	JUO 983	71	KGK 803	25	KW 474	34
HTB 656	37	JJD 499D	110	JUO 992	118	KGK 959	114	KW 6052	57
HTC 661	108	JJD 511D	118	JUS 774N	80	KGM 664F	49	KW 7604	34
HTF 586	37	JJD 524D	76	JV 9901	57	KGU 142	25	KWE 255	51
HTF 644B	44	JJD 539D	110	JVB 908	48	KGU 284	22	KWT 642D	33
HUD 476S	46	JJD 551D	92	JVF 528	46	KGU 290	117	KXW 171	114
HUO 510	118	JK 8418	108	JVH 373	83	KGY 4D	88	KXW 22	114
HUP 236	72	JK 9915	108	JVH 378	83	KHA 301	20	KXW 435	96
HUY 655	65	JKC 178	89	JVH 381	109	KHA 311	109	KXW 488	114
HVM 901F	38	JLJ 403	65	JVO 230	45	KHA 352	20	KY 9106	33
HVO 937	39	JMC 123K	110	JVS 293	72	KHC 367	88	KYV 781X	81
HVU 244N	38	JMN 727	57	JVU 755	37	KHH 378W	105	KYY 529	109
HVU 247N	118	JMS 452E	80	JVV 267G	110	KHU 28	67	KYY 615	109
HWO 334	55	JN 5783	40	JVW 430	23	KHU 326P	67	KYY 622	102
HWV 294	69	JNA 467	37	JWB 416	51	KHU 624	104	KYY 628	117
HWY 36	109	JNB 416	26	JWS 594	48	KHW 306E	55	KYY 647	109
HX 2756	87	JND 629	109	JWU 307	101	KHW 630	66	KYY 961	78
HYM 768	88	JND 646	37	JWU 886	33	KID 154	24	L247 FDV	46

Reg	No.	Reg	No.	Reg	No.	Reg	No.	Reg	No.
L929 CTT	102	LOI 1859	111	MLL 817	102	NDP 38R	111	NUD 105L	70
L932 CTT	112	LOU 48	62	MLL 952	78	NDV 537G	74	NUW 567Y	88
LA 9928	36	LOW 217	98	MN 2615	87	NEA 101F	55	NVK 341	72
LAA 231	62	LRA 801P	39	MNC 525W	97	NEH 453	23	NWA 257K	44
LAE 13	67	LRN 321J	94	MNS 10Y	81	NEL 119P	111	NWO 462R	111
LAK 309G	33	LRN 60J	67	MNW 86	33	NFM 67	67	NWU 265D	33
LAK 313G	33	LRV 992	98	MO 9324	19	NFN 84R	77	NWW 89E	76
LAX 101E	110	LRV 996	70	MOD 823P	72	NFS 176Y	50	NXL 847	95
LCD 52	28	LST 873	116	MOD 973	71	NFW 36V	35	NXP 775	78
LDJ 985	44	LSU 381V	112	MOF 90	20	NG 1109	32	NXP 997	88
LDP 945	105	LSX 16P	49	MOO 177	77	NGE 172P	80	NZE 598	53
LDS 201A	49	LTA 729	71	MOR 581	62	NHA 744	55	NZE 620	53
LDS 279A	78	LTA 748	71	MPU 21	69	NHA 795	55	NZE 629	53
LED 71P	44	LTA 772	41	MPU 52	23	NHN 250K	92	O 9926	54
LEN 101	76	LTA 813	95	MPX 945R	104	NHU 2	66	OAE 957M	104
LEO 734Y	63	LTA 946	71	MRB 765	115	NJA 568W	97	OBN 502R	96
LEO 735Y	63	LTC 774	37	MRT 6P	30	NJO 703	46	OC 527	54
LEV 917	84	LTF 254	82	MSD 407	80	NJW 719E	55	OCH 261L	111
LF 9967	90	LTN 501	42	MSD 408	80	NKD 536	89	OCK 985K	28
LFJ 847W	72	LTU 869	53	MSF 122P	80	NKD 540	89	OCK 988K	77
LFJ 862W	74	LTV 702	104	MSF 465P	80	NKJ 849P	79	OCK 995K	85
LFM 302	118	LTX 311	109	MSF 750P	49	NKR 529	65	OCK 997K	86
LFM 717	118	LUC 210	25	MTC 540	93	NKU 214X	86	OCU 769R	92
LFM 734	118	LUC 250	109	MTE 635	33	NKU 245X	34	OCU 807R	92
LFM 753	67	LUC 381	109	MTE 639	48	NLE 534	109	OCW 8X	112
LFM 767	33	LUO 692	118	MTJ 771S	89	NLE 537	88	OD 5489	103
LFR 529F	85	LUS 524E	49	MTJ 84	115	NLE 603	78	OD 5868	103
LFR 540G	85	LVK 123	72	MTL 750	18	NLE 643	117	OD 7500	103
LFS 288F	49	LWB 377P	111	MTT 640	115	NLE 672	25	ODK 705	82
LFS 294F	49	LWB 388P	51	MUT 253W	87	NLE 673	109	ODL 400L	32
LFS 296F	99	LWR 424	109	MV 8996	108	NLE 882	78	ODV 287P	111
LFS 480	48	LYF 104	109	MXX 23	55	NLE 939	102	OED 217	22
LFW 326	35	LYF 316	109	MXX 261	78	NLJ 268	65	OEM 788S	89
LG 2637	52	LYF 377	117	MXX 283	109	NLJ 272	65	OFC 205	46
LHA 870F	20	LYM 729	92	MXX 289	114	NLP 645	41	OFC 393	46
LHC 919P	64	LYR 533	33	MXX 292	109	NMA 328D	52	OFC 902H	70
LHL 164F	76	LYR 542	57	MXX 332	101	NMS 358	80	OFM 957K	60
LHN 784	57	LYR 672	109	MXX 334	25	NMS 366	48	OFN 721F	77
LHN 785	83	LYR 854	114	MXX 364	88	NMY 634E	116	OFR 970M	86
LHN 860	62	LYR 910	25	MXX 410	102	NMY 646E	116	OFS 777	48
LHT 911	84	LYR 915	101	MXX 421	109	NMY 655E	78	OFS 798	48
LHW 918	67	LYR 969	114	MXX 430	102	NNB 125	37	OHK 432	35
LHY 937	109	LYR 997	23	MXX 434	101	NNB 547H	96	OHU 770F	67
LHY 976	66	M627 HDV	102	MXX 481	77	NNB 589H	96	OHY 938	66
LIL 9929	50	M939 XKA	38	MXX 489	101	NNC 854P	118	OJ 9347	20
LJ 147	65	MAH 744	30	MYA 590	25	NNU 123M	39	OJD 172R	25
LJ 500	65	MAL 310	45	MZ 7396	53	NNU 124M	39	OJD 192R	34
LJF 30F	51	MAP 340W	99	NAC 416F	46	NNU 234	65	OJD 903R	80
LJF 31F	64	MBN 177	94	NAE 3	69	NOB 413M	56	OJF 191	87
LJH 665	118	MCK 229J	76	NAG 120G	49	NOC 600R	103	OJI 4371	86
LJW 336	20	MCN 30K	92	NAH 135P	77	NOE 544R	56	OJO 727	69
LJX 198	82	MDJ 555E	44	NAH 941	77	NOE 576R	111	OLD 589	88
LJX 215	82	MDL 880R	32	NAT 766A	110	NOV 796G	55	OLD 714	35
LKT 991	85	MDL 954	109	NBB 628	28	NOV 880G	103	OLJ 291	41
LLU 670	114	MDT 222	57	NBD 311F	101	NPD 108L	111	OLV 551M	89
LLU 732	114	MFM 39	109	NBN 436	64	NPD 128L	111	ONE 744	28
LLU 829	28	MFN 898	76	NBU 494	37	NPD 145L	27	ONF 865H	96
LLU 957	96	MFR 306P	94	NCD 559M	111	NRA 78F	39	ONO 49	23
LLU 987	96	MHU 49	67	NCK 106J	94	NRG 154M	29	ONO 59	35
LMA 284	37	MHY 765	51	NCK 338J	94	NRG 26H	80	ONU 425	69
LMJ 653G	40	MJ 4549	73	NCS 16P	49	NRH 802A	64	OOX 825R	21
LMS 168W	81	MJA 891G	38	NDB 356	118	NRN 397P	86	OP 237	20
LMS 374W	50	MJA 895G	110	NDH 959	57	NRN 586	94	OPV 821	99
LN 4743	29	MJA 897G	38	NDK 980	37	NSF 757	80	ORB 277	55
LN 7270	90	MKB 994	89	NDL 375G	80	NSJ 502	49	ORC 545P	45
LNA 166G	96	MLL 555	109	NDL 637M	32	NTF 466	42	ORJ 83W	38
LNN 89E	45	MLL 570	76	NDL 656R	50	NTT 661	74	ORS 60R	50
LOD 495	115	MLL 682	114	NDL 769G	63	NTU 125	95	ORU 230G	66
LOG 301	20	MLL 722	109	NDM 950E	110	NTW 942C	23	ORV 989	70
LOG 302	20	MLL 740	25	NDP 31R	111	NTY 416F	49	OSC 711	49

OSJ 620R	83	PRN 79K	94	RN 8622	93	SLT 58	25	TE 8318	34
OSJ 629R	50	PRN 906	94	RNA 220J	96	SMK 676F	110	TEC 599N	65
OSJ 636R	116	PRX 187B	99	RNA 236J	100	SMK 686F	92	TET 135	51
OSK 831	92	PRX 200B	99	RNE 692W	112	SMK 701F	44	TF 6860	33
OST 502	24	PRX 206B	99	ROD 765	82	SMK 716F	110	TF 818	35
OT 8283	62	PSJ 480	44	RPU 869M	111	SMK 732F	92	TFA 987	110
OT 8592	62	PSJ 825R	51	RRM 148M	77	SMK 734F	85	TFF 251	69
OT 8898	62	PSL 234	103	RRM 386X	81	SMK 747F	110	TFN 980T	77
OT 8902	62	PSX 189Y	112	RRN 405	85	SMM 90F	78	TGM 214J	49
OTA 632G	102	PTC 114C	38	RRN 428	94	SMS 120P	50	TGY 102M	111
OTA 640G	95	PTD 640S	96	RRS 46R	50	SND 455X	97	THM 515M	111
OTB 26W	64	PTE 944C	38	RRU 903	65	SND 460X	97	THM 692M	60
OTT 43	95	PTF 718L	94	RRU 904	65	SND 501X	97	THX 220S	111
OTT 55	41	PTF 727L	94	RSC 194Y	81	SNS 823W	112	THX 646S	78
OTV 137	57	PTT 106R	104	RSD 973R	80	SO 3740	47	TJ 6760	93
OTV 161	45	PTW 110	23	RSG 825V	81	SOA 658S	21	TJO 56K	70
OU 7951	85	PUA 310W	112	RSJ 747	101	SOA 674S	101	TKU 467K	34
OU 9286	79	PUF 165H	99	RSK 615	109	SOE 913H	55	TMS 403X	81
OUM 727P	18	PV 817	30	RTC 645L	44	SOI 3591	83	TMS 585H	49
OV 4090	54	PV 8270	30	RTT 996	72	SOU 456	62	TNA 496	37
OV 4486	54	PV 9371	30	RU 2266	65	SOU 465	62	TNA 520	37
OVF 229	77	PVH 931	58	RU 8678	47	SPT 65	92	TNB 759K	96
OVL 465	35	PW 8605	90	RU 8805	71	SPT 963V	73	TOB 377	20
OVL 473	101	PWL 413	46	RUF 186	71	SPU 985	86	TOB 997H	103
OWC 182D	101	PWL 999W	70	RUF 37R	99	SR 1266	26	TOJ 592S	117
OWC 720M	111	PWS 492S	84	RV 3411	70	SRB 424	26	TPD 109X	101
OWE 116	51	PY 6170	108	RV 4649	70	SRJ 328H	38	TPJ 61S	88
OWE 271K	56	Q124 VOE	55	RV 6360	42	SS 7486	48	TRJ 109	44
OWS 620	48	Q507 OHR	67	RV 6368	70	SS 7501	48	TRJ 112	38
OZ 6686	53	Q995 CPE	104	RVO 668L	111	SSA 5X	81	TRN 481V	94
PAJ 829X	93	RAG 400	80	RWB 87	51	SSF 237H	49	TRN 731	94
PAU 204R	80	RAG 411	49	RWC 637K	111	SSN 248S	80	TRU 947J	110
PBC 113G	87	RAG 578	48	RWU 534R	83	SSX 602V	50	TRY 122H	87
PBC 734	26	RAL 795	109	SAS 859T	80	STJ 847L	86	TSJ 272	82
PBC 98G	87	RB 4757	82	SB 8155	20	STL 725J	110	TSJ 47S	80
PBJ 2F	77	RBC 345G	100	SBD 525R	101	STO 523H	45	TSK 736	115
PBN 668	109	RBD 111M	101	SBF 233	55	SUK 3	55	TSO 16X	81
PCG 888G	98	RBD 319G	101	SCD 731N	99	SV 6107	93	TTD 386H	38
PCG 889G	98	RBW 87M	70	SCH 117X	45	SVA 438	65	TTR 167H	98
PCK 618	94	RC 2721	35	SCH 237	21	SVF 896G	110	TTT 781	82
PCN 762	92	RC 4615	54	SCN 268S	92	SVS 281	105	TUG 20	72
PCW 203J	92	RC 7927	20	SCS 333M	49	SVV 587W	101	TUJ 261	51
PDH 808	55	RC 8472	105	SCS 335M	86	SWS 671	48	TUO 74J	74
PDJ 269L	44	RC 8575	105	SCS 366M	49	SWS 715	48	TUP 859	72
PDL 515	32	RC 8575	57	SDA 757S	56	SWV 155J	92	TV 4484	57
PDL 519	32	RCH 629L	39	SDK 442	37	TAX 235	109	TV 9333	57
PDU 125M	26	RCK 920	110	SDL 638J	32	TBC 164F	18	TVS 367	48
PDU 135M	56	RCM 493	59	SDL 268L	32	TBC 50X	87	TVT 127G	44
PFE 542V	35	RCP 237	88	SDX 33R	64	TBD 279G	69	TWH 809K	64
PFN 865	45	RCS 382	49	SDX 57	23	TBK 190K	70	TWL 928	46
PFN 867	77	RCU 588S	92	SEO 209M	63	TCD 374J	99	TWM 220V	89
PFR 346	85	RCU 838S	92	SFC 610	46	TCD 383J	99	TWW 766F	33
PFR 554H	85	RD 712	68	SFV 421	94	TCD 481J	99	TWY 8	76
PFR 747	100	RDB 872	67	SG 2030	28	TCD 490J	99	TXJ 507K	38
PFW 935	109	RDH 505	55	SGD 407	23	TCK 465	94	TYD 888	48
PHA 370M	56	REN 116	38	SGD 448	80	TCK 726	94	TYJ 4S	99
PHJ 954	23	RFE 416	35	SGD 500	80	TCK 821	80	UAS 954	109
PHN 699	118	RFM 453F	44	SGD 65	80	TCO 537	92	UBD 757H	101
PHN 831	92	RFM 641	42	SGR 935V	72	TDH 912	21	UBN 902	64
PJX 232	33	RFM 644	42	SHA 431	55	TDJ 612	44	UCS 659	49
PJX 35	76	RFU 689	69	SHA 645G	55	TDK 322	51	UCX 275	21
PKG 587M	111	RGS 598R	77	SHN 301	92	TDK 686J	118	UDT 455F	58
PKH 600M	111	RHS 400W	50	SHN 80L	39	TDL 564K	32	UEO 478T	63
PKW 434J	110	RKC 262	89	SJ 1340	48	TDL 566K	111	UF 1517	19
PND 460	37	RLN 230W	112	SKB 168	89	TDL 998	88	UF 4813	19
PNF 941J	96	RLN 237W	104	SKB 224	89	TDT 344	115	UF 6473	19
PNU 114K	39	RLS 469T	50	SKB 695G	89	TDV 217J	102	UF 6805	19
POR 428	62	RMS 400W	81	SKL 681X	77	TE 5110	53	UF 7428	19
POU 494	79	RN 7588	93	SLT 56	88	TE 5780	82	UFC 430K	46
PRN 145	94	RN 7824	37	SLT 57	88	TE 7870	114	UFF 178	48

Reg	No.	Reg	No.	Reg	No.	Reg	No.	Reg	No.
UFJ 292	92	VDV 817	74	VVP 911	55	WW 4688	57	YD 9533	73
UFM 52F	59	VER 262L	46	VW 203	71	WWH 43L	96	YDB 453L	96
UFP 233S	87	VF 2788	30	VWM 83L	89	WWJ 754M	58	YDK 590	37
UGB 196W	81	VF 8157	30	VY 957	37	WWM 904W	89	YDL 135T	32
UGR 698R	111	VFJ 995	109	VYO 767	101	WWY 115G	100	YDL 315	88
UHA 255	55	VG 5541	95	VZI 44	53	WX 2658	64	YF 714	71
UHA 941H	56	VH 2088	82	VZL 179	53	WX 3567	28	YFM 269L	111
UHA 956H	55	VH 6217	65	WAJ 112	49	WYP 203G	110	YFM 283L	69
UHA 963H	110	VHB 678S	80	WBN 955L	96	WYW 6T	25	YFR 351	85
UHA 981H	56	VHF 57V	89	WBR 246	33	WYW 82T	64	YFS 310W	81
UHG 141V	81	VIB 5069	112	WBR 248	92	WZJ 724	53	YG 7831	90
UHY 359	67	VJG 187J	77	WCG 104	79	XAK 355L	34	YHT 958	67
UHY 360	66	VJO 201X	70	WDA 4T	117	XBO 121T	50	YHY 80	68
UHY 362	103	VJW 882L	32	WDA 700T	21	XBU 17S	38	YJG 807	77
UHY 384	66	VK 5401	42	WDA 835T	56	XBU 1S	96	YL 740	46
UK 9978	21	VKB 711	89	WDA 956T	103	XC 8059	87	YLG 717F	33
UKA 23V	89	VKB 841	89	WDA 986T	21	XCH 425G	110	YLJ 286	28
UKA 562H	89	VKB 900	89	WDF 569	55	XCV 326	109	YMA 99W	44
ULS 716X	50	VL 1263	34	WDK 562T	118	XCW 955R	94	YNA 321M	96
ULS 717X	50	VLT 140	41	WEX 685M	76	XDH 516G	55	YNU 351G	110
UMA 370	37	VLT 143	116	WFM 801K	34	XDH 519G	22	YNW 33X	104
UMO 180N	111	VLT 163	116	WFN 912	27	XDH 56G	55	YPT 796	72
UNB 524	109	VLT 216	117	WG 1620	47	XDH 72	20	YR 3844	87
UNB 629	37	VLT 235	116	WG 2373	80	XFG 25Y	112	YRC 194	45
UO 2331	103	VLT 237	116	WG 3260	47	XFM 42G	49	YRC 420	111
UOA 322L	39	VLT 242	116	WG 4445	80	XG 9304	48	YRT 898H	28
UOU 417H	79	VLT 25	78	WG 8107	47	XGM 450L	80	YSD 350L	49
UOU 419H	79	VLT 250	109	WG 8790	48	XHA 482	55	YSG 101	49
UP 551	42	VLT 268	114	WG 9180	48	XHA 496	55	YSL 334	116
UPB 312S	101	VLT 281	116	WH 1553	34	XHO 370	62	YT 3738	22
UPE 203M	101	VLT 298	114	WHA 237H	92	XJA 534L	96	YTE 826	28
URE 281	109	VLT 44	23	WHL 970	76	XKO 72A	110	YWB 494M	46
USV 324	99	VLT 85	114	WHN 411G	92	XLG 477	33	YWL 134K	70
UTC 672	37	VLW 444G	101	WJY 758	33	XLV 140W	44	YYB 118	100
UTC 768D	44	VM 4439	37	WKG 284	110	XM 7399	87	YYJ 914	49
UTF 732M	94	VMO 234H	101	WKJ 787	95	XMS 252R	50	YYS 174	80
UTG 313G	110	VMP 10G	80	WKO 132S	111	XMS 422Y	81	ZC 714	53
UTN 501Y	73	VMP 8G	49	WKO 138S	111	XNG 770S	30	ZD 7163	53
UTU 596J	55	VNB 101L	38	WLT 371	116	XNX 136H	20	ZH 3926	53
UTV 229	82	VNB 132L	96	WLT 506	20	XO 1048	25	ZH 3937	53
UU 6646	25	VNB 173L	96	WLT 529	105	XON 41J	21	ZH 4538	53
UUA 212	92	VNB 177L	96	WLT 529	58	XPK 51T	101	ZI 9708	53
UUA 214	33	VNB 203L	96	WLT 900	114	XRD 23K	110	ZJ 5904	24
UUF 110J	71	VO 6806	40	WLT 902	114	XRU 277K	66	ZJ 5933	53
UUF 116J	99	VO 8846	45	WNG 864H	56	XSL 945A	49	ZL 2718	53
UUF 328J	99	VOD 123K	110	WNO 478	23	XSN 25A	49	ZL 6816	53
UUF 335J	99	VOD 545K	74	WNO 556L	77	XTA 839	74	ZO 6819	53
UVL 873M	35	VOD 550K	74	WOW 993T	110	XTC 530H	80	ZO 6857	53
UWH 185	64	VOD 88K	74	WP 6114	64	XTF 98D	118	ZO 6881	53
UWX 981F	100	VOI 8415	83	WPG 217M	111	XTP 287L	70	ZO 6949	53
UXD 129G	101	VPT 598R	72	WRA 12	51	XU 7498	90	ZO 6960	24
UZG 100	53	VR 5742	37	WRJ 448X	97	XUA 73X	76	ZS 8621	24
UZH 258	24	VRD 186	22	WRL 16	104	XUF 141	98	ZU 5000	24
VBD 310H	100	VRD 193	58	WRP 767J	101	XUO 721	74	ZU 9241	53
VCO 772	112	VRF 372	100	WS 4522	47	XUS 575S	80	ZV 1510	92
VCO 802	112	VRU 124J	66	WSD 756K	80	XVU 341M	96	ZY 1715	24
VD 3433	47	VSB 164M	80	WT 7101	33	XVU 352M	38	ZY 79	53
VDL 264L	32	VSC 86	48	WT 7108	42	XVU 363M	96		
VDV 107S	111	VSS 158M	80	WT 9156	82	XVX 19	23		
VDV 123S	74	VTU 76	33	WTS 266T	50	XW 9892	22		
VDV 137S	102	VTY 543J	92	WTS 270T	80	XWS 165K	49		
VDV 752	118	VUD 30X	70	WTS 708A	92	XWX 795	58		
VDV 753	118	VUP 328	72	WUA 832	109	XYJ 418	33		
VDV 760	51	VV 8934	35	WUH 173T	111	XX 9591	25		
VDV 798	74	VVK 149G	92	WV 1209	30	YBD 201	115